Edinburgh writer Alan Robertson first became interested in Joe Harriott through reading Ian Carr's book on contemporary British music, *Music Outside*. He listened to Harriott's music and became fascinated by the man, his life story and his aesthetic achievements. Following his interest to its logical conclusion, he interviewed a great many people and wrote his first book: the biography of Harriott published by Northway in 2003. Following publication, and having been contacted by other people who had known Joe Harriott well, he could not resist pursuing the subject further. The new material casts much additional light on the man, the musician, and the problems he encountered as a Jamaican in Britain in the mid-twentieth century.

Gary Crosby, the contributor of the foreword, is a leading British jazz bass player who has done much to develop young jazz talent through his bands 'Jazz Jamaica All Stars' and 'Tomorrow's Warriors'.

'Robertson's research is meticulous and far-reaching and his panorama of comments ... provides a valuable insight into a towering and tragic figure. *Fire in his Soul* is an important work: a detailed assessment of a seminal but long neglected artist.'
Kevin Le Gendre, *Independent on Sunday.*

'Robertson tells Harriott's story warts and all and has produced a wonderful read.' Stephen Graham, *Jazzwise.*

'a long overdue and welcome homage to a sadly neglected and original musician.' Derek Ansell, *Jazz Journal International.*

'Robertson opens up Harriott as a musician and man and shows him as a proud, self-directed and lonely seer of jazz, a black musical prodigy in a white British underworld of the music where it was so much more easy and comfortable to be an imitator.'
Chris Searle, *Morning Star.*

'a compelling and rather sad story of the life of one of Britain's most important jazz musicians, a musician who was admired by fans, musicians and critics alike. One that was not always treated with the dignity and acclaim that he should have been afforded.'
Bill Smith, *Coda.*

'should be read by anyone interested in the survival of the artistic impulse in a largely indifferent, sometimes overtly hostile environment.' Chris Parker, *JARS.*

'The sparky and unpretentious attitude of working musicians shines through, providing a stream of canny observations.'
Ben Watson, *The Wire.*

'Robertson's fine biography follows Harriott from childhood prodigy to emigration from Jamaica into a UK that welcomed, but ultimately failed to nurture, his massive talent. The clear style combines with thorough research to give valuable insight into this complex and innovatory musician.'
Steve Millward, *Manchester Evening News.*

'Un libro davvero importante!'
Enrico Betteinello, *www.allaboutjazz.com/italy.*

Alan Robertson

JOE HARRIOTT

FIRE IN HIS SOUL

Second Edition

northway publications

Published by Northway Publications
39 Tytherton Road, London N19 4PZ, UK.
www.northwaybooks.com

Edited by Ann and Roger Cotterrell.

Cover design by Adam Yeldham, Raven Design.

Cover photos courtesy of Max Jones Archive. Back cover: Joe Harriott with Michael Garrick (piano), Ian Carr (trumpet), Don Rendell (tenor) and others, probably late 1960s.

The publishers acknowledge with thanks the kind permission of copyright holders to reprint the photographs used in this book. Permissions have been sought in all cases where the identity of copyright holders is known.

A CIP record for this book is available from the British Library.

ISBN 978 0 9557888 5 7

First published 2003.
Second edition (revised) 2011.

Printed and bound in Great Britain by Berforts Group Ltd, Stevenage.

Contents

foreword

Mojo – the man who killed Yellow Bird

One day, when I was practising trumpet at the age of fifteen, a visiting family friend, Uncle Deacon – a DJ from Jamaica and the man with the hippest record collection in England – put his head around the door and laughed: 'Wha! So yu a go join Joe 'Arriott an' dem bwoy dem down a Hundred Club and Flamingo.' London's Oxford Street and Wardour Street, liquor, gambling, wild women, wine and song were all conjured up in my mind. Whether my mind's eye was true or not, the image made me practise harder that evening than ever before. 'Yellow Bird' – that British stereotype of the Caribbean – began to sound out of tune.

The second time Joe Harriott – or 'Mojo' as he was nick-named – entered my life was on hearing a tape of Joe talking to John Dankworth about 'free form'. Now I could add intellect and awareness of abstract art and form to the mystique of Mojo as there were not many people I knew from his generation who could speak so eloquently on such subjects. Listening to the tape made me feel very proud and inspired; not only did he come from the same city as my parents, but also we shared a common aim:

Kill Yellow Bird ... dead ... stone dead.

Mojo's assimilation and transformation of Charlie Parker into the abstract free form music of the great Joe Harriott Quintet of the 1960s is an important legacy as are his liberation of form, ideas about collective improvisation, and his gift to non-American musicians of confidence to play jazz without feeling inferior to their US counterparts. Mojo didn't feel that musicians had to go to America to create good jazz. It was not so much where you were, but more the power of the mind that mattered.

His premature death and, to some extent, the hitherto lack of importance attached to his artistic achievements and tenets, confirm to me the absolute need for a support system for creative young musicians of African-Caribbean descent to thrive and contribute to a multicultural jazz community. Mojo's legacy encourages us to strive to kill Yellow Bird.

Coleridge Goode, Tommy Jones, Herman Wilson, Ian Carr, Frank Holder, Sonny Bradshaw and others who worked with Mojo all have their own stories. It is clear, from speaking to those who knew him – if indeed anyone ever got close enough to him to really *know* the man – that though he was admired by those who worked with him, he was not an easy person. A passionate musician yet a lonely, troubled soul, emotionally detached, longing to be accepted as a serious artist, he found himself worn down by a system that refused to accommodate him. Who knows? Maybe if he had been around in the age of the Jazz Warriors, the support system that was so lacking in his time might have sustained him.

Was Mojo ahead of his time? Perhaps. Until now there has been a distinct paucity of information about this important figure, most of it being passed down by word of mouth. So it is not before time that Alan Robertson has gifted the world a biography of Joe Harriott, celebrating his life and achievements, and acknowledging his generous contribution to the jazz scene.

Fire In His Soul gives us an opportunity to learn more about this great musician, draw our own conclusions and perhaps encourage us to understand, and maybe love, The Man Who Killed Yellow Bird.

Kill Yellow Bird ... dead ... stone dead.

Gary Crosby
London, 2003.

introduction to
the second edition

My biography of Joe Harriott was first published in 2003, thirty years after the great alto saxophonist's death. The publication of this new enlarged edition also marks a significant Harriott anniversary. It is sixty years since his arrival on British soil in May 1951. I made my own arrival that month via Simpson's Maternity Pavilion in Edinburgh so 2011 gives me two sixtieth anniversaries to celebrate.

Some might question why there is a need for a new edition of a biography whose subject died in 1973. The simple answer is that following publication numerous people contacted me both to comment on the book and to bring to my notice their own part in the musician's life. Their stories provided a far more detailed picture of the enigmatic and rather secretive man I had written about. I anticipate that in some quarters there will be hostility to revealing certain details of Joe's private life. Whilst researching the first edition I experienced reluctance on the part of some contributors to be critical of Joe. One said after making candid yet truthful remarks, 'But don't put that in your book. Joe's not here to defend himself.'

The negative aspects of Joe's personality are not in doubt and are not constructs of mere gossip. I believe that inclusion of this new information is essential if we are to understand the true nature of this superbly gifted musician. Offstage, he was a seriously flawed individual who was exploitative in his human relationships with men as well as women. It is easy to understand how Joe, whose childhood was disrupted when he was removed from family and placed into care, had difficulties in forming warm and giving relationships. I do not doubt some products of care homes do become well-adjusted, caring individuals but it is apparent that a large percentage do not. Instead they struggle with addiction, mental turbulence, violent tendencies or homelessness.

I became aware of him in my mid-teens when he was joint leader of Indo-Jazz Fusions. My interest in jazz deepened during my twenties and it was my reading of *Music Outside*,[1] Ian Carr's book on British contemporary jazz, which provided the 'hook' that eventually led me to research and write this biography of Harriott.

Carr wrote of British modern jazzmen: 'For the heroic few who do continue to be totally committed to the music after they have reached their forties, there is often a terrible price to pay. The saxophonist Joe Harriott and his long-time associate the drummer Phil Seamen both died ... in their early forties. Phil Seamen was worn out by drug addiction, but Joe Harriott, one feels, was defeated and worn down and out more directly by the system, the hostile environment. From being one of the leading pioneers of free jazz and the co-creator of the Indo-Jazz Fusions which made such an impact in the 1960s, for the last two years of his life he had been reduced to the obscurity of the provinces where he wandered about working as a soloist with local rhythm sections.'

In those few lines referring to Joe, Carr started a curiosity in me which culminated in this book. I wanted to know as much as I could about Harriott. How good a musician was he? If he was as good as Carr suggested, why did his life have such a sad conclusion? Listening to his music seemed the right way to start.

I managed to acquire a vinyl double album of *Indo-Jazz Fusions* from a collector friend at a time when one could expect to pay £75 for it at a record fair. It was great to hear the emotionally charged sound of Joe's alto sax within this Indian setting, but I now yearned to hear the legendary free jazz of the Harriott quintet. It appeared that none of the band's 1960s albums featuring free jazz had ever been reissued. Only in the late 1990s did *Free Form* and *Abstract* become available again, issued on CD for the first time. On finally hearing the albums, I found their impact undiminished by the passing of time. I was utterly stunned by the music and the quality of the musicianship. Joe Harriott had proved worth waiting for.

It was evident that his achievements were largely neglected. Here was someone very special, yet how many people, even among jazz fans, had heard of him? A book should have been written about Joe much earlier. In the continuing absence of one, I decided to make my contribution to bring his name to the fore again.

Joe Harriott was a virtuoso of the alto saxophone, a visionary in the development of jazz, and ultimately a victim of neglect by an unappreciative arts establishment. His wonderful technique and individuality on alto sax should have been enough to ensure legendary status in British jazz. Even more significantly, he embarked on a quest to create new forms of music, to fashion beautiful art from a musical palette no one else had used. In many histories of jazz, even of British jazz, there is a gap where his name should be prominently featured. That he should become a 'forgotten man' seems inconceivable when one looks at what he achieved.

First was his concept of free form jazz in which he dispensed with the traditional rules of ensemble jazz playing. The gifted colleagues in his quintet experienced more freedom in group-improvised music than anyone had previously considered possible, given the quality of the music. The results were far removed from the anarchy and chaos one might have expected. Indeed, one is struck by the beauty of many of Joe's compositions and, given the unplanned spontaneity of the music, it is astonishing how often it really swings.

In the mid-sixties he engaged in a second groundbreaking project. With Indian violinist, arranger and composer John Mayer, Harriott created Indo-Jazz Fusions to attempt a marriage between jazz and Indian classical music. Like free form jazz before it, this was met with much ill-considered criticism, scorn and derision. But today his work with Mayer can be recognised as part of the genesis of world music: a genre so accepted today it seems always to have been with us.

So this book is not a story of heroic failure against insurmountable odds; rather it is a celebration of Joe Harriott's achievement in the face of artistic hostility and jealousy. It applauds his triumph despite his inauspicious beginnings, and it vindicates his unswerving belief in his musical vision. In addition, I intend it to pay homage to all those artists in jazz and in other fields who find sufficient faith and courage to follow their convictions rather than pursuing more tempting mainstream options which offer professional stability, financial security and the refuge from constant challenge. Individuals like Joe really have no other course. They are driven by their passion to discover and create. They are genuine artists for whom material concerns are often relegated at great cost to themselves.

Harriott stood tall, not just physically at 6 foot 2 inches, but as a towering artistic presence. He rarely delivered anything less than his best. His audiences were never short-changed. He was routinely described as 'difficult to get to know', but it is my good fortune that he made an indelible impression on many people and won a legion of friends the length and breadth of Britain. Not all found his personality to their liking, but a considerable majority of the musicians and non-musicians who talked to me about Joe treasure their memories of times spent with him. I hope you feel you can share their pleasure as you read their memories. If you are new to the subject of Joe Harriott, and reading his story leaves you wanting to hear his musical legacy, one of my main objectives will have been realised.

Any description of music, however erudite, is a poor substitute for listening to it. Accordingly, I have avoided lengthy descriptions of Harriott's compositions and performance. I hope, if you are not already familiar with the wonderful music Joe Harriott left us, that you will have the opportunity to make your own response to it. Sadly not all of his great recordings have been reissued. *Southern Horizons*, *Movement*, *High Spirits* and *Hum Dono* remain serious omissions from his catalogue.

1.

very much taken with his instrument

That Joe Harriott's origins are extremely sketchy is in no small way due to the man himself. He shed no light on his background throughout his time in Britain and actively avoided the subject even among his closest friends, many of whom had no idea he had been raised in an orphanage. The information I have about his life in Jamaica comes largely from Joe's sister, his brother and a daughter.

Joseph Arthurlin Harriott was born in Kingston, Jamaica on 15 July 1928. His middle name was formed by adding an appendage to his maternal uncle Arthur's name. His brother Ivanhoe's name was similarly formed from that of his paternal uncle, Ivan. 'They made mine Ivanhoe so I would be different,' Ivanhoe explained. 'We stayed at 3 Diagular Road, in East Kingston, off Windward Road, which was a major road. Going in one direction it took you out to the suburbs and the countryside. In the other, it took you to [the parish of] St Thomas.'[1]

Joe's mother, Muriel Scarlett, was born in Panama and he was the eldest of her four children. His birth was followed at two yearly intervals by those of Theresa Josephine, Ivanhoe Valentine and Velma. Joe and Theresa shared a darker skin tone than their siblings. Joe retained a special affection for her and in adult life was more likely to speak of her than any other family member. Tragically, Theresa contracted polio and died aged twenty-four.[2] Of his father, Ivanhoe told me, 'I didn't know my father's real first name. Everyone called him by a nickname, 'Rafael'. Rafael Garfield Harriott he was called. He was never there.' Velma, basing her comments on family photographs, added: 'My mother was dark. Rafael was a very tall black man with a lighter complexion.'[3]

Trumpeter Dizzy Reece, also from Jamaica and a close associate of Harriott in later years, suggested that Joe's ancestry might be found somewhere other than Kingston. He told me he thought it likely that Joe's origins were in the parish of Clarendon,[4] citing many Reece and Harriott families associated with the area. He mentioned that he knew of at least one relative, Chester Harriott, the father of television chef Ainsley. Chester played piano and sang, later settling in England. Though Chester told me he believed Joe and he were cousins, there is considerable doubt that they were. Val Wilmer, whose knowledge of West Indian musicians is unparalleled, has written that she found no evidence linking them. Research by the BBC into Ainsley's ancestry for the television programme *Who Do You Think You Are?* followed a separate thread entirely. Had there been a connection to Joe it seems unlikely that it would have gone unnoticed or passed without mention.[5]

After Joe's father died, his mother, now with a new partner whose surname was Gray, became pregnant with her fourth child, Velma. Velma told me: 'My Mum died. When I was three weeks old she passed on. She was a Catholic. On her dying bed she told her sister to look after us girls. She left the two boys for the Catholics to look after.'[6] This must have been in 1934, some four years before Joe entered the Alpha School which was run by Catholic nuns. The intervening years are unaccounted for although it seems certain that he and Ivanhoe were separated.

Ivanhoe knew that his mother died in her twenties. 'Some fever – nobody told me the details. The government took I and Joe to the Sisters of Mercy and my mum's sister took the two girls, Theresa and Velma. She kept them and clothed them.' He added that, although he too entered the Alpha Home, he did so four or five years after Joe first went there. Ivanhoe was first sent to Maxfield Park Children's Home which catered for younger boys.

Sister Susan Frazer, now the Director of the Alpha Boys' School in Kingston, confirmed that Joe entered the register of the school on 6 July 1938, just over a week before his tenth birthday.7 Run by the Sisters of Mercy, the school and orphanage in South Camp Road provided a complete environment for the boys. Alpha School's concentration on music has been so consistent and successful that, since its founding in the late nineteenth century, it has produced many first class musicians of international reputation. While prior events no doubt left their mark on Joe's personality, the move to Alpha shaped the course of his life.

When Ivanhoe first arrived at the school, Joe was already dedicated to his music. 'We were never close. He was so busy with his instrument all the time. If you wanna find Joe, you listened for the music. He didn't play games like the others. He only would be perfecting his music.

'Everything was done by ringing a bell. To wake you up, they rang a bell. Breakfast, they rang a bell. Devotion, they rang a bell. I used to hear those bells all the time.' He admitted, 'I was a pain in the ass. I ran away and they brought me back. I went to the country, to my aunt's, but they were frightened they'd be prosecuted. They talked to a policeman and he told them that it would be better if I went back and I did. After a couple of years they [his aunt and uncle] came and got me.'8

Although Ivanhoe did not complain to me about his time at the school, his niece Pauline said that the boys 'were treated very badly. Joe would be more easy-going and had it easier because they realised he was good at music. His younger brother fared worse than Joe. He was more stubborn. They beat Uncle more than Joe.'9

Sister Mary Ignatius Davies, generally known as Sister Ignatius, was a seventeen-year-old novice nun with the Sisters of Mercy the day Joe was passed into their care. She described the climate of the school: 'Musicians have usually benefited from the principles and dedication imparted under the most rigorous disciplinary conditions.'

For many generations of deprived and often orphaned boys,

Alpha offered a route out of poverty and an alternative lifestyle to that of crime. Careers beckoned in orchestras and bands of all kinds. It must be said, however, that anyone seeking to further a career in classical or jazz music would have found it impossible to do so without leaving Jamaica. In the words of the Sister: 'The music in Jamaica was very poor, but the school, it inspired them.'[10] Of that, there is no doubt. From music tuition at Alpha came brilliant musicians like Tommy McCook and Don Drummond, the originators of Ska, recognised as Jamaica's own music and the forerunner of reggae.

The Alpha Boys' Band, formed in 1892 as a drum and fife corps, is described in the school's current information leaflet as, 'a seed hidden in the soil of Jamaica. Who could have visualised that that seed would have grown into the sturdy tree that the band is today?' The first band members played by ear as it was beyond the school's finances to employ a bandmaster. In 1908, brass instruments were obtained through the efforts of a Bishop Collins and the brass section was arranged by Sergeant Kniff of the West India Regiment. From then on, the school benefited from the growing base of trained pupil musicians available to return as tutors. Today there are three major bands on the island: military, regimental and constabulary, and former Alpha brass band members provide the backbone of each one. The Alpha band is an integral part of the musical culture of Jamaica.

'The Alpha is the best school in the world for boys from poor families,' attested trumpeter Eddie 'Tan Tan' Thornton, who arrived at the school as, in his own words, 'a bad boy'. The personal focus for his gratitude was Sister Ignatius, for whom he transformed himself. 'She give me confidence. I was her number one guy.' The Sister had what would now be termed good interpersonal skills. Whatever the demerits of some other members of staff all those years ago, speaking to her in recent years, I felt she exuded gentleness and generosity. Eddie remembered her with affection: 'You meet her, you fall in love with her.' Dizzy Reece went as far as to describe her as 'sexy'.[11]

Sister Ignatius eventually became head of the school and held the position for many years until her death in February 2003.

Within a short time of his arrival at Alpha, Joe began learning the clarinet under the tuition of bandmaster Vincent Tullock, a past student of the school. Tullock was strict but effective. Sister Ignatius thought 'he was very good and saw that the boys got on. They were poor but there was more respect than today and they really wanted to make something of themselves. It's easier today. Life was harder then.'

She remembered Joe clearly. 'He was very neat, tidy. A quiet fellow. He didn't come tall. When he was sixteen he started to grow tall. He did play cricket. Everybody played cricket in Jamaica then. He was not much taken with sport but very much taken with his instrument. He would practise and practise.'[12] Band practices were held each weekday evening and an incentive for some boys in learning an instrument might well have been that it allowed them to escape from cleaning toilets or kitchen chores. On Sundays the boys were often assembled to play at functions in the local community.

From around the age of eleven Velma eagerly attended concerts whenever Joe appeared with the Alpha Boys' Band. 'He used to come to the Catholic Fair and played in a churchyard with a music stand. He went all over the country to play music and people came from all over to hear Joe. We used to look for him.'[13]

In addition to musical tuition, the boys received vocational training. Eddie 'Tan Tan' Thornton told me that Joe learned printing and bookbinding each afternoon and showed a particular talent in the latter. Eddie knew that Joe's natural ability and his total application to music meant it was unlikely he would ever use his bookbinding skills. 'Joe was number one guy for study. He was very intelligent. He could have gone to college or university.'[14] Velma agreed: 'Everything he did, he did well. The Alpha bandmaster sent his son to Joe to learn. He said about Joe: "It was a gift."'[15]

The boys' musical education was thorough. They learned theory, composition and arrangement through the study of the classics. In his teens Joe took up tenor and baritone saxophone, finally beginning to specialise on alto sax. He told Val Wilmer: 'There were maybe eight or ten of us, and I was the one who started teaching them to play because I was the senior in the band. We used to get all the stock arrangements in the Swing Series, things by people like Lionel Hampton and Benny Goodman.'[16]

The young musicians had a voracious appetite for American jazz. Alphonso Son Reece, two years Joe's junior and soon to be known to everyone as 'Dizzy', was the son of a former silent film pianist. Dizzy's first instrument was baritone horn at eleven years of age, switching to trumpet at fourteen. He recalled that: 'There was quite a lot of jazz in Kingston and a lot of good musicians. There were plenty of records too. I listened to everybody and went through all the periods.'[17]

Just as Joe found himself teaching saxophone to Harold McNair[18] who would later become known as a fine jazz instrumentalist, Dizzy passed on his trumpet knowledge to younger pupils like Eddie Thornton. 'Dizzy and Joe were two good friends,' said Eddie. 'Very tight.'[19]

Sister Ignatius recalled Joe playing in the Carlyle Henriques band when he was about fifteen. She remembered that at sixteen he experienced a spurt in growth, acquiring his tall, lean build in his final year at Alpha. In 1945, seven years to the day after he arrived at the school, he left and began making his living playing music at every available opportunity. Keen to learn, he continued to study classical music and played with a local symphony orchestra as well as dance bands. His first professional jobs were with Jack Brown's swing band and Eric Deans' big band. Velma said, 'Eric Deans was an outstanding music man. Joe joined him but he wasn't properly paid. I think some English musician heard him and told him he should come to Britain.'

This may have planted a seed that grew in Joe's mind. Both bandleaders played swing in the styles of Glenn Miller and Count Basie and would eventually leave Jamaica: Brown for New York and Deans settling in Manchester. Harriott was a committed Charlie Parker disciple by this time, and adept at producing Parker-like lines played at breakneck pace. In 1948 he worked with the Jamaican All Stars. A year later, tenor saxophonist Andy Hamilton, then leading the Silvershine Band in Jamaica, invited the young Joe to join his band and stay with him in Port Antonio, some sixty miles from Kingston. 'He didn't have his own saxophone at that time but he was a very good musician.'[20]

London-based baritone saxophonist, Harry Klein, told me that in either 1949 or 1950, 'I was on the *Mauretania* in the ship's band and we went to Kingston, Jamaica. The passengers were a lot of wealthy people and we were invited ashore with them for a function at the Myrtle Bank Hotel where a five or six piece marching band provided the music. When I met Joe later in Britain I said, "I saw you playing in a marching band." He said, "It wasn't me."'

But Harry remained convinced that it had been Joe. 'I believe he thought being in a marching band was demeaning, beneath him.'[21] Sometime in 1950, bandleader and trumpeter Sonny Bradshaw first met Sister Ignatius. He was forming a seven piece band and needing a sax player. She told him she knew the perfect person and arranged for him to meet Joe Harriott. Sonny paid tribute to the Sister after her death. 'She had the sense of being able to spot the musician in the young boy and spotting talent. We didn't have a school of music then. Alpha was the School of Music.'[22]

Ivanhoe Harriott recalled that Joe also played keyboard, clarinet and guitar. 'He could play anything, but the saxophone was the love of his life. Joe would go to Sonny's house rehearsing so many hours. To me it seemed really boring.' Sonny significantly influenced Joe. 'He sorta directed him,' Ivanhoe said.[23]

In fact, Bradshaw was the person most responsible for introducing Harriott to jazz arrangements: he played them in Sonny's band in which the musicians wore Dizzy Gillespie berets and cream serge suits. Sonny himself remembered that Joe 'left Alpha and came straight to me. He had to play my arrangements with the Sonny Bradshaw Seven. I had to write every damn thing. We did progressive arrangements based on American recordings. Joe, Herman Wilson on trombone and myself on trumpet formed the front line. We were together for some time. We had a car that seven of us travelled in with the string bass strapped on top. We played all over Jamaica. Jazz was the dance music of the time.

'When Ozzie Da Costa approached me to [let him] take Joe and Herman with his band to Europe, I gave him permission because it was a good opportunity for them. And it proved to be so, because they never came back.'[24] But although Joe did not return after leaving Jamaica he never forgot his debt to Sonny. Throughout each turn of his career he would send him copies of his recordings.[25]

Andy Hamilton recalled: 'When Harriott was back home he used to have a big following as a young man. He was slim with a long neck and he always smile and, you know, his playing! When he plays a saxophone is like he is telling a story. So we all listen to what he is doing. He got something, that's all. He built himself.'[26]

Jamaicans, like other citizens of the new British Common-wealth, had played their part in winning the war against fascism and from 1948 West Indians were specifically targeted and encouraged by the British Government to come and help rebuild the country. The Labour Government had been elect-ed in 1945 with a radical manifesto that promised more equali-ty in 'a land fit for heroes'. The new National Health Service and the trains and buses of Britain's public transport required a huge injection of labour as well as investment.

For West Indians the attraction was purely financial. With high unemployment in Jamaica, Britain offered work and seemed to promise a standard of living unattainable at home. With affordable sea passage provided, thousands of West Indians accepted the invitation, some naively expecting utopia. The former troopship *S.S. Windrush,* advertised as sailing 'about 23rd May 1948', offered Cabin Class accommodation at £43 and Troopdeck at £28. Embarking on a journey hindered by engine problems, Dizzy Reece and calypso vocalist Lord Kitchener were among eighteen *Windrush* passengers listing 'musician' as their occupation.[27]

That many passengers were unprepared for the reality of life in Britain was shown by the clothing worn by some, more suited to the tropics than the temperate English weather. But another factor was even less welcoming than the weather. Racial discrimination, largely unchecked by law, met them soon after arrival. As *Windrush* passenger John Richards put it, 'They tell you it is the mother country, you're all welcome, you all British. When you come here you realise you're a foreigner and that's all there is to it.'[28] Finding rented accommodation was a major source of grief and British West Indians were often faced with 'No Blacks' statements in property advertisements. For black musicians, the prospect of 'life on the road' placed them in the unenviable position of continually meeting discrimination as they sought accommodation.

But, by 1950, Dizzy Reece was thriving, finding work plentiful in London and on the European scene where he often played with visiting American jazzmen of the calibre of tenorist Don Byas and pianist Walter Bishop. Around that time, Joe Harriott, realising his earnings from music would be severely restricted if he remained in Jamaica, decided that he too would pursue a musical career in Britain. With a Jamaican passport it was easier to come to Britain than America, perhaps the more obvious choice for a jazz musician. It has been said that, once he had decided on the move, he began to save money for it, even undertaking menial work including washing dishes in restaurants. But Eddie Thornton was dismissive of this story. 'Joe would never wash dishes. He was too proud.'[29]

Around the same time, Ivanhoe Harriott moved from his aunt's home to stay with Joe, now living with a young woman called Edith Grant. 'That was when the pregnancy occurred,' Ivan told me. Joe Harriott became a father when Edith gave birth to a girl, whom they named Pauline Theresa. In a peculiar coincidence, one of the first nurses to speak to Edith after the birth of her daughter turned out to be Joe's sister, Theresa.

When Edith discovered that the trainee nurse's name was Theresa Harriott she asked, 'Do you have a brother who is a musician?' Theresa quickly realised that the baby girl bearing two of her names was her brother's daughter. Looking back on it years later, Velma saw divine forces at work. 'That's how God worked that we would have Pauline to look after.'

Despite the arrival of a new family around him, when an opportunity to travel to Europe came his way, Joe seized it. He was invited by pianist and singer Ozzie Da Costa to join his band, which was bound for Germany to play for U.S. servicemen stationed there.[30]

When Joe left Jamaica behind, he bade farewell to Edith and his thirteen-month-old daughter, Pauline. Speaking of the relationship between Joe and Edith, Pauline told me, 'They weren't married, but they were very close. They met at the school gates. She was seventeen. I have love letters she got from him. But I'm not letting you see them! My mum was upset by him. She waited on him six or seven years.'[31] Velma, too, felt abandoned by her oldest brother. 'He told my aunt he was going. He did and he just forget about us. He went and we were just forgotten. Eleven years after he left he started to send Ivan and me money. Then nothing again.'[32]

Pauline, however, did not grow up feeling resentful. She drew positive conclusions from the episode. 'As I was brought up, I was always aware of my father. My uncle and the others in the family called him "Honey". That was the name they always called him by. It was always, "If Honey knew you was climbing that tree," and so on. He told my mother he didn't want me coming over to live in Britain because it wasn't a nice place to be growing up in, with racism and everything. He wanted me to remain in Jamaica.'

The story that Joe had won a scholarship to go to America or Britain was common currency in Jamaica around the time he left and Pauline grew up believing it. As well as love letters to Edith, Joe would send regular postal orders made out to Pauline around 1955 and 1956. 'My mother would take me down to the post office and lift me up to the counter. This was my father's way of making sure I would have to learn to write my name so I would get my presents. As a little girl I loved my little clothes, painted shoes and little bag.'33 Another sign of Joe's desire to influence his daughter was the music lessons he paid for. The piano tuition was eventually terminated, Pauline believes by her mother, possibly in reaction to realising that Joe was never going to return, or because the payments dried up.

When Edith herself decided to begin a new life in Britain, Pauline was brought up by Joe's female cousin, Verica Watkis McLeod, where she was surrounded by the comfortable lifestyle of a woman who was a midwife and dispensed medicines. 'I was brought up with three maids in the house,' said Pauline. 'I had a very happy childhood. I had a pet goat, Gregory, and a pet cow, which used to try to come in the house. There was a special tree I used to climb, where I would sit surrounded by mangoes, fascinated by birds' nests, ignoring the shouts of "Pauline!" from my aunt. She would say, "I'm going to make a tape of me shouting your name and let it play and play and play."

'I usually played with the banker's children, and the matron's children. Each Monday morning we waited for the school bus at 6 a.m. to take us to school where we stayed until Friday at 12 noon. After that we could go swimming in the Milk River baths where the water came from the rocks with healing powers. Anything good I have about me, I got from that time. My father wanted me to go and live with them. He wanted me to have that lifestyle. They all thought the world of "Honey" and I knew I was loved.'34

Pauline stayed at the McLeod household until her mother Edith, who had since married, decided that life in Britain would be best for her daughter. At the age of thirteen, Pauline joined her mother in London.

From that time it was clear that life was going to be different. As she struggled with laden bags on a shopping trip she complained at the weight, only to be given a reality check by her mother. 'We don't have no maids here!'

2.

the London scene 1951

An early morning flight from Kingston touched down in Miami and was followed an hour and a half later by a second flight on to New Jersey. There the Ozzie Da Costa band members were accommodated in some style in spacious hotel rooms for their overnight stay. Then, on 14 May 1951, they embarked aboard a liner carrying holidaymakers, business people and students coming to study in Britain. After sailing for seven or eight days during which the musicians played some hour-long concerts, the ship called in at Cork. Here they were given a tour of the Irish city, for most of them their first experience of Europe. After sailing on to Southampton they made their way to London. As fate would have it, the Da Costa band's stay in the capital was extended while travel documents were applied for and the paper work processed.[1]

Hearing of Joe Harriott's arrival, Dizzy Reece quickly made contact and took him round everywhere – an ideal introduction from one who'd made his own London debut three years earlier. Sitting in with London jazz bands whenever the opportunity arose, Joe began drawing much favourable attention from Ronnie Scott and other modern jazz musicians in London. He withdrew from the planned trip to Germany, risking opprobrium from other Da Costa band members when he opted to stay behind. Da Costa himself no doubt felt Joe showed a lack of principle in doing this, given that the German engagement he reneged on had been the means of his passage to England. But Harriott had been quickly convinced that he should make his stay in Britain permanent and was eager to capitalise on the immediate impact he had made on the scene.

I

In the many interviews I conducted, the widespread opinion was that Joe had done all the necessary groundwork to equip himself as a top instrumentalist by the time he came to Britain. Apart from this preparedness, he always had the energy and inclination to play unpaid jam sessions that would regularly go on well into the early hours of the morning. He connected with people on the bandstand with more ease and satisfaction than he generally did off it. Setting time aside for daily practice was not for Joe. The hours of solitude others spent on scales and arpeggios had little appeal for him and anyway, he didn't need it. His technique was without peer on alto saxophone. But if he entertained the idea that his mastery of the instrument would secure him a comfortable living, he was guilty of an entirely unfounded optimism.

The hottest jazz music of the immediate post-war years was bebop. Its heroes were Dizzy Gillespie, Charlie Parker, Bud Powell and the highly individual pianist, Thelonious Monk. Bebop's epicentre was New York City. This new jazz form had some followers in Britain but the greatest barrier in the UK to much wider promotion of bebop was the British Musicians' Union edict restricting appearances by American artists. This had been introduced in response to the protectionist action of their US counterparts which had dated from the Depression. Performance licences were restricted for all foreigners and only issued on a reciprocal basis.

On one occasion this reciprocity allowed the Ted Heath Orchestra to visit the States while Stan Kenton's band played to British audiences. But the plain fact was that the American public was hardly salivating at the prospect of an influx of British dance bands.

In reality the arrangement meant UK musicians had only two alternatives if they wanted to hear the new bebop music. Occasionally, imported 78 records could be bought in London's specialist record shops. But to hear jazz live was, of course, the ideal. Many British musicians made it to New York's jazz clubs by plying their trade in dance bands on board transatlantic liners like the *Queen Mary*. The nickname they adopted was

'Geraldo's Navy', after the bandleader who arranged bookings of musicians for the Cunard liners. Four of these 'sailors' were future musical associates of Joe's: Bill Le Sage, Tony Kinsey, Ronnie Scott and Benny Green. Within as short a time as possible after disembarking, the British musicians would be ensconced in a jazz club, taking in, along with the cigarette smoke, the potent sound of bebop.

On British soil, Joe's first work was with Pete Pitterson's band, which also played bebop. Born in Kingston seven years before Joe, Pitterson was a fine jazz trumpeter. Like most jazz musicians in the 1940s he had depended on employment with dance bands, like those of Ivor Kirchin, Vic Lewis and Tommy Sampson, for his main income. Working for Pitterson proved fortunate for Joe as the trumpeter gave him the benefit of his experience, advising him on how best to further his career.[2]

Pitterson's drummer, Tommy Jones, remembered the first concert Harriott played on British soil at the Conway Hall in Holborn, London: 'We were the first black band to play bebop. We played on a Sunday. That was the first time Joe played out for the public: it was reported in the *Melody Maker*.'[3]

Around this time, Joe visited the Sunset Club in London's Carnaby Street, a haunt of Jamaican musicians, and it was there that he encountered for the first time his namesake, the pianist and singer Chester Harriott. Chester had come to Britain after winning a scholarship to study music at Trinity College, London. Although their paths would rarely cross, they played together at the club.[4]

In late August 1951, drummer Laurie Morgan was travelling home on a Saturday late-night bus when he met Jamaican trumpeter 'Bushy' Thompson. Thompson was keen that Morgan should take in the playing of a recently arrived Jamaican altoist who would be at the Sunset Club the following day. 'I went the following afternoon,' said Laurie, 'and was knocked out by him. I took him down to Feldman's and it was there he really took off. He never spoke to me again, and our paths didn't cross. He'd have made it without me, but I was the one who got him started, I suppose.'[5]

On 26 August, billed as a 'new arrival', Joe sat in with other British musicians at the Feldman Club in the basement of 100 Oxford Street. Soon to be known as the 100 Club, it was home at that time to the younger, modernist persuasion of UK jazzmen. In wartime, when it was called Mack's Restaurant, the venue had been a certified air raid shelter. On the club's opening night, 24 October 1942, the advertising read, 'Forget the Doodle bug – Come and Jitterbug at the Feldman Club'. Bill Le Sage, who often played there, described its origins: 'Old Man Feldman started up a Sunday night club there, mainly for his sons – Victor and his two brothers. Carlo Krahmer, who started the Esquire label later, was there on drums and Tommy Bromley on bass.'[6] Feldman senior saw the club as a showcase for his sons: Robert on clarinet, Monty on accordion and Victor, also known as 'Kid Krupa', a child prodigy on drums, vibes and piano. For the abundantly talented Victor, certainly, it had delivered the prominence he merited and Harriott's appearances, too, impressed many people including Krahmer.

As in the case of every bebop alto sax player of the time, Joe's debt to Charlie Parker was evident. Val Wilmer later recorded Harriott's reflections on his 'debut': 'I don't suppose I was playing as well as I could. I expect it was partly true to say I sounded like Parker, but you can't play *like* him.'[7]

The impression he made was obviously favourable enough. Within a week he was a member of bassist Joe Mudele's sextet where he remained for over a year. Mudele told me: 'We were playing in a place run by Rik Gunnell.' (This may have been the Two Way Club, so named because of Gunnell's attempt to bring traditionalists and modernists together under one roof. It shared the same address as Feldman's.) 'There was Joe [and] a black trumpeter who used to play with Ted Heath and Honey Brown was singing. [Gunnell's Club] didn't last long.'[8]

Gunnell was a colourful character. Formerly a Smithfield meat market porter and ex-boxer, he was an opportunistic wheeler and dealer. It was said he didn't even like jazz but enjoyed the 'ambience' jazz clubs offered. Many of the clubs associated with him were, like the Two-Way Club and the later Club Basie and Blue Room, short-lived. He had much more success with his Flamingo Club all-night sessions.[9]

Joe was much impressed by some of Mudele's musical experiences. The bassist told me, 'this is no big thing ... but when I played the Club Eleven in the original Dankworth Seven we went for a week to Paris in 1949 to hear Charlie Parker and Miles Davis. They were playing at the Salle Pleyel and used to go jamming at the Club St. Germain. One night I played 'Cherokee' and 'Out of Nowhere' with Charlie Parker. This made a big impression on Joe. He would often mention it.'

Harriott raised his profile by performing in public at every opportunity. This extended to playing New Orleans jazz as well as bebop. He may have been unaware of the violent antipathy between many followers of these musical styles. For musicians to move between one style and the other was not at all a common practice. Joe and Welsh pianist Dill Jones were rarities in that they enjoyed playing in both modernist and New Orleans ensembles. Drummer Tommy Jones remembered a traditional jazz night in 1953 at the Royal Festival Hall. The event was one of Harold Pendleton's early forays into concert promotion. A clearly bemused Pendleton saw the two modernist namesakes, Tommy and Dill, take the stage with an otherwise traditional line-up. 'What are you doing here?' he asked them. But there was nothing incongruous about their participation when they began to play.[10]

Trumpeter Mick Mulligan's band was of the New Orleans persuasion and on Tuesday nights Joe often sat in with them in a dive called the Club Faubourg in Old Compton Street in Soho. Mulligan's vocalist, George Melly, remembers this era when some patrons could not tell the difference between racist abuse and harmless fun. A city publican, 'an enormous fat man with the sensitivity of a rhinoceros,' frequently turned up at clubs where Melly and the band happened to be playing. One night he staggered into Le Metro, while Harriott was sitting in with them. 'As soon as the guv'nor's eyes focused enough for him to realise that it was 'un homme de couleur' who was taking the chorus, he leapt up and capered across the front of the stand shouting, "Walla! Walla! Walla!" Joe didn't bat an eyelid.'[11]

But Harriott was certainly hurt and angered by racial abuse. Mulligan recalled, 'I remember him being very sensitive about colour. You had to say 'coloured' then. The term 'black' wasn't used. If you did use it, it caused offence.' Ian Croal was a bass-playing student in Edinburgh when he met Harriott in 1961. He recalled the bitterness in Joe's voice as he reflected on events ten years before: 'When I came over on holiday people welcomed me but the mood changed when I decided to stay.'[12]

During the sixties, at a jazz and poetry event, Harriott mentioned to poet John Smith that he was thinking of uprooting and going to live in Switzerland, a country he had been highly impressed with while on tour. The Swiss he met had never seen a Jamaican before. Smith suggested that Joe would find himself treated an equal. His instant response was: 'I don't want to be equal. I want to be superior.'[13]

He continued to do gigs with New Orleans and blues bands, as well as in his preferred medium of modern jazz. 'At that time Joe was just hustling around to get on the scene,' said Frank Holder, who was then a singer and percussionist with the Johnny Dankworth Seven. 'Joe had arrived and he wasn't long in the country. I don't know who booked it, but he was booked to play opposite the Dankworth Seven. The job was in High Holborn at the Holborn Hall, or something like that. But Joe came on and exploded! For a moment you would think that he blew John into the ground because this guy came with such a different approach. That was the first time I met Joe.'[14]

Coleridge Goode recalled the first time he heard Harriott. 'It was 1951 at a concert in the King's Cross area [St Pancras Town Hall]. I was with Tito Burns' band, the leading group there.' The band Joe was with played in the interval. 'He was quite outstanding. The influence of Charlie Parker was in his playing. It was always there. It never left him.'[15]

In Harriott's playing though, there was much more than imitation. His chosen instrument allows the individuality of the player to shine through. As Dave Gelly states in his book *Masters of the Jazz Saxophone*, 'a saxophone can sound virtually any way the player wants it to.' He quotes the *Harvard Dictionary of Music*: 'Being intermediate between the timbres of wood and brass, it may pass from the softness of the flute to the broad, mellow tone of the cello to the metallic strength of the cornet.' Gelly, an accomplished saxophonist himself, explains: 'It was jazz which discovered the truly magical quality concealed inside the saxophone: that it resembled the human voice. A voice expresses the style, mood, origins, age and all-round personality of its owner, and the same is true of the jazz saxophone.'[16] Harriott's associates would very often attest to the truth of that in his case. His saxophone sound was instantly recognisable and the true voice of the man.

While his playing revealed his roots in the Caribbean, his style from the early days had a fiery quality apparent to every serious listener. From the very beginning his music was invested with passion, carrying more than a suggestion of inner turmoil. Harriott made it clear that this 'voice' was unalterably his own. 'I try to think for myself and to put my own stamp on my playing but it is hard to escape your environment. The players who have really evolved styles of their own are the first and last words on their subject.'[17] Joe's stamp was firmly indented.

Tall, lean and debonair in appearance, he was very straight-backed and had a grace in movement which was complemented by his mannerliness. In keeping with the accepted notion of what a professional musician should wear, Harriott favoured a well-cut suit, often dark brown in the fifties but invariably dark blue or black in later years. He always wore a smart white shirt and dark tie and often sported a folded handkerchief in his breast pocket. Saxophonist Ken Baxter, who became a good friend to Harriott in the late fifties, remembered him looking at his most impressive in the white jacket that he occasionally wore.[18] He was scrupulous about keeping his hair short. His beard and narrow moustache were always neatly trimmed. A lit cigarette was a virtually permanent feature.

Andy Hamilton remembered that Joe liked to smoke cigarettes a lot. 'I don't mean drugs. He's a very clean fellow. When one is out, another one in.'[19] Even when he was playing, he would often find a way to attach his cigarette to his saxophone so that it was available for immediate access during someone else's solo.

In a surprise decision, the Ministry of Labour granted permits to two American and two European musicians to appear in concerts organised by the National Federation of Jazz Organisations at London's Royal Festival Hall in 1952. The Americans, who would perform in a traditional jazz and blues concert on 28 June, were blues guitarist and singer Lonnie Johnson and pianist Ralph Sutton. For the modern jazz concert two days later, the NFJO had invited trumpeter/pianist Rob Pronk from Holland and Swedish altoist Arne Domnérus. British musicians would provide support.

The fallout was immediate from the Musicians' Union. Despite the fact that advertising, including press announcements, had gone ahead and that Lonnie Johnson was lined up for a nationwide tour, the MU banned any of its members from taking part in either concert. Hostility against their Union's policy was widespread among jazz musicians but most would not countenance disobeying a Union directive. A number of British-based musicians, however, did risk notoriety in supporting the banned concerts. Two prominent 'blacklegs' were Joe Harriott and the drummer from Kenny Graham's Afro-Cubists, Dickie De Vere. With a brace of names to choose from (his real one was Paul Rainberg), Dickie appeared that night as Buddy Reece.[20]

Cab Kaye and his Cabinettes opened the second half of the 'modern' concert. When Kaye spoke to *Melody Maker* shortly before the concert he seemed relaxed about the politics of the evening. Wearing a singlet and munching gooseberries, he was sure that the stance taken by Joe, De Vere and himself was correct. 'We've all had some great jobs in Holland and Sweden. We ought to show some hospitality to these men in return.' Pianist Tommy Pollard added his support, 'We've played in their countries. Surely it's not too much to let just two fellows in as artists.'[21]

As one of the Cabinettes that night, Harriott was among some familiar faces: Dizzy Reece, tenorist Sammy Walker and drummer Tony Crombie. Their 'rumbustious' performance was well received with cheers ringing out above the applause. However, not everyone was enthusiastic. According to *Melody Maker* reviewer Mike Nevard, Joe didn't have a chance to shine as the performance was, 'more like cabaret stuff; bubbling vocals, with solos kept to the minimum.'[22]

There were ramifications later when Humphrey Lyttelton, a pillar of the British jazz scene, announced his resignation from the NFJO. This protest, in response to the organisation's breaching of Musicians' Union policy, induced other British musicians to follow suit. Lyttleton supported his Union even though he was, personally, deeply unhappy with the ban on foreign artists. Indeed, three years earlier, in 1949, he had decided that he would be prepared to go to jail rather than miss the chance to play with Sidney Bechet when Bechet visited London that year.[23]

A week after the concerts, the MU still threatened action against Harriott and other members deemed to have acted against Union instructions. Significantly though, the Union's general secretary, Hardie Ratcliffe, seemed to be retraining his sites on targets other than the participating musicians: 'The whole trouble resulted from failure of the National Federation of Jazz Organisations, and the Ministry of Labour, to consult the Union.... The NFJO entirely ignored the Union until June 25, when only a few days before the [first] concert, they admitted an error by expressing deepest regret that previous contact with the Union had not been made.'[24] The story then drifted from the front pages of the music press and no punitive action seems to have been taken against Joe, Dill Jones, Dizzy Reece or anyone else who performed at the concerts.

*

A significant event on the London music scene took place on Sunday 31 August 1952 when Coventry Street's luxurious Mapleton Restaurant opened a jazz club in its basement. 'Jazz at the Flamingo' was born when Jeff Kruger and his father Sam, who had been organising Jewish dances there, decided it would make a great jazz venue. The new club began with the Johnny Dankworth Seven and a reformed Kenny Graham's Afro-Cubists on the bill and *Jazz Journal* described the opening as one that would be long remembered. 'No fewer than 1,500 fans queued for hours in the hope of admission. Some forty policemen and three walkie-talkie sets were called into action to control the crowds.' The club soon built up 'an enviable reputation for good jazz in the most comfortable and deluxe surroundings the average fan has ever experienced.'[25]

The comfort seems debatable because *Melody Maker* gave a very different report of the opening night. 'Inside, the atmosphere was as torrid as a stoke hole of a ship.... Compere Tony Hall pleaded in vain for the pressing throng to give the band boys breathing space, but, like King Canute, they wouldn't budge an inch. A few hep cats tried to dance; most preferred to stand still.'[26]

Within a short time the 'stoke hole' had a resident band, with a title allowing unlimited changes in the identity or number of the personnel. This was the Jazz at the Flamingo Unit: 'comprising among others, the alto "giant" Joe Harriott, former Club Eleven pianist Tommy Pollard, and young up-and-coming stars like Terry Brown (trumpet) and Benny Green (baritone).'[27] The Flamingo's 'Unit' soon proved so popular that outside engagements beckoned. Following a hugely popular appearance at a Sunday Swing Session at the Lyceum, the band was enlisted to play at the Palladium alongside the Ted Heath band on 15 February 1953.

Joe also played with Dizzy Reece's Headliners, a nine piece band which appeared with Ronnie Scott's group at St Pancras Town Hall on 1 February. Trombonist Chris Barber remembered that, later in 1953, he played with Harriott for the first time, at the Recital Room in the Royal Festival Hall. 'Joe first played with the band when it was Ken Colyer's band. The perceived wisdom was that he wouldn't enjoy it much but he did. Then he guested with us, the Chris Barber band, at odd concerts we did in the Purcell Room where we had a regular series of shows.'[28] Their friendship and musical collaboration continued over the years bringing benefit to both.

A new venue for Harriott in London's West End was the jazz club of the plush Bagatelle Restaurant, which opened in early December 1953. Previously the entertainment had generally been a cabaret. The opening jazz night featured the resident band of Les Baker with his wife, vocalist Joyce Clarke, and during the evening they gave way to guest artists Joe Harriott and Mike McKenzie, a Guyanese pianist who had been in Britain since 1949. In keeping with the formal atmosphere of this venue, Joe and Mike donned dinner jackets and bow ties.[29]

In 1953–54, traditional jazz multi-instrumentalist Dave Keir often enjoyed Joe's company in London when they frequented a Greek restaurant called The Rex in Old Compton Street. Lots of musicians would meet there, including Chris Barber, Humphrey Lyttelton, Monty Sunshine and Lonnie Donegan. The business was run by a Greek Cypriot called Solomon who provided tasty but cheap food accompanied by bouzuki music. 'Joe was probably an introvert' recalled Dave, 'but I always found him a very nice guy.'

Harriott would often talk to Keir about Charlie Parker, who had recently been encouraged by a musical instrument maker to feature a plastic sax called the Grafton Acrylic. 'The body was white or cream with gold key work on it and it was advertised with the slogan, "a tone poem in ivory and gold". The Grafton had advantages in maintenance. The coil springs were less likely to break than straight springs. You could also undo about four screws and all the keys came off. The whole thing could be repadded in about ten minutes. Knowing Joe to be a great Parker fan, I asked him if he didn't fancy one.'

Joe's answer was typically unequivocal, 'No. If I get a bash in mine, I can get it straightened out. If I drop that and it cracks, it's finished.'[30]

3.

building a reputation

In 1954, Harriott made his first record. The EP[1] *Cool Jazz with Joe*, recorded in the second week of February by the Joe Harriott Quartet, featured Dill Jones on piano, Jack Fallon on bass and Phil Seamen on drums.

Two years older than Harriott, Seamen had worked in big bands and already had a substantial reputation. Their careers would be intertwined over many subsequent years. Fallon had arrived in the UK in 1946 with the Canadian Air Force and had made a big impression as a modern-style bassist.

The notes by James Asman for the EP referred to Dill Jones and Joe as 'recognised giants' of British jazz. Unlike most of his jazz contemporaries, Jones enjoyed playing in various settings from blues and barrelhouse to thoughtful modern jazz. The latter was the mode which the Harriott recording required. Asman wrote that Joe's 'declamatory blowing on alto has long since put him in world class.'[2]

He continued to guest with many bands including Britain's first rhythm-and-blues group, led by jazz drummer Tony Crombie, and Kenny Graham's Afro-Cubists. London-born Graham was a talented multi-instrumentalist and an innovative composer-arranger. His band featured Dizzy Reece on trumpet and Joe on alto when it recorded four tracks for Esquire on 27 April 1954. *Jazz Journal* reviewer Alun Morgan preferred the compositions on the Afro-Cubists' earlier *Caribbean Suite* recorded the previous year but liked the coupling of Reece with Harriott.[3]

Word was spreading around the country about Harriott's talent but Joe did not always seem to understand how publicity worked to his benefit. As Harry Klein pointed out, 'the National Jazz Federation helped him to become established, but he was a funny fellow. They put his picture on the cover of *Jazz News* (the NJF's own publication) and he promptly went in and demanded £100 for using his image. They were trying to do him a favour.'[4]

Bassist Spike Heatley was starting out on his musical career in 1954. He played with Harriott in ad hoc groups and in Bill Le Sage's trio. 'One of the places I recall playing with him was the Bull's Head at Barnes. I was a beginner and quite overawed by him. I always seemed to be apologising. Joe said to me: "You've nothing to apologise for. You're a great player." I didn't believe it, of course. He was a very nice man, very considerate. All my memories of Joe recall him like that. I had the highest regard for him.'[5]

Gradually, Harriott made contacts that would stand him in good stead over the next few years. One was with the flamboyant independent record producer, Denis Preston. In the autumn of 1954, Joe was booked to play on a session organised by Preston which produced four 'highlife' tracks destined for the African market. The band, Buddy Pipp's Highlifers, included West Indian and West African musicians and the music was a happy and relaxed result of the meeting of two cultures.

Preston undoubtedly saw great potential in forming a working relationship with Joe as he developed his centre of operations, Lansdowne Recording Studios near London's Notting Hill Gate. At the end of the nineteenth century, the studios had been the workplace of English painters Charles Ricketts and Charles Shannon. In this building, which Preston acquired on borrowed money, he would later produce almost all of Harriott's recorded output as a leader. Preston's wife was West Indian and, apart from his commitment to jazz, he had a special fondness for Jamaican music and made many records featuring Caribbean singers and instrumentalists.

Within the personnel for the Buddy Pipp session were Joe's former employer and adviser Pete Pitterson and English jazzmen Bruce Turner and Tony Kinsey. Pianist Mike McKenzie co-wrote two titles with conga drummer Buddy Pipp.

Jazz writer Roger Cotterrell, on a visit to the Lansdowne Studios in 1974, had the chance to hear these rarities by courtesy of Denis Preston, and thought the vocals 'dire'. An instrumental track, 'Akee Blues', marked Joe's debut as a recorded composer and Cotterrell thought it 'a particularly attractive performance'.[6] A dispute arose over ownership and the masters were destroyed. However, this vintage recording can be heard on the excellent double CD compilation *Killer Joe* featuring many of Joe's recordings from the mid-1950s.

Outwith drummer Tony Kinsey's temporary identity as a member of Buddy Pipp's Highlifers, his trio had been building its own reputation around London: first at Vi Hyland's Studio 51 Club and later through a residency at Jeff Kruger's Flamingo Club. Kruger acted as promoter for many artists who appeared there, arranging gigs for them elsewhere in Britain and abroad. Harriott was one of the musicians who eventually benefited.

In spring 1954, tenor player Tommy Whittle who had been playing with the trio left to form his own band. Kinsey had heard Joe's alto in many Soho jam sessions and invited him to be Whittle's replacement. 'Joe's playing came as a tensed surprise to the fans who had become used to the easier flow of Whittle,' wrote one commentator. 'His alto was often hoarse in its urgency and he presented a strikingly new sound to British jazz.'[7]

Soon after Harriott joined Kinsey, Kruger arranged a prestigious booking for the group at the Paris Jazz Fair. An Anglo-French band exchange meant Michel Attenoux and his orchestra could accept a booking at the Festival Hall in London while Kinsey's men would play at the famous Salle Pleyel concert hall in Paris.[8]

On the flight to France, Kruger found himself seated next to Harriott, who had a terror of flying. He reminisced, 'I had many conversations with Joe – always short and always fragmented and I never learned much about his background. The longest conversation I had was on [that] small plane crossing the English Channel. It was, to say the least, pretty bumpy for a while. Joe let me know in no uncertain terms he did not appreciate this kind of travel and [he asked], in future, would I ensure a smoother passage.'9

Bill Le Sage played piano and vibes in the group and both he and Kinsey were not only technically gifted instrumentalists but also prolific, inventive composers. Both had been members of 'Geraldo's Navy'. Kinsey had learned much about leading groups as a member of the Dankworth Seven. He was shrewd and knew the pitfalls. And as a realist he didn't believe all he read in the music papers: a definite advantage given some reports that related to his group.

'Kinsey Triumph in Paris Leads to Bid for US' read the *Melody Maker* headline on 12 June 1954 following the performance at the Salle Pleyel. An accompanying photograph showed a smiling Joe and Thelonious Monk in relaxed mood with Mary Lou Williams seated behind them. *Melody Maker* enthused over the performance of the Kinsey trio with Harriott on 5 June, as the French celebrated the tenth anniversary of the Allied landings in 1944. 'With less than fifteen minutes at their disposal they went on stage at the Salle Pleyel and conquered the turbulent, iconoclastic patrons of the Third International Salon du Jazz in a manner for which they must receive the congratulations of every British lover of jazz.'

Playing just three short numbers, 'they succeeded in shattering once and for all whatever doubts may still exist on the continent and in America as to Britain's ability to produce modern jazz on a par with that of any other country in the world. There were boos, – yes, but only ... when it was realised that they were not to be allowed to play a fourth number. Equally complete was their success among the international cognoscenti backstage.'10

Dick Edwards, owner of the Ringside Jazz Club in Paris, considered Kinsey 'the answer to his search for the perfect drummer'. The band was also wanted by the Mars Club in Paris and a leading Barcelona hotel. Harriott was offered an Amsterdam concert. But because of the group's commitments at the Flamingo, all these offers had to be turned down.

Inspired by the response to the Kinsey group from international stars like Mary Lou Williams and Gerry Mulligan, Jeff Kruger tried to book the band for the American Jazz Festival on the 17 and 18 July at Newport, Rhode Island. He contacted the festival's producer George Wein and hoped that the Musicians' Union would allow a reciprocal exchange.[11]

The Salle Pleyel performance promised so much in upping the international profile of the band. The Ringside Club was a regular haunt of visiting American jazzmen in Paris and Dick Edwards was keen to book Harriott and the Kinsey trio to play there. He wanted a reciprocal agreement with his own resident group featuring the brilliant Martial Solal, then labelled 'the most promising pianist in Europe'.[12]

The Ringside booking and the visit to the USA failed to materialise but Joe took part in three recording sessions with Kinsey in May, September and December 1954. The tracks, recorded for Esquire, were released as singles and EPs. Bill Le Sage and bassist Sammy Stokes[13] completed the line-up for the sessions. In Le Sage's view, recording with Harriott 'was so good, for everybody. Like all the really great players, Joe was great to work with.' 'Joe was a real catalyst,' Kinsey added. 'A fountainhead. Destined to become a leader – which is what happened.'[14]

Peter Newbrook of Esquire Records[15] remembered the sessions: 'Joe was very professional, inventive, very quick to catch on. A lot of it was improvised. He'd jump right in and know what to do. He reminded me of Dizzy Reece. What was great about Joe was ... he was so excited. He never played 'down'. He was always 'up' when he was playing.'[16]

The 'Tony Kinsey Trio with Joe Harriott' sessions reappeared on a 1987 LP titled *Jump for Me*. But Joe's name now took precedence over Kinsey's, the group being presented on the LP as 'Joe Harriott with the Tony Kinsey Trio'. Kinsey expressed mild annoyance over this revision of history as the group was never billed as such.[17]

In his sleevenotes for *Jump for Me*, Stan Britt wrote that, 'each of the titles allows the listener to appreciate [Harriott's] tremendous gifts as a soloist ... obviously Parker-based' but with 'a style and sound which makes him very much his own man.'

Roland Ramanan commented in a review: 'One of the first things that strikes the listener is the sound that Harriott produces from his instrument. More than just 'good tone' it charges each note he plays with absolute conviction ... Joe's playing clearly inhabits the harmonic terrain of Parker, but there are many beautifully jagged peaks that are purely his own.'[18] The trumpet-playing Roland Ramanan's father was a player of absolute conviction, too. He was Joe's great front line partner of later years, Shake Keane.

In January 1955 *Melody Maker* reported that the Kinsey trio were about to sign a recording contract with Decca and would probably 'accompany [the popular vocalist] Lita Roza on sides to be made in February.' The members of the group, smiling and smoking cigarettes, were pictured in overcoats and mufflers posing inexplicably with a goat on a lead. The accompanying text read: 'The group, in festive mood was just off to play a date in Paris on New Year's Eve.'[19]

Kinsey told me with unconcealed scorn: 'That wasn't in Paris. That was miles the other side of Paris in eastern France! What a journey that was in a van right across France!' By the time they arrived at the gig, the intense cold and the group's far from comfortable van had robbed them of any lingering 'festive mood'.[20]

But opportunities continued to arise. 'Tony Kinsey and his bassist Sammy Stokes have been singled out for the unprecedented honour of accompanying Oscar Peterson and Ella Fitzgerald on their forthcoming tour of Britain,' reported *Melody Maker* in February. 'And as a gesture to the Tony Kinsey Quartet, Harold Fielding, who is presenting the US jazz giants here is lengthening his programme by twelve minutes to give the group its own spot.'[21] Harriott and the Kinsey band expected to appear at ten concerts starting with the Albert Hall on 22 February.

Once again the band was to be disappointed. 'In the event,' Kinsey recalled, 'Norman Granz decided he wouldn't let us play as a group so just Sammy and I did it but I insisted they had to pay the rest of [the band] ... They paid Bill and Joe while Sammy and I went off and worked with [Ella and Oscar].'

This brought another *Melody Maker* headline: 'Norman Granz vetoes Kinsey Four backing Ella Oscar Concert.' Granz insisted that, 'this is not to be construed as detrimental to the Tony Kinsey Group. Rather do I feel that the concerts should remain recitals by my two artists as originally arranged.' To rub salt into the wound, the recording dates with Lita Roza, planned for February, had to be postponed because of the tour.

Tony said of Granz: 'That's what it was like in those days. He was a great person to work for. He was alright with us as well, but for the Americans he was superb to work for. He was a bit of a dictator. He had this vision for his American artists and that was it, you know. British guys had to take second place.'

The *New Musical Express* Poll in January 1955 showed Harriott's increasing popularity with the jazz public. Johnny Dankworth led the alto section with 1582 votes and Harriott was in third place with 286 votes. Kinsey was fourth in the drums section. Joe continued working with Kinsey in the spring of 1955 until illness struck. It was the first instance of what was to become a pattern. A lung infection was diagnosed and Harriott became a patient of Pinewood Sanatorium, a tuberculosis hospital in the Berkshire countryside.

He was back in action by 17 May to record a Decca album *Presenting the Tony Kinsey Quartet*, on which Joe's tour de force, 'Fascinating Rhythm', can be heard. Returning to a number he had recorded with Kenny Graham, he achieves, with apparent ease, a quite staggering pace. This recording makes clear that he was free of any respiratory problems following his illness.

Kinsey recalled this particular number with affection.

'I remember one great event that we had at the Albert Hall. The BBC used to put on a concert every year of the best bands. We had this special arrangement by Bill Le Sage of 'Fascinating Rhythm'. It was great, and really fast. And we just walked across this long stage. The drums were set up and they were announcing the quartet and we just went straight into this rather tricky rhythm. In that place which was so echoey at the time, it was difficult to control fast tempos especially. But never any problem with Joe. He was fantastic.'[22]

On 27 May, Harriott was in the studio again, this time for his own *Joe Harriott with Strings* EP recording, set up by Denis Preston. Thus he became the first British jazz artist to feature on a recording accompanied by strings. Sammy Stokes and Phil Seamen provided familiar support, with Max Harris on piano, and the ballads recorded were 'I'll Remember April' and 'Easy to Love'. Laurie Johnson, later a highly successful TV theme composer and arranger, arranged and directed the six piece string section.

Preston explained: 'This was directly inspired by Norman Granz's Parker with strings recordings, and I thought it an appropriate exercise for an artist so heavily influenced by the legendary Yardbird.' Indeed, he saw himself as the British Norman Granz and enjoyed the comparison, going so far as to tell Max Jones he thought he was a better producer than Granz but obliged to work with lesser musical talents than the American had at his disposal.[23]

But Harriott was not a lesser talent. Preston found from the start that Joe was dedicated to producing his best at every opportunity. 'His approach in the recording studio was always thoroughly professional, and his work never fell below his own high level of competence, and on a good day could be outstandingly exciting.'[24]

A month later, on Tuesday 21 June, Joe recorded another EP, *The Joe Harriott Quartet*, for Preston at Lansdowne Studios, this time for the Columbia label. Phil Seamen, Joe, Max Harris and Sammy Stokes produced a record particularly cherished for the quality of Harriott's ballad playing. Harris, who had few opportunities to work with Joe, found him, 'a delightful man with a good sense of humour. I still listen to that record today. Not to listen to myself, but to listen to Joe.'[25]

Seamen, innovative and much admired, was always Harriott's first choice on drums. He had worked for Nat Gonella in the 1940s and described Nat as a major influence in his becoming so adept in sight-reading at an early stage in his career. 'He was the greatest guy. He was a father to me. Nat made me stay behind after the band rehearsal and practise my parts. If I made a mistake I got a clip round the earhole. Sharp and swift!' This disincentive to make mistakes produced rapid progress. 'We used to get Tommy Dorsey arrangements which had Buddy Rich drum solos written out. Believe you me, if you've ever seen a [written out] Buddy Rich drum solo, it looks like fly shit.'[26]

On the Columbia EP, 'Dicky Bird' is a straightforward Harriott bebop composition and 'My Old Flame' is a beautiful rendition which shows Joe's mastery of the ballad. His tone conveys the sentiment of the song with more than a hint of anguish. The Parkerish, up-tempo 'What is This Thing Called Love' showcases Seamen in a wonderful solo. But the real revelation is the exquisitely tasteful 'Don't Blame Me'. This plaintive ballad has been recorded by many great sax players, but no one does it better than Harriott.

Also in June 1955, Rik Gunnell opened the Americana, an all-night jazz club, at the Flamingo's original home, the Mapleton Restaurant. From midnight until seven in the morning, patrons were guaranteed jazz and cabaret acts for ten shillings (50 pence) inclusive. Appearing on the opening night were Joe and the Eddie Thompson Trio.[27] Thompson had studied at the same school for the blind as George Shearing, who was six years his senior. He was an entertaining pianist whose guide dog would habitually take up residence under the piano as he played.

Joe was fond of him. On one occasion he arrived to play the Flamingo to find Eddie on the stand for the first set with Max duly in position under the piano. Eddie had just started a number without playing the verse. Joe put his sax down, cupped his hands to his mouth and shouted, 'What about the verse?' Eddie laughed, turned and said, 'I know who that is. Hey, Joe!'

The long-envisaged recording of Lita Roza with the Kinsey group finally took place at the end of July. The results were issued on Decca's London label album, *Listening In The After-hours* whose title contrived to produce the mnemonic L-I-T-A. The Liverpool-born singer had a wide fan base. Two years earlier she had had a number one record in Britain with *How Much is That Doggie in the Window*. More significantly for the Kinsey dates, she had strong jazz leanings as her tenure with the Ted Heath Orchestra testified. Her repertoire was drawn from the great American songwriters such as Johnny Mercer, Hoagy Carmichael and Irving Berlin.

Lita said of the album: 'Isn't Joe Harriott marvellous? The record was made in a hurry. Decca were wondering how to use the Kinsey group and they asked me how I felt about recording an album with them. I said, "Great!" I always liked working with small groups and I loved the way Joe Harriott played with such emotion. Some musicians are great technicians but, like some lyrics and tunes do, Joe could bring tears to my eyes the way he played. Behind me, he was just so ... I forget I'm singing when I listen to him. Listening to the records today it's Joe I hear playing. I don't hear the lyrics. It was amazing how mellifluous Joe was. Gorgeous, gorgeous.'[28]

Harriott's solos are attractive but, as this was Roza's date, he is very restrained. On most tracks he breathily caresses the melody and Kinsey uses brushes throughout. Le Sage probably wrote the arrangements and seems certain to have been behind the trademark changing rhythms on 'That Old Black Magic'. Although Tony Middleton correctly asserts in his sleevenotes that singer and band sound as though they have long worked together, the truth is that they met up just for the recording sessions. Thoroughly professional as always, the Kinsey group made an album that exuded style and empathy with the vocalist.

By now, Joe's Kinsey colleagues and others were familiar with some of his quirky ways. Phil Seamen noted Joe's regular misquoting of the RAF sign-off 'Roger and out'. Sharing a cab one night with him, Phil smiled quietly when Joe said 'Roger and Alf' on paying the taxi driver. Seamen adopted the saying and so strengthened Joe's belief that he was using a common idiom. Joe routinely used the expression in his time with Kinsey. Tony said, 'Whether he meant it as a joke or he'd just misheard it, we were never sure, but it used to crease us up every time.' Sammy Stokes couldn't resist asking Joe what it meant. Joe replied with obvious sincerity that it was what RAF pilots said on the radio when they reached the end of what they had to say.

By August 1955, Joe was about to deliver his 'Roger and Alf' message to the Kinsey band. It was time to sign off and seek new musical adventures.

A week before leaving Kinsey to join Ronnie Scott, Joe made another quartet EP called *No Strings* with Lennie Bush[29], Seamen and Harris. Again under Denis Preston's supervision, this time it was made for the Nixa label. Harriott's composition 'Just Goofin'' made its first appearance on record along with the relaxed 'Joe's Blues', a fast 'Just Friends' and the beautiful ballad 'Everything Happens to Me'.

Jazz Journal's reviewer 'P.T.' preferred Joe's up-tempo playing, arguing that at slower tempo, 'one realises the limitations of his style and technique ... Joe has a long way to go before he can be termed anything more than a good performer with a nice feeling for modern jazz plus a good rhythmic attack.'[30] My impression is that Harriott barely gets into his solos here before they end. More flexibility on the recording times would have allowed him to stretch out and play more naturally. Seamen's one drum solo is similarly throttled at birth.

On 29 August 1955, after around eighteen months with Kinsey, Harriott joined Ronnie Scott's newly-formed eighteen piece orchestra. Ronnie commented, 'I admire Joe's playing very much. He should fit in with the new band very well. He will, of course, be strongly featured as a soloist.'[31]

Harriott and the band's baritonist Benny Green soon became good friends. In some small part this was because, while touring, Joe's habitual post-gig all-nighters meant that his room-mate, Green, regularly had a room to himself and a good night's sleep. According to Dominic Green in his biography of his father, 'Benny found [Joe] ... a relaxed, charming companion, showing none of the irascibility for which he was renowned.' Importantly, Benny had a deep respect for Joe's musicianship. With Harriott he felt, 'the rare sensation of true musical exultation which one may experience when playing next to somebody whose trains of musical thought are fresh and exciting. I cannot remember having enjoyed this uplift very many times in my entire career as a musician, but it is a sensation always well worth the waiting.' He named Joe, Ronnie Scott, Tony Crombie, Victor Feldman and Dizzy Reece as the musical associates regularly able to give him this sense of wonder.[32]

'On the many occasions when I had the pleasure of playing alongside him,' Green wrote later, 'I never failed to notice the tremendous physical energy he put into his saxophone playing, the way he would worry over some tiny knotty point of technique, practising hours and days and weeks to overcome it, how ready he was with advice and how eagerly he engaged opinions about the problems of playing the saxophone. In one band in which we worked together I saw him play 'Summertime' almost every night for four months without ever ceasing to admire the surging tone, the flying fingers and the great talent for minting melodic phrases.'[33]

Benny described how he and Joe became familiar with the cellar at 39 Gerrard Street which would become the first of Ronnie Scott's clubs. 'This place had been ... a "near-beer joint" ... owned by small-time thugs. And then it became a taxi driver's haven and then it became a place where you could pick up birds. There were prostitutes working down there. And they used to have a little house piano and Joe Harriott and myself

[went] down there once or twice at one, two o'clock in the morning if we wanted to learn a new tune.... It was a dreadful stinking place. It smelled and there were no facilities. It was just a very nasty hole.'[34]

Scott had scheduled ninety hours of rehearsal time for his new band but knew, as any musician does, that the true potential might be achieved only after being on the road for weeks. Tony Brown in *Melody Maker* described the first rehearsal of Ronnie's big band at Studio X, a large single-roomed wooden building in Dineley's Rehearsal Rooms in Marylebone. Brown highlighted the problems with allusions to childbirth, some probably unintended. 'There are so many problems at the birth of a big band,' ran his headline, seeming to cry out for an epidural rather than celebratory champagne. Photos imply the trauma. Joe scratches his chin while he and Green 'ponder over a tricky passage'. Ronnie 'deliberates a knotty point' and Norman Stenfalt lies, like an exhausted expectant father, slumped over his piano gazing bemusedly at his music.[35] Scott should probably have just refused *Melody Maker* access at this pre-natal stage.

The band's formation certainly raised expectations. Jimmy Deuchar, Victor Feldman and Stenfalt were available to write as well as play for it. Among the other members with Harriott were Hank Shaw, Ken Wray, Dave Usden, Derek Humble and Phil Seamen. Altoist Dougie Robinson joined on returning from playing on the French Riviera with Geraldo. Tony Brown noted that Scott was 'out front' because 'he has the authority rather than the reverse. He sees no necessity to emphasise this. He gets what he wants.... A languid pencil tapping on his music stand induces attention; his rather weary, "Hold it," stems an ensemble flood of sound; "Let's take it again from letter G," is sufficient to smother musicianly ribaldry arising from missed cues and the like.'

Brown saw the band's debut at the Samson and Hercules Ballroom in Norwich in mid-September.[36] But it seemed to him under-rehearsed, nervous and accident-prone. 'Over-blowing upsets balance within the sections and between them. Bad

balance robs dynamics of their force, sometimes destroys them
utterly.' Once again, the frustrated midwife appears: 'It was a
painfully premature delivery; but the infant was lusty enough:
it will thrive.'

Brown tried to look forward positively: 'Many thoughtful
people would select Ronnie Scott, Dougie Robinson and Joe
Harriott as among the best dozen saxophonists in the country
today. A section that contains this trio has boundless possibilities. Phil Seamen is regarded in the profession as our most
swinging drummer. With the Scott band he produces a prodi-
giously loud beat – but a beat none the less.' He singled
Harriott out. 'Soloist of the evening was unchallengeably Joe
Harriott. Every time he rose to play, Joe was urged [on] by the
noisy enthusiasm of the onlookers. He didn't allow this to
upset his musical poise. Right at the end of the evening, he
played a long 'Lover Man' that was full of ideas.... Harriott
seems destined to rise to heights in the Scott ranks.'

In October, the band recorded for Esquire ('Bang', 'With
Every Breath I Take', 'Night in Tunisia' and 'The Big Fist'). The
individual talents were greater than the sum of their parts,
however, and working in Scott's orchestra was not a success for
the ambitious and impatient Joe. Phil Seamen, a famously
volatile character, would be described in today's parlance as a
'wind-up merchant'. A build-up of ill-feeling between Seamen
and trumpeter Dave Usden reached boiling point onstage at a
Hogmanay engagement in Morecambe. Blows were exchanged
on the bandstand as the dismayed revellers' rendition of 'Auld
Lang Syne' threatened to be drowned out by the roared abuse.

Ronnie later admitted regret at forming the orchestra. He
called the project 'one of my worst ever'. As leader, he seemed
powerless to control the increasing mood of anarchy including
'differences in interpretations of the scores by saxophonists
Dougie Robinson and Joe Harriott. That was a pain especially
as I was a member of the same section.'37

Harriott had too much pride and self-belief to be happy as
subordinate alto sax to Dougie Robinson. Pete King remembered: 'Dougie was a very fine lead alto player and the leader of

the sax section which is why we wanted him from Geraldo's band. The leader has to have the say. At that stage, I don't think Joe would have had much experience of working in a big band. He wasn't exactly the kind of guy you'd want in the sax section. I think he wanted to be solo. Joe was a very fine player indeed.'[38]

Writer John Fordham remarked that the 'less charitable' thought that the band's 'most intense and creative activity was its poker school, famed for the unblinkingly dispassionate physiognomy of Harriott.'[39] Trumpeter Hank Shaw, later a member of Joe's quintet, endeared himself little to his colleagues by his prudent habit of immediately posting his winnings home. Scott disbanded the orchestra early in the New Year, realising that it had failed to gel in the way his nine piece band had.

The big band lived on sartorially at least. After its demise, Harriott and Seamen sometimes turned up independently at pubs and clubs wearing the navy-blue small-checked suits of the Scott orchestra. Among the company there would be a rush to shout 'Snap!' first.[40]

Joe worked with Seamen's quintet from January to November 1956 with pianist Johnny Weed, guitarist Dave Goldberg and bassist Stan Wasser.

He never recorded with this group[41] but in March he played on three tracks by a George Chisholm sextet including Seamen and Joe Mudele. Chisholm, a brilliant trombonist, risked offending jazz purists by using zany humour, 'mugging' and blowing raspberries to establish himself with wider audiences on prime time programmes like *The Goon Show* on radio and television's *Black and White Minstrels*. The blend of virtuoso instrumental performance and comedy followed a tradition that worked successfully for Louis Armstrong and Fats Waller. But Joe would never have tolerated such behaviour in any group bearing his name and must have been happy that his engagement with Chisholm was for a recording session rather than a television variety date.

In July 1956, he recorded for MGM under his own name again with Seamen, Johnny Weed and, on bass, Major Holley. The two numbers were a Harriott composition 'Blues Original' and 'My Heart Belongs to Daddy'.

Someone destined to play a significant part in Joe's life was Margaret Tynski. Previously an enthusiast for classical music concerts and a ballet supporter, she had been introduced to the London jazz scene by her fiancé. On first seeing Joe (playing with Tony Kinsey in 1954) she felt drawn by his magnetism and 'knew from that evening that somehow a relationship would ensue.'[42]

January 1957 saw her first step towards making this a reality. 'The first time I spoke to Joe was at an all night session at the M Club in Leicester Square. It was always well attended by the American Forces who travelled to London from their base in Ruislip. The black Americans were the most incredible dancers, the like of which we had not seen in this country. Joe had finished his set and was leaning against the bar with a drink, taking in the scene. I seized the opportunity to tell him how much I had enjoyed a recently broadcast BBC Radio programme featuring him, which of course led to conversation. He said he would be playing at the Queen Elizabeth Hall. "Why don't you come and bring your boyfriend?"

'I did not admit that he was my husband of a few weeks. That was the beginning of a long relationship. I have a memento of that all-nighter. My husband sketched a black American dancing, with Joe in the background, playing alto.

'We did attend the Queen Elizabeth Hall performance. We were near the front and Joe spotted us in the audience. At the end of the performance Joe beckoned us to the front where he had come down from the stage and was packing his sax away. We stayed with him some time in conversation, during which time he had surreptitiously slipped me his telephone number. From there onwards I travelled to London regularly to meet him. He also visited me at my home.'

*

In spring 1957, Harriott rejoined Tony Kinsey. He and tenorist Bob Efford replaced Don Rendell and Ronnie Ross in Kinsey's quintet. They made their debut at the opening night of the Flamingo Club's new premises in Wardour Street on Sunday 7 April. The Jazz Couriers featuring Ronnie Scott and Tubby Hayes also made their first public appearance at the same event. *Jazz News* enthused about the new club. 'Here in the long low room, expensively decorated and dimly lit, some of the best modern jazz in Europe can be heard. The club has a good dancing area and tables are available in the "wings".'43

Kinsey was pleased to have Harriott back. He told *Melody Maker* that Joe was 'one of the greatest saxophonists in Europe,' and added that 'the basic sound of the group will not alter much.' It would still feature originals by members of the quintet and, 'as Bob Efford has never played with a regular jazz group this will give him the chance to develop into one of the country's leading jazz stylists.'44

A Flamingo patron wrote that on 18 April, 'I heard the wonderful Tony Kinsey Quintet for the first time in person and it was such an enthralling experience that I shall never forget it. All the Kinsey groups have been very good, but this one is superb! Every member reached [such] a standard of swing, ideas and emotion as to put the others, English and American to shame.'45 The band went on to win the *New Musical Express* award for the best small jazz group of 1957–58.

Looking back on those times, Kinsey told me, 'There was another club, the Cafe Anglais, next to the Odeon in Leicester Square. It's a restaurant now, but we worked there a lot. I always remember Joe there. Every time we did a gig, Joe would always show up early and sit for an hour playing the piano, swinging away. Course, I was setting up my drums, getting ready, and he was sitting there just grooving away on the piano. I can see it now. He wasn't a great pianist technically but he could play tunes and he could swing a bit.

'Sometimes we'd play at the Cafe Anglais, then come back and play the all night session at the Flamingo. The Flamingo in Wardour Street wasn't a bad room. It was rather big and bare but with the lights out and the spotlights on it was quite nice. I've got some pictures of us playing down there with the Ellington guys, Paul Gonsalves, Clark Terry. We were the regular group and we played our regular arrangements but if there was a band in town, like when the Ellington band was in town, they'd make for the place after the gig because their concerts finished at ten o'clock or half past nine. They'd come in and do us the honour. You don't sit there thinking this is special. It's just great, because everything is right.

'The better the people that you're working with, assuming one is able to do it oneself, the better it'll be. That's what we used to have with Joe. I mean there was this rapport I felt with him which was just incredible. Joe was a natural swinger which is the essence of jazz. Joe was perhaps the greatest saxophone player I had ever worked with. But I didn't sort of think like that. I just thought, well, that's good. And you'd come off and it was forgotten. People say you're only as good as your last performance. I think you're only as good as your next performance.'

Kinsey remembered visiting Americans wanting to play with Harriott at Rik Gunnell's Star Club. 'Alan Clare worked there regularly. And after a gig we'd sometimes go up there and there'd be sessions with some of the American players in town. Thad Jones used to come in regularly when he was with the Basie band and he'd always ask, "Where's Joe? I want to play with Joe." It was a good club.'[46]

The quintet made a live recording for Decca on 16 May 1957. The rider 'Joe Harriott appears by courtesy of Denis Preston' indicated that he was now contractually tied to Lansdowne. Joe's front line partner, Bob Efford, according to Flamingo compere Tony Hall, was 'a modest un-pushing personality', nevertheless capable of fierce emotion in his playing. Being paired with Harriott enhanced his work. Efford felt Joe was a very special talent. 'Playing with him brought out the best in me,' wrote Efford, 'for which I will always thank him.'[47] The album title, *A Jazz at the Flamingo Session*, is misleading. Although the session was identical in content to a typical

Flamingo set by the quintet, it was recorded at the Railway Arms pub next door to the Decca West Hampstead studios. (The pub was wired directly to the studio and this imaginative arrangement made a quality recording possible with a live audience. A year earlier Tony Crombie's Group recorded their own *Jazz at the Flamingo* there for Nixa.) The cover of the Kinsey album pictures the band at the Flamingo: Joe 'sitting out' while Bob Efford plays a solo. Kinsey wears a v-neck sweater; bassist Peter Blannin is casual in an open-necked checked shirt, with Le Sage and Efford in light greyish suits. Joe by contrast, wears a suit of dark blue or possibly charcoal grey and looks utterly immaculate in a dazzling white shirt matched with a silvery tie.

Along with a title by Kinsey, two from Le Sage and two others from the Ellington repertoire, Joe's 'Just Goofin'' was included on the album, marking his debut as a composer on Kinsey recordings. The gentler 1955 version recorded by Harriott's quartet for Nixa had become, in Tony Hall's words, a 'flag waver', played at a cracking tempo. Hall marvelled: 'I wouldn't swear to it, but I counted twenty-two solo choruses by Joe, twenty by Bob and I think eighteen by Tony himself.' The audience, specially invited Flamingo Club members, responds boisterously to Joe's solo and cheers like a boxing audience at Kinsey's closing flourish. Summing everything up, Hall wrote that, 'the earthy-sounding altoist's return was extremely welcome' and had 'brought a new vitality to the Kinsey quintet.'[48] But in June 1957 Harriott left Kinsey for the last time to front drummer Allan Ganley's quartet.[49]

Margaret Tynski remembers visiting Joe around this time at his flat at 154 Portnall Road. 'Joe had just bought Duke Ellington's LP *A Drum is a Woman* which he was eager for me to hear.' Margaret discovered in October 1957 she was pregnant. Still living in a marital relationship, she was anxious that the child could be Joe's. As it transpired, it was not. 'After the birth of my daughter I told Joe I would not see nor contact him again. However, after about six months we resumed the affair with Joe frequently asking me to pack my bags and come to town. He had no scruples at persuading me to leave my husband and daughter. And I was besotted.'

As well as playing gigs with the Ganley group, Joe recorded the EP *Gone Ganley* with them in November. Ganley was delighted with his new altoist, writing in the sleevenotes that Harriott 'is the most consistent player I have ever worked with. I've yet to hear him play a bad chorus.' Allan's recollection years later was: 'Yes, I did work with Joe. We made an EP down the Mapleton. We were never close. He was a fabulous musician, though, so inspiring to work with.'[50]

Roger Cotterrell saw the Harriott–Ganley partnership as mutually beneficial. 'On this EP,' he wrote, 'Harriott's playing has a swaggering exuberance no doubt inspired in part by the swinging, technically impeccable drumming of Ganley. At this stage in Joe's development, when he was essentially a soloist rather than a group musician, regular work with the Kinsey and Ganley groups, both of which used fairly tight arrangements closely controlled by the drummer-leader, was no doubt a help to him in imposing a sense of form and group discipline.'[51]

In the same month as the Ganley recording, Joe almost recorded on a Dizzy Reece date for Tempo Records. Dizzy and Joe were similar in several ways. Both were Jamaican and had attended Alpha School. Each had a strikingly original tone and was recognisable after only a few bars. Both were capable of being immovable once taking up a position in an argument. Jazz producer Tony Hall described Dizzy as 'a warm, generous, emotional person. Temperamental, too. At times to the point of cussedness.'[52]

Frank Holder remembered that Dizzy 'carried his trumpet around in a brown paper bag with green moss on it.'[53] Thinking he could help the young trumpeter up the career ladder, Holder had proposed him as a recruit to the Dankworth band. 'He turned up two hours late for an audition for fourth trumpet and John told him, "You don't work for us."' The impression had not been of a dedicated professional.

Professionalism was a quality that Harriott personified. This extended beyond his musicianship. He made a point of presenting himself as immaculate, well-mannered and punctual. Joe had a Jamaican tailor, his trousers cut in the typical Jamaican style of the day, loose at the thigh, tapering to the ankle with a turn up.[54] Holder remarked that in his appearance and spoken sophistication, Joe reminded him of Billy Eckstine. In contrast to Harriott's sophisticated, intellectual personality, Dizzy was a streetwise type – literally streetwise, as *Jazz Monthly* writer Jack Cooke remarked. 'Dizzy taught me how to hang around street corners without being noticed.'[55] More positively, Dizzy was a mover and shaker, capable of creating his own opportunities for being noticed. As had been the case when Joe first came to Britain, Reece was a good person for Harriott to have as a friend, an innovator with entrepreneurial skills. 'I was the first one,' Reece remembered, 'to open a club after midnight. It was the Zanzibar Club and the authorities were all against it.'[56]

Their differing approaches to life may have been significant in what happened on the morning of 29 November 1957. Harriott was in the studio rehearsal rooms with Reece, Phil Seamen, bassist Lennie Bush and pianist Norman Stenfalt. This session eventually provided two EPs for Tempo under the supervision of Tony Hall. Hall told me, 'They were supposed to be rehearsing in the morning when Dizzy and Joe had a big fight. They didn't particularly like each other at the best of times. It would be more verbal than physical. Joe was a prickly sort of guy. I don't know what it was about and I didn't ask. It was probably more to do with how he [Joe] felt when he got up in the morning.'[57]

When Dizzy was asked about the argument, he remembered it differently, even associating it with a different session. But he explained, 'I used to hear tenor in my head and I wanted Joe to play tenor. And Joe sounded very good on tenor. It would be down in history now, but he didn't want to do it. We didn't have an argument, really.'[58]

There is agreement that Harriott departed the scene before

the session began and Dizzy called in a replacement, tenorist Sammy Walker, another former Alpha boy. Walker had been improving his technique playing on the continent, like his compatriot Bogey Gaynair. Walker played, as Hall put it, with a 'natural jazz sound and a general feeling for the blues'[59] but the numbers recorded are tantalising when one imagines how Joe might have contributed, particularly on the beautiful ballad favoured by Thelonious Monk, 'Sweet and Lovely'. Another track, Reece's composition paying homage to Thelonious, 'A Variation on Monk', would have brought out the spikiness in Joe's playing to great effect.

Hall, who had previously written enthusiastically about Joe's work with Tony Kinsey, had reservations about him which went beyond his personality: 'I found him too Parkerish,' he told me.[60] He had lavish praise for Dizzy who was in top form. Hall wrote in the notes included with Reece's *Progress Report* CD: 'I find it difficult to write about Diz without feeling a little biased. To me personally, he is possibly the most original and individual musician on the British scene. A musician who, given the chance to go to America and work there, could easily develop into one of the world's great jazz trumpeters.'[61] Reece got the chance and seized it, leaving for New York in October 1959.

As a footnote, in 1961 Joe's quintet performed Dizzy's 'A Variation on Monk' for a BBC radio concert in a series, hosted by Steve Race, called *Jazz for Moderns*. Race said that Harriott's solo 'made the happy grin spread all over the face of producer Terry Henebery'.[62] A second Reece composition, 'Shepherd's Serenade', opened the programme. This recognition of Reece's compositional skills and the fact that Joe later recorded Dizzy's 'The Rake' and 'Shepherd's Serenade'[63] seem to refute any suggestion of lingering bad feeling. Harriott could easily have drawn upon his own considerable stock of compositions rather than play those of a contemporary he disliked.

4.

a fence over which few are prepared to step

By early 1958, Harriott had decided he was ready for a regular band of his own. The formation of his quintet in March allowed him to develop his own ideas for a group. The band's repertoire at first was essentially bebop and featured several Horace Silver numbers. Although the music was not original, and Joe was still heavily influenced by Charlie Parker, the band's sound had a charged, emotional quality.

Jack Cooke told me that Harriott had wanted Phil Seamen as the quintet's drummer from the start, as he was 'technically and instinctively the best drummer of the time, but then everybody wanted Phil. His ability to sight read the most difficult charts led to him being in great demand from studios and theatres despite his heroin addiction and frequently outrageous behaviour.'[1] Phil was unavailable so an alternative, 'Benny' Goodman, took the drum stool. Goodman's real first name was David but nobody used it.

For the first weeks the quintet included Edinburgh lawyer and former wartime squadron leader Pat Smythe on piano.[2] This talented musician was also a scratch golfer, good enough to play as an amateur in the British Open. He had moved temporarily to London to test the water for a career in jazz and worked with Dizzy Reece's quartet in early 1958. But Smythe soon returned to Edinburgh, completed his law studies and became a practising solicitor in his father's law firm. His replacement, Harry South, was a gifted composer and arranger as well as a fine jazz pianist.

Bassist Lloyd Thompson's stay in the band was as brief as

Smythe's. His replacement was Jamaican bassist Coleridge Goode. Goode was much in demand for session work at this time as well as playing in pianist Alan Clare's trio at the Star Club in Dean Street. The club was humorously dubbed the 'Scar Club' by those who recognised a number of razor-carrying gangsters among the regular guests.[3] In the war years, Coleridge had broadcast with Stéphane Grappelli and had recorded with Django Reinhardt during the legendary guitarist's visit to London in 1946. He liked the simultaneous singing and bowing style of Slam Stewart and featured this in his own solos.

Drummer Bobby Orr had joined Clare's trio on returning from touring in the USA. Goode remembered Harriott running an eye over the rhythm section one night in the club. It was obvious that Goode and Orr had already developed a good rapport musically and socially. 'Joe came in, played with us and asked us to join the quintet,' the bassist remembered.[4] For Goode the move was agreed swiftly. By the end of March he had joined up with Harriott and, except for occasional absences, maintained his position throughout the existence of the quintet. Orr would join later.

The trumpet position was secured by Hank Shaw, prudent poker player from the days of Ronnie Scott's big band. Goode remembered Hank arriving for gigs on the pillion of his girlfriend's motor scooter – never an option for a bass player. The self-taught Shaw had been a founder member of Club Eleven, the pioneer group of London beboppers at the end of the 1940s.

In April, the quintet, still including drummer Benny Goodman, took up a fifteen-day residency at Frankfurt's Storyville Club, a venue popular with American servicemen, – perfect timing for a fledgling band to develop their musical tightness before a knowledgeable and receptive audience. Singer Doris Steel remembered a surprise encounter. 'I was with a Dutch or a Swedish band. I think it was 1958. I remember meeting Joe in a hut in a forest in Germany. It was a hut with a bar, not at all luxurious, but dark like a shed with wooden tables. The drivers all knew it. I saw this black guy sitting there and I said, "you look like Joe Harriott." He said, "that's funny. I *am* Joe Harriott."'5

Meanwhile, the National Jazz Federation had opened their new headquarters, the Marquee Club, in London's Oxford Street on 13 April 1958. Chris Barber, a founding director of the NJF, pooled his music business acumen with accountant Harold Pendleton, the Marquee's owner who was already a seasoned jazz promoter. The opening night featured pianist Michael Garrick's new quartet, modelled on the Modern Jazz Quartet, and trumpeter Kenny Baker's band.

In this circular-shaped room, the decor was more like that of a child's playroom than a jazz club. The bands played underneath a low, garishly striped 'circus' awning. The wall decoration of large cog designs added to the peculiarity. Fans danced and absorbed the atmosphere. Photographs taken on the opening night confirm that before the sixties the young were, in attitude and fashion, like miniature versions of their parents. Wide-pleated skirts and Puritan-style white collared dresses were much in evidence. The men, on and off the bandstand, wore suits and white shirts.

The Harriott quintet appeared weekly at the Marquee, beginning a long, fruitful association with the venue. The NJF in this period had ten thousand members and the club often attracted a capacity crowd of 800 including members of the next generation of British jazzmen, such as drummer John Marshall. 'When I was still at school,' Marshall said, 'I used to go and see [Joe] at the Marquee on Saturday night. I liked both Bobby [Orr] and Phil [Seamen]. Phil was more of a character, a legend.'6 Michael Garrick, who would feature repeatedly in Harriott's later career, first made the altoist's acquaintance at this time because the Garrick and Harriott groups began to work regularly on the same bill at the Marquee. He was much impressed hearing Joe's band over the following weeks and months: 'I thought, "My goodness, we sound a bit puny compared to this."'7

In May 1958, Benny Goodman left to work with Laurie

Metcalfe's band on the liner *Mauretania* and Bobby Orr joined the quintet. Born in Cambuslang, Lanarkshire, the son of a pipe major, Orr had played drums from the age of three. Taking up the trumpet at sixteen, he quickly showed talent in this too. By his mid-twenties he was playing with bandleader Basil Kirchin but a year of hard-blowing jazz caused serious lip problems. He told me, 'I lost my chops and went back to drumming.'[8]

Remarkably, his drumming career took off like a Formula One racing start and Bobby soon joined Jack Parnell's band. 'Some of the finest drummers in the country have played in my band. Phil Seamen, Allan Ganley, Kenny Clare,' declared Parnell. 'Top line boys, every one. Yet I don't think I have ever been happier playing… with anybody than I am with Bobby. He fits in beautifully with my ideas. He plays with a real hard driving beat. But above all, he has that quality which so many drummers lack and which is impossible to teach. That quality is taste.'[9]

Jack Cooke recalled that, around this period, Harriott was beginning to develop radical musical ideas: 'I can remember being in the old Marquee one Friday afternoon in 1958 when Joe and Dizzy Reece were trying with some success to get out of the idea of playing on chords and into the kind of free melodic playing that Ornette Coleman was just beginning to put on record, though at that time none of us had heard him, or hardly even heard of him.'[10]

Pat Smythe also thought Joe began working on his free form ideas with Dizzy Reece in 1958. Smythe had worked with Dizzy's quartet during that year and was in a good position to know. In 1973 he told Roger Cotterrell about the Harriott–Reece rehearsals and emphasised that Joe had not heard Coleman's music before the quintet began playing free form. The 'collective thing' was predominant for Harriott but Coleman 'was still working with soloist conceptions'.[11]

Joe confirmed these accounts during an interview with Brian Nicholls which appeared in the Dave Brubeck UK tour programme in January 1961. 'I started this before Coleman started his music to any effect – over two years ago, in fact. I tried some experimental stuff with Dizzy Reece; but there were difficulties in presenting it as a so-called new form of music, and so the ideas were shelved for the time being. But not forgotten. Now I think I've found much of the solution, and the fact that this has coincided with the publicity that Coleman's getting can be called fortunate or unfortunate – whatever you wish.'[12]

Trumpeter Shake Keane knew as early as 1958 that Harriott was thinking his way towards something revolutionary. 'We used to talk quite a lot – if Joe could be said to talk – before I joined the quintet. We used... to try to "unscrew the inscrutable". That is, we used to deal in all kind of metaphysical aspects of all kinds of occult situations and whatnot. Well anyway, in the middle of this, we sometimes used to speculate on what would happen if you played jazz without chords. And we once invented a system called the monochordial system. I mean, this was invented around the breakfast table over fried bread and eggs. The monochordial system ... in which you rely on ascending and descending diminished chords and you try to do what you can with those and try to keep some sort of jazz feeling. Well, this was years before we started playing free form.'[13]

Frank Holder occasionally guested as percussionist with the quintet. 'I lived not far from Joe Harriott,' he recalled. 'In his early days of writing he rang me and said, "Frank, I've got an idea. I'd like you to come round and see what you think of it." When he explained I said, "I know where you're at. Great!" He'd already made up his mind, anyway, and I said, "Yeah, fine." The idea of this free form stuff ... Ornette Coleman hadn't come on the scene, really. It wasn't a question of where Joe had heard anything ... from him or anybody. He just created this thing.

'He said to us, everybody in a way would be soloing, in that you're not playing the changes as everybody plays. You know what the changes are, but you're playing your own line. The others are listening to that line and playing their own line. Mind blowing, I'm telling you! It was amazing how we all just fell into it, just like that. And they were so excited about it. It used to blow our minds.'[14] But it was almost another two years before free form entered the repertoire of the Harriott quintet.

By July, the quintet was playing both Saturday and Sunday nights at the Marquee. Fellow resident performer, eighteen-year-old Ceylonese singer Yolande Bavan was pictured in *Melody Maker* accompanied by the band.[15]

Alongside the photo of a debonair Joe accompanying the beautiful vocalist, was a reminder of attitudes outwith the jazz scene. 'Mecca's Grand Casino, Birmingham,' it was reported, 'was this week brought into line with the Locarno, Nottingham, and Locarno, Sheffield, in refusing admittance to Negroes unless they take their own partners.'[16] The head of the Mecca dancehall chain was quoted: 'This is not a bar but a restriction. Our job is to keep order in our halls. We have noticed that when a coloured man asks a white girl for a dance and is refused he generally becomes abusive. This happened a month ago at Sheffield when six coloured men were involved in a knife fight. So on went the ban.'

Inevitably, there were times when Joe felt vulnerable to subtle acts of racism, as Margaret Tynski experienced: 'Once in a restaurant, Joe ordered our meal. We waited and waited for this to arrive. Joe was pushed for time, annoyed, and said to me, "Come on, we're going." With that, we left. I was embarrassed, not having experienced a situation like that before. Joe may have thought the delay deliberate; a black man with a white woman. There were a lot of hostilities in those days. People did stare and make obvious remarks. Joe would be aware of it and ignore it but I am sure it hurt.'

On 25 August, Harriott collapsed and was rushed to hospital. It was a recurrence of his chest troubles. He was suffering from bronchial pneumonia, pleurisy and a lung infection. He spent three and a half months recovering, once again in Pinewood Sanatorium. The band had been due to start their annual break the week following his collapse and were thrown into some confusion over how best to continue their residency after the holidays. Coleridge Goode assumed leadership of the quintet and called in baritonist Harry Klein to take Harriott's place. The choice of instrument was not as odd as it appeared. Although alto and baritone are further apart in pitch than tenor and alto, both are in E flat making transposition of scores unnecessary.

One night at the Marquee, a teenage Peter King took Joe's place. For the young altoist, the thrill of the opportunity was tempered by serious apprehension. 'I was terrified, even though Joe wasn't there. I felt a huge responsibility to play well. It all went OK, thank God! Joe was simply one hell of a great alto player and an idol of mine.'[17]

During his enforced absence Harriott wrote what would be one of his most recorded titles, 'Count Twelve'. He also began work on an ambitious piece called 'Pinewood Suite' which, in contrast, was never recorded. Also during this period he continued the quest for his own definitive approach to jazz. He felt the time had come to escape from the confines of the musical structures of modern jazz. Unshakeable self-belief, and his drive to be recognised as a truly original thinker, turned this hiatus in his playing career into an opportunity and he immersed himself in music theory. From this time he began working towards the 'abstract' or free form musical ideas, which would become his greatest achievement. But it would be over a year before he began to try them out with his band.

At the time of Harriott's illness Shake Keane interviewed him for the BBC's Caribbean Service and heard of his ideas. Later, Keane told broadcaster Peter Clayton: 'Joe had a way of going roundabout this, that or the other. He would say for example, "I would play something and you would 'overshadow' me." By overshadow he meant counterpoint. It took a little while for me to understand Joe's personal vocabulary, but... I have a feeling, you know, that he invented the term 'free form'.'[18]

On release from hospital in the first week of December,

Harriott needed a period of recovery and often spent time at the flat of a girlfriend, a nurse at Paddington General Hospital. Joe told the music press he would debut the 'Pinewood Suite' on his first outing with the quintet and he was determined to have it ready. His girlfriend watched fascinated as, totally absorbed, he set about completing his composition. His behaviour at that time hinted at his later self-neglect and she had to remind him to eat as the hours went by, so engrossed was he in composing and arranging.[19]

Joe discussed his treatment for tuberculosis with Margaret Tynski: 'TB hospitals in those days were isolation hospitals. He told me of the unpleasant treatment, having fluid from his lungs drawn off by hypodermic needle. I joked with him at the time and said, "Joe, you need to find yourself a nice West Indian nurse." He laughed and said, "What do I want with a West Indian nurse?" His many lady friends, as far as I know, were all white. After leaving hospital he became neglectful at taking his medication.'

As a consequence of his illness, Joe had given up his flat at Portnall Road and on leaving hospital had moved to a more spacious ground floor property at 94a Clifton Hill in St John's Wood, NW8. This attractive home, in a terraced Victorian villa, comprised a living room, bedroom, kitchen, bathroom and w.c. The large living room had an upright piano Joe occasionally played.

To the rear was a walled garden with a lawn, some trees and shrubs and a small patio outside the bedroom window. The front gate at the left side of the house gave access to a sloping path between the house and the Clifton pub. At the foot of the path you turned right to reach the door. Not surprising for someone known for his immaculate appearance, Joe liked the flat in order and would clean the linoleum and carpets using dustpan and brush as there was no vacuum cleaner. The landlord, an Eastern European called Charles Gellnik, owned numerous properties in the area. His office was in Blenheim Terrace and Joe called there each month to pay the rent.

A friend, Kenny Baxter, looked in on the gradually strengthening patient. 'I visited him as much as I could and got shopping for him. I don't think Joe ever really recovered from this illness. He became more reclusive.'[20] Still in recuperation, Harriott returned to the Marquee but during early January 1959 he had to limit his playing to solo piano. He was a competent pianist, capable of some good blues numbers and particularly fond of playing 'Body and Soul'.

On Friday 30 January the band, with Harriott now fully active, played a programme at the Marquee featuring the debut of 'Pinewood Suite'. The National Jazz Federation celebrated Joe's return by announcing that Marquee Club members and NJF members would be admitted free to this gala night. For the occasion, the quintet was augmented with baritonist Ronnie Ross and Joe's recent interviewer, trumpeter Shake Keane. Frank Holder and Bobby Breen provided additional percussion on bongos and congas respectively.[21]

'All that period we were at the Marquee... we got a fiver each night,' said Bobby Orr. 'In those days you could buy the whole band a drink for a pound... The back door was onto the Coach and Horses in Poland Street... I'd go out there and my suit was wringing in sweat, soaking. I used to run out there for a couple of large [drinks]...and back in again. I mean we really worked hard. The appreciation of the audience was fantastic.'[22]

Back in full-time activity, the quintet set off on 20 February for Italy and the San Remo Festival. Shaw and Goode left by car intending to follow the route of the Monte Carlo Rally while Joe elected instead to travel by train with Orr and Harry South. On the Saturday opening day, Harriott led his band in a set of straight hard bop. On stage they made an unfortunate start and Goode had to play into a mike when his bass amplifier blew up. But despite this ominous opening the band, according to a possibly partisan *Melody Maker*, was 'the hit of the festival'.[23] They certainly made a big impression on one influential audience member, Horace Silver, one of Joe's favourite musicians. Silver made it a mutual admiration society after hearing the Harriott quintet. 'We got on fine with Silver and later he sent us some of his compositions,' recalled

Coleridge Goode.[24] Bobby Orr enthused: 'He sent us the parts when he got back to the States. ['Señor Blues'] had a 12/8 feel. It was fantastic!'[25] After the show the band took part in an all-star jam session at a plush restaurant in the mountains just outside the town.

On 5 May, Harriott recorded his *Blue Harriott* EP to be issued by Columbia. This studio date, again supervised by Denis Preston, included three Harriott originals: 'Count Twelve', 'Still Goofin'' and the relaxed, swinging 'Jumpin'' with Joe'. 'Señor Blues' was also included and the tone of Joe's alto in unison with Shaw's clarion-like trumpet gives the quintet's version a sharper, more dynamic attack than that of the Horace Silver band. All four tracks swing well and feature good solos. 'Still Goofin'' soon became the quintet's signature tune.

Melody Maker's headline on the EP's release was: 'Harriott enters the top bracket.' Columnist Bob Dawbarn enthused: 'Harriott gets better and better. This is excellent alto playing by any standards. Harriott plays throughout with great confidence and drive – still very much along the paths trodden by Charlie Parker, but with sufficient individuality to avoid all charges of copying.' The whole band won his admiration but 'Shaw has never played better on record.' Dawbarn's only worry was that record buyers might be 'still prejudiced against the local product.'[26]

In October 1959, Joe headed with Dill Jones for the Storyville Club in Frankfurt to play with American trumpeter Chet Baker[27] who was enjoying some respite from the attentions of American narcotics agents. On returning home Harriott led his quintet on 26 October at the 1959 Jazz Jamboree at the Gaumont State, Kilburn. This annual charity evening was organised by the Musicians' Social and Benevolent Council and, on this occasion, featured fourteen bands covering every aspect of British jazz.

Fans had become accustomed to jazz circuses like the Jamboree, in which a large number of groups were given brief exposure to the audience. But, when it was announced that the Modern Jazz Quartet would make a second tour of Britain,

Bob Dawbarn in *Melody Maker* expressed the hope that this might herald a new era in which the quality of the individual spots would outweigh the quantity.[28] Harold Pendleton of the National Jazz Federation, the moving force behind the tour, gave cause for hope when he told him, 'I have viewed the tendency toward jazz circuses with abhorrence, and I don't propose to join in. I want people to have ample opportunity to hear the MJQ – after all, the Federation has always been proud of the concerts it has put on.'

It was confirmed that from 21 November until 6 December 1959, Harriott and baritonist Ronnie Ross would guest with the MJQ on tour. Pendleton said, 'This time I want to know if people will pay to hear six top-rate jazzmen. If we prove this is so, no doubt other promoters will follow our lead ... British artists are getting good – the Americans realise it even if a lot of our people don't. Take Joe Harriott. I think he would give any American altoist a run for his money.'

John Lewis, the MJQ's pianist and musical director, had met Harriott and Ronnie Ross two years previously while touring the UK for the first time. Ross had been with the MJQ's supporting band, the Don Rendell quintet and, for the 1959 tour, Lewis himself had asked for the services of Joe and Ronnie. As he introduced each concert, Lewis praised the British saxophonists, both of whom participated fully alongside the Americans and had solo features performing titles of their choice. Harriott avoided frenetic, lengthy solos, playing exquisitely on ballads like 'Lover Man' and MJQ standards like 'Bags Groove'. The MJQ were wildly popular and some Harriott fans thought that Lewis' patronage was evidence that the altoist's world class status was at last recognised.

Critic Benny Green was less enthusiastic. He criticised both the quartet's performance and their trademark formal attire at the opening concert at the Royal Festival Hall on November 21. John Lewis' effort to make jazz socially acceptable might be 'an excellent idea. Better morning coats and gloom than tales of Al Capone and bootleg days. The snag is that this courting of respectability has drained away so much of the vitality of their music that there is little left but a few flickers of animation from the brilliant vibraharpist, Milt Jackson, and occasional passages reminiscent of Bach, of all people.' Green continued: 'The National Jazz Federation augmented the quartet with two British saxophonists whose comparative vulgarisms tore the unity of the quartet to shreds, although it was hardly their fault. The quartet plays music from the twilight corridors of a dream, and saxophones have no place there.'[29] Audiences did not share Green's opinion. Illicit recordings of concerts at the Usher Hall in Edinburgh and Manchester's Free Trade Hall register wild applause after each piece.

Bassist Dave Green was at the Festival Hall concert. 'I was about seventeen. I remember Joe got thunderous applause. Joe was a great fiery player and after the reserve of the MJQ, it was wonderful! The band was very restrained. That was their whole thing. Then Joe came on roaring and the audience were absolutely potty about him! I'll never forget that. Joe played fantastically.'[30]

Jazz enthusiast Barry Fleming was also there. His diary entry read: 'We walked across the footway to the Royal Festival Hall. The MJQ were beyond adjectives. Ross and Harriott both played well although Joe had it rough with the acoustics.' According to Barry's notes, Joe's showcase was 'Autumn in New York' and he was joined by Ronnie Ross on 'Bags Groove', 'Body and Soul' and 'Night in Tunisia'.[31]

Like Harriott, Lewis was a man of impeccable manners, immaculate appearance and strong musical convictions. But his aim of drawing jazz closer to the European classical music tradition was completely different from Joe's. Where Lewis was dispassionate and delicate in his approach to music, Harriott was naturally fiery and bold.

Despite these differences, 'John Lewis really loved Joe Harriott,' according to Chris Barber. Barber was in a position to know as he, Harold Pendleton and Lewis remained firm friends until the pianist's death.[32]

Barber's trumpeter Pat Halcox recalled hearing Joe say he

had felt restricted in playing with the MJQ.[33] Ideally he would have liked to introduce his free form music in this setting but Lewis didn't want the improvisation to go that far. By the end of his time with the MJQ, Harriott confessed to feeling a little bit frustrated.

After the tour, he returned to working with the quintet. Bobby Orr was married on 12 December 1959 and his wife immediately discovered the disadvantages of life with a jazz musician. Bobby had to sell a trumpet and a twenty-inch cymbal to get funds to leave immediately on a 'working honeymoon' to Frankfurt where a return booking for the quintet beckoned at the Storyville Club.[34] 'Frank Holder was driving. There was Harry South in the car and his wife, and me and my wife, Frank Holder and his wife ... so there were six of us in the car! I think it was about three weeks we were there. It was like a modern club, you know – drinking bar upstairs – but it was mainly a jazz club, people sitting at tables listening to the jazz. It went on until two or three in the morning. We played every night.' It was during this trip that Joe began giving his band members his ideas about playing free. As Coleridge remembered it: 'We decided that when we came back to London we'd experiment with various ways of doing that.'[35]

On the way back from the Storyville residency, Frank Holder was driving late one night through Belgium on the way towards the English Channel. The car was not quite as cramped as on the outward journey: Frank's wife, Harriott, and Bobby Orr and his wife were the passengers. Harry South and his wife were in another vehicle. Holder had to think twice as he saw a driver approaching him on the same side of the road. Frank agonised over which option to take – into the oncoming traffic or off-road to avoid collision. He tried to move between the streams of traffic but everyone felt the impact as the oncoming car struck their vehicle on the right side of the front bumper. As they registered the shock of the collision, they realised they had escaped serious injury.

Frank recalled that Joe reacted quickest, leaving the car and running up the road to the offending driver's vehicle. Opening the door, he hauled the driver out to exact immediate retribution. 'Joe was in a terrible state and I had to pull him off the other guy who was about sixty and really stoned. The police arrived and I had to 'walk the white line', as well as the other guy. But it was so obvious that they didn't really need to test him. He was so stoned.' They had narrowly avoided going off the road and down a steep incline, but what struck Holder most about the whole incident was the extremely agitated condition Harriott was in. Joe explained that he had been in a bad car accident before. He didn't specify details but said his whole life had sped before him on that occasion as it had again on the dark Belgian road.

Frank and his weary passengers resumed their journey homeward but the damaged car could not negotiate tight corners in the towns. Holder, a body builder with a powerful frame, stopped the car and set about the damage with his feet and hands, pulling the bumper away from contact with the wheel. This allowed them to get back to the ferry. In the resulting court case Holder had to go to Belgium to give evidence helping to convict the other driver of causing the accident.[36]

During the trip there had also been a collision of a musical kind. Harriott's free form ideas were controversial in the quintet and, as a result, the band's personnel altered soon after returning. As Goode put it, with much understatement: 'I don't think Harry or Hank were too enamoured with it, although Bobby was fine.'[37] Frank Holder said, 'Hank was a hard bop trumpeter, Kenny Dorham influenced. He felt he was being edged out.'[38] When I asked Shaw to recall his tenure as Harriott's trumpeter, all he was prepared to tell me was: 'My memories of Joe Harriott are not happy ones.'[39]

Hank left the quintet on 6 February 1960 and, in the following weeks, several trumpeters deputised. Coleridge Goode recommended Shake Keane as a permanent replacement and Harriott gave his approval, conditional on a successful month's trial. Keane had played with Joe on various occasions previously. But he needed to be persuaded by Coleridge to take on the challenge of joining the quintet because he did not consider himself primarily a jazz musician at this time. With some assistance from his bassist friend, he began learning the trumpet parts, finally joining the group in mid-March. The highly varied musical experiences he had behind him were an advantage for the next stage of his career.

Ernie Garside saw advantage for the Quintet in the enhanced social harmony: 'There didn't seem to be any tension between anybody when Shake Keane joined the band. He would fit in and "didn't get out of his pram". He was an imposing figure, about 6 feet 4 inches and was built like a wrestler. He had a beard and all that. He looked fierce at first glance except for his eyes. Because of his size he used to frighten the kids and horses but he was a gentle giant, a beautiful chap.'[40]

Shake, whose love of literature led to his nickname, was born Ellsworth McGranahan Keane in May 1927. 'I was one of a family of seven, all playing trumpet, taught by my father after a firm grounding in part-singing hymns,' he explained. 'No one was serious about jazz, and no one in St Vincent was a professional musician.[41]

'I didn't come to Britain with the expressed purpose of getting into music particularly, although music had been part of my life, all my life. But I had been a secondary schoolteacher in St Vincent and I wanted to do a degree in English. I thought it better to do it outside the West Indies. For one thing the University of the West Indies was far away from St Vincent. About a thousand miles away northwest by sea.

'So when I came to England in '52, it was to study at London University. I had some idea that I could work for my degree and make a little money playing on the side, as I did at home. I never planned anything – everything has happened to me. I joined a nightclub band in 1952, and when it folded I went on tour with Mike McKenzie's group, which made me some contacts. I never played the jazz clubs much. I hated the look of the one I went to, and didn't go back to a club for years.'[42]

Interviewer Peter Clayton once asked Keane what had made it worthwhile coming to London, apart from the opportunity to make music with the quintet. He was quick to answer: 'It was mostly playing the flugelhorn. It was an instrument that I didn't know before, although I felt always [about] the trumpet [that] really, as musicians say, I didn't naturally hear it in my head. And I was searching all over the place, using large-bore trumpets and deepening the mouthpiece. And one day Coleridge Goode, the bass player with Joe Harriott – I wasn't with Joe Harriott then – he said to me, well, why don't you try the flugelhorn? And it was the most satisfying sound to me. Very deeply. And through the flugelhorn I was able to, for want of a better expression, express myself fully.[43] And that is what I really look back to. From there, other things, you know. But that is where I start when I look back.'[44]

As Keane's trial period gave way to permanency some fans lamented Shaw's departure. Frank Holder noted this with Harold Pendleton. 'It so happened I was taking Harold in my car, down to the [Bath] Festival. And Harold, of course, liked – as we all liked – Hank Shaw. He said, "What's this I hear that Hank is not playing the festival?"

'Frank answered Pendleton: "I'll tell you something.... If this guy, Shake Keane, doesn't blow your mind within the first four bars, then I don't know what I'm talking about!" Sure enough the band went on and he took off.'[45]

The festival attracted a radio outside broadcast unit which recorded half an hour for BBC *Jazz Club*. The broadcast on 26 May included the quintet playing 'Round Midnight' and 'Cookin' at the Continental.'

Keane was a genial man, even deploying good natured banter to confront his local newsagent over small ads for accommodation displayed in his shop. The two men were friendly, but Keane would point out the 'No dogs. No blacks' stipulations in some ads. 'What's this doing in your shop, then?' he would ask whenever he spotted a new offensive postcard. The embarrassed shopkeeper was left squirming each time as he resorted to the 'what-can-I-do-about-it?' response. In the 1950s and 1960s, these pernicious ads were commonplace, and, at the time, within the law.[46]

Shake used humour to ridicule racism. Baritone player

Harry Klein was once called upon to dep in Mike McKenzie's band. Klein recalled waiting to be introduced to the other band members, all of whom were black. With consummate timing, Shake asked Harry: 'Aren't you scared we might eat you?'47

Bobby Orr encountered Shake's puckish humour. 'We'd go into the pub at the interval. I was dressed up and had a new tie on. He had this thing he did. He would say, "I love your tie." If he said he loved your tie – you had to give him it, swap ties with him. And he had a rotten old tie on! Yours might be a brand new one, like one my wife had just bought me. Later on, someone else would come up and say it and the ties were on the move again.'

'But eventually you'd get it back?' I asked.

'Not a lot,' said a wistful Orr.48

Drummer Colin Barnes got depping opportunities because of Orr's growing reputation. 'A lot of people remember Phil Seamen with Joe, but Bobby was a wonderful drummer, just as creative as anybody. He was starting to draw a lot of notice and offers of work. He would phone me some Saturday mornings to do the Marquee gig with Joe the same night. It was a great experience for me. Joe played with unbelievable passion.'

'I remember Shake in the Coach and Horses having brandy with cheroots or a cigar during the break. I still have one of his old ties somewhere that he swapped for one of mine. Cole and Joe went back a long time and there were arguments between them. Coleridge did this Slam Stewart thing on bass. Joe didn't like it and said he was going to ask Cole not to do it. But there was immense loyalty there too. Cole was someone that when you looked at him, you couldn't imagine him being young. It was something about the dignity and the authority he carried.'49

Dignity was an essential factor in the manner with which Harriott presented his music to the public. Promoter Ernie Garside recalled: 'After the show Bobby Orr did this thing playing with pencils on his teeth' (usually Mozart's 'Turkish Rondo'). He'd go right up next to the mike. He didn't do it in concert. Joe didn't like anything like that. It smacked of showmanship.'

In April 1960, the group, now including Keane, made four tracks for an EP entitled *A Guy Called Joe*. 'Caravan' was recorded on 8 April and featured Frank Holder's bongos. Further tracks recorded on 21 April were Harry South's compositions, 'Liggin' and 'Southern Horizons', Joe's own 'Tuesday Morning Swing' and the standard 'You Go to My Head'. Together with the recordings previously issued on the *Blue Harriott* EP, these eventually made up the balance of material included in the quintet's first LP, *Southern Horizons*.

Jazz News reviewed *A Guy Called Joe*: 'We have many fine musicians in Britain. Often when one of them turns in a particularly inspired performance patriotic critics get out their dictionaries and start challenging any Americans to beat us. The truth is that we have a handful of musicians in this country who, with a little more experience, could open a few eyes in the States. Of these Joe Harriott is undoubtedly one. Joe's only fault being that if challenged by another soloist he becomes a little frantic in his efforts to outdo him.'[50]

Early in May, a further change in the quintet occurred when Orr announced that he was leaving to replace Tony Crombie in Ronnie Scott's quintet. Orr was much in demand and later said of himself, 'I was the flavour of the month, the new face on the scene.'[51] *Jazz News* quoted his reasons: 'I felt I needed a change, and when the offer came ... I took it. I've enjoyed playing with Joe, but I want to keep improving my playing, and the only way I can do that is by playing with as many groups as possible.'[52]

Harriott's new drummer was Tommy Jones whose previous experiences included work with trumpeters Pete Pitterson and Leslie 'Jiver' Hutchinson. Immediately prior to joining the quintet he had played with Jimmy Deuchar and Tubby Hayes and depped on a few dates with Joe.

Next to go was Harry South who left for Ronnie Ross's and Bert Courtley's Jazztet. Again, citing his period with the Harriott quintet as a good experience, Harry said the time had come 'for a musical change'. Another reason was that he wished to write for the new group and it seemed unlikely that as many opportunities would arise with the Harriott quintet given the direction Joe had decided to take.53

His departure allowed Pat Smythe to return to the quintet. Smythe had decided to commit himself to music and had given up his legal career in Edinburgh, succumbing to the lure of the London jazz scene. His widow Heather told me, 'He wasn't a good lawyer – I don't know what he did! He got such silly cases like people slipping on hotel mats and whatever.' Pat had quickly come to regard the legal system with cynicism. He told a friend, 'the law is frightened to deal with reality.'54

Some friends regarded his attitude to the whole business of living as detached. He had had to equip himself mentally to risk death constantly in his wartime role as an RAF pilot and he conveyed an outward impression of nonchalance. Heather Smythe laughed when I spoke of this perception. 'He was a fairly anxious person, but I'm sure that he would be delighted if that's what people thought. He was deeply affected by the war, suffering terrible breakdowns fairly immediately after it ended. It went on and on.'55

'He was so quiet-spoken,' Ernie Garside said of Pat. 'I thought if he had had his cigarette in one of those cigarette holders he would have been just right in one of those English films.'

London Symphony Orchestra bassist Dave Willis worked often with Smythe and found him 'a completely self-contained guy. Very dour. Very Scottish. Master of his own thoughts. Master of his own thing. He was like an island, unapproachable. His playing was absolutely studied like Bill Evans. He'd taken on [Evans'] mantle, slightly hunched over the piano.'56

Smythe so loved Evans' playing that whenever the American pianist appeared at Ronnie Scott's, he listened to him on every possible night. Bassist Spike Heatley said, 'I was at Ronnie's playing support with Selina Jones, along with John Marshall and Brian Lemon. Initially we'd been booked to support the Francy Boland band and they held us over to do the Bill Evans booking, too. All the bassists – Jeff Clyne, Dave Green and Dave Holland – were at the left hand side listening to [Evans' bassist] Eddie Gomez. I used to see Pat there each night. He wasn't with the others. Pat used to secrete himself away with a small beer and take everything in.'[57]

A website dedicated to Smythe's memory describes him perfectly: 'Often in his playing there were Debussy-like references and he was particularly receptive to new ideas and experimentation despite the natural lyricism so evident in his playing.'[58] His diffident exterior concealed an adventurous spirit – as well as a thorough knowledge of the classical and jazz piano repertoire.

With new key figures, Keane and Smythe in place, Harriott's quintet was now very different from the one he had started with in 1958. It was the vehicle be needed to develop his ideas of free form, or, as he called it, abstract music. This cerebral, audaciously talented group of individuals now embarked on making music that challenged listeners as well as players. Yet it is impossible to ignore that, even in some of the abstract compositions where the beat is not fixed, there are occasions when the whole band swings joyously. Trumpeter Stu Hamer heard them and was much impressed: 'Joe, Shake, Coleridge, Tommy Jones ... they blew the arse off everybody else! Many were jealous, especially the London clique.'[59]

The band could build such tension in a number that the climax exhilarated the listener. On record the music is consistently beautiful, achieving such 'tightness' that listeners suspect telepathic communication. It didn't happen by accident. Many rehearsal hours were required to reach the understanding achieved by the quintet members. As Shake Keane noted: 'A student came to hear the group the other night and seemed quite disappointed – he was expecting anarchy!'[60]

In America, the dramatic change in jazz had occurred in parallel. Texan alto saxophonist Ornette Coleman had ignited the scene with 'free jazz'. His first albums *Something Else* and *Tomorrow Is the Question* announced the arrival of a revolutionary new talent. Some critics were scornful but others, such as Nat Hentoff, voiced support. Coleman could also count on the enthusiasm of prominent musicians such as John Lewis and Gunther Schuller. Reedmen John Coltrane and Eric Dolphy were experimenting in other ways too with monumental influence on their contemporaries.

Harriott and all who worked with him were angered by claims that he had jumped on an Ornette bandwagon. Joe later protested that he had conceived the idea of free form during a five week hospital stay early in 1960. 'I had time to think then, and I sort of looked at the music scene as I knew it and came to the conclusion that I just had to do *something*.'[61]

In fact, as noted earlier, there are grounds for claiming that Harriott's free form ideas can be traced back as far as 1958. In any case, it is clear that before writing any of his revolutionary new music, Joe found inspiration in the worlds of literature and art as well as music. The works of American poet and essayist Ralph Waldo Emerson and painters Pablo Picasso and Paul Klee came under particular scrutiny. Ian Carr remembered Harriott coming back to his place after a Newcastle concert. 'He'd just been to a Picasso exhibition. He said he had looked around the room at the paintings on show and he realised, "That's what I'm trying to do. Paint pictures."[62]

Margaret Tynski remembers this Picasso enthusiasm. 'Shortly after I left Joe,[63] he saw me in Old Compton Street and asked me to go home with him. He wanted to talk things over, etc. In the living room was an easel with a canvas on it. He had been painting bars of music in very bright colours, his imagination fired by a Picasso exhibition. This was obviously influenced by his latest girlfriend. I guess she was an artist, or that way inclined, as the bedroom fireplace, which was attractive and Victorian, had been painted over in very bright colours. Joe seemed proud of his artistic efforts, showing me the work on the easel, and said, "What do you think of this? I'm painting music with colours." I was not impressed. I don't know how long that phase lasted.'

Early in the 1960s, jazz photographer and journalist Val Wilmer discussed with Joe his new concept, which he called abstract music or free form. 'He was quite intellectual. I remember when I went to see him he was talking about Paul Klee the painter, and Picasso. In fact I had to go home and brush up on my Klee. At that time I couldn't understand why he was comparing his music to abstract painting. Of course, I can now. I did afterwards, but at the time I was too young to appreciate it, I think. He thought of himself as an artist.'[64]

Coleridge Goode acknowledged some awareness of Coleman's ideas but said, 'we felt our approach was different. Ornette's thing was sort of fragmented somehow, while we wanted to get more of an ensemble feeling. Our music was certainly distinct from Ornette's. At first, anyway, there weren't any records of his; we just read things about him in *Melody Maker*. We made our first [free form] record in 1960 and when we did hear Coleman it wasn't too close to what we were doing.'[65] Challenged that some thought him a Coleman copyist, Joe responded, 'No, we really aren't copying him. Whilst I can appreciate his work, I would never accomplish anything by just copying him. And, in point of fact, I listen to his records when I get the chance in order to make positively sure that I'm not going too closely in his direction.'[66] Harriott's promoter friend, Ernie Garside agreed. 'When he played his 'out' stuff, as we call it, I know it was on a parallel and at the same time as Ornette, but Joe's stuff was different. It wasn't quite so offensive. I had it explained to me by all the guys. "We bounce off each other" and all that. It somehow was logical. The way they were going on, Joe and them, that could have been forever.'[67]

Jazz writer Richard Williams also thought Harriott's and Coleman's innovations were distinct. 'The basis of the group's success was Joe's brilliant composing. Tunes like 'Calypso Sketches' welded a rhythmic and melodic effervescence to a very delicate kind of impressionism which made sense of Joe's claim that he wasn't in the least influenced by the contemporary innovations of Ornette Coleman.'[68] Something entirely new had arrived in jazz and Harriott was its inventor.

Above Contrasting images of Joe Harriott as a young man (*left*, with a tenorist friend, courtesy Max Jones Archive; *right*, photo by M. Scott, courtesy *Jazz Journal International*).
Below 'Destined to be a leader': Harriott and the Tony Kinsey Trio (Kinsey, drums; Sammy Stokes, bass; Bill Le Sage, piano and vibes) at their regular stomping-ground, London's Flamingo Club, in 1954 (courtesy Tony Kinsey).

Above 'Never any problem with Joe. He was fantastic.' The Kinsey Trio with Harriott at a Royal Albert Hall BBC concert, London, 1954 (courtesy Tony Kinsey).

Below Sparring partners and parallel lives: Harriott in drummer Phil Seamen's group c.1956. Major Holley is on bass and Dave Goldberg the guitarist (courtesy Max Jones Archive).

'One of my worst ever projects': The ill-fated Ronnie Scott Orchestra of 1955. Scott is at the far left. Hank Shaw is at the right end of the trumpet section, Phil Seamen on drums and Norman Stenfalt on piano. Ken Wray is third from left in the trombone section. Saxophones (left to right) are Pete King, Dougie Robinson, Harriott and Benny Green (courtesy of Peggy Burton).

Above Harriott's first quintet rehearsing in late 1959 or early 1960. Left to right: Harry South, Coleridge Goode, Hank Shaw, JH, Bobby Orr (photo courtesy Redferns).

Left Turning up wherever music could be played: JH with Bill Haig on piano, Coleridge Goode, bass, and Bill Bond, drums. Southend, late-50s or early-60s (courtesy Bill Bond).

Below With the MJQ's drummer Connie Kay and baritonist Ronnie Ross, MJQ's UK tour, November–December 1959 (photo Bill Wagg).

5.

so far nobody has thrown anything at us

Quite apart from the free form developments, Harriott remained much in demand in conventional jazz contexts. In November 1960, he was selected to join sixteen of Britain's finest jazz performers in showcasing Harry South's compositions and arrangements on BBC radio's *Jazz Club*.[1] And what a showcase it proved to be! Fifty minutes of first class performances from a line-up including Jimmy Deuchar, Ken Wray, Tubby Hayes, Ronnie Scott and Ronnie Ross. The programme opener found Harriott on familiar territory with 'Southern Horizons'. 'The broadcast,' said producer Terry Henebery, 'gave a deserving arranger the chance of displaying his talents. The writing was marvellous and the band excellent.'

In the same month a major development occurred for Harriott's own group. On 12 November, no doubt to Joe's delight, Phil Seamen made his debut appearance with the quintet, joining them at the Marquee Club in place of Tommy Jones who returned to freelancing. Harriott now had the ideal musicians to record his next album.[2]

Seamen had recently worked with Tubby Hayes' quartet and as a featured drummer at the Blue Note Club in Paris. 'Phil didn't last a great long time with anybody because his personality was too strong,' explained Ernie Garside. One Seamen idiosyncrasy was to re-christen people. 'Phil had names for everybody. I remember there was a girlfriend he had. He told me her name was Doris. After a considerable time had passed I remember asking him what her surname was. He answered, "Karloff".'[3]

His colleagues in the Harriott band did not escape his wit. 'Every time he farts,' Phil said, referring to Joe's smoking habit, 'there's a fall of soot.' Goode, probably because of his seniority and dignified bearing, was dubbed 'Uncle Remus'. Harriott was 'Blind Lemon', recalling the name of a legendary 1920s blues singer. But these names compare favourably with Seamen's title for trumpeter Maynard Ferguson, famed for hitting unbelievably high notes. Maynard became 'Strain'ard', bringing to mind connotations as much lavatorial as musical.[4]

Phil arrived one night at the Marquee's door just as Michael Garrick was also arriving. Stopping dramatically in his tracks before the benignly smiling, bearded Garrick, he feigned amazement and theatrically exclaimed, 'Good God! Jesus Christ!'[5]

Joe and Phil were opposites in many ways. While Harriott liked to project an image of self-control and enjoyed being leader, the anarchic Seamen loved debunking authority. The two undoubtedly respected each other's talents yet a silent war ran throughout their long association. 'Joe doesn't have a chip on his shoulder,' Phil liked to joke, 'he's got a bloody telegraph pole!'[6]

Seamen sometimes had studio and theatre work. For a memorable period he was the drummer with the pit band for the English production of *West Side Story*. Ronnie Scott often referred to a famous occasion when Phil fell asleep in the pits. As he slumped forward, striking the gong, he had the presence of mind to call out loudly: 'Dinner is served.' At the end of the show's premier in Manchester he said to the City's mayor, 'I don't know about you, Mayor Ponsonby, but I had a ball.' Phil's bizarre chapter in musical theatre ended in farce, as Jack Cooke told me. 'He got fired when his pet Alsatian, Billie, half-ate the star's Chihuahua.'[7]

Joe was eagerly anticipating the first recording of his abstract music. Just how important Phil was to his plans is clear from letters he wrote to Margaret Tynski, who was away demonstrating Cona Coffee Makers on a two-week promotion in Bournemouth. In one dated 17 November 1960, Joe wrote,

'We played at the I.C.A. The music was well received. The members played very well, I think, and many people there were pleased to hear our new music. Very satisfying feeling.

'We are playing Cambridge tonight, and the Marquee and Flamingo on the weekend. Next week, Wednesday, we record the new music ...'

Four days later he wrote to her, 'This is the latest news. Last night we played the Flamingo, which went well.

'At the end of the session Phil told me he is going away into hospital for a "cure" as it's known. He is a drug addict. So he's going in for treatment. As you know, we record for Denis Preston this Wednesday and next week and Phil is going in next Monday. So I spoke with Denis today and will record this Wednesday and this Saturday. I will be in the studio from 1 a.m. until 5 [a.m.] Saturday. I am making sure that we do the recording before Phil goes in. He says he will be away two weeks but I think they will keep him in longer.... He has suggested someone to play for him while he is away so I'll just have to manage as best I can.'

The Harriott quintet's first 'abstract' LP, *Free Form*, came out on the Jazzland label with the title modishly printed in lower case. The sleeve design was by Ken Deardoff, whose work had previously appeared on Bill Evans' classic Riverside albums. The front pictured a sculpture in monochrome showing a wooden frame supporting varied objects. These included a cast iron, mechanical money bank with an arm designed to feed pennies into the gaping mouth of its black face. A peculiar reference, indeed. The reverse side was very different with black, seemingly random brush strokes, suggesting the work of a demented Japanese calligrapher. The apparently random nature of both pieces of cover art was presumably meant to suggest similar trends in the music.

'In the constantly changing and shifting world of jazz, experimentation is a necessity not a luxury,' claimed the sleevenote. 'Not all attempted change takes root and becomes part of the living fabric of jazz, but without the bold adventurers there would, in time, be very little besides stagnation.' Harriott was quoted: 'If there can be abstract painting, why not abstract music? There is a dividing line in my mind about what we are doing, but I think the best way of expressing this is to say that, while it has form, while the themes are structural, our approach to it is abstract. We make no use at all of bar lines, and there is no set harmony or series of chords, but there is an interplay of musical form and we do keep a steady four in the rhythm section.'[8]

Jazz Monthly's reviewer Burnett James saw the distinctiveness of Harriott's approach 'The attack seems to be less on the chord itself (as with Ornette Coleman) than on the chord progression. A similar challenge to the tyranny of the bar line is actually less new than it may at first sight appear. But the way in which it is done is also significant.'

James astutely pointed to a difficulty. 'Certainly, until these ideas gain wide currency and acceptance it will be impossible for a group of players to come together for the pleasure of making music spontaneously in 'free form'.' But he added, 'I can say that I have enjoyed this record a good deal. The 'free' interplay within the group as a whole, as well as between the soloists individually and with the rhythm section, is constantly intriguing ... in this 'abstract' music, Phil Seamen's drum solos do not sound merely dull and tiresome. Perhaps the reason is that a drum solo is by its nature 'abstract', and in this context it has a relevance that escapes it when the principal note is one of emotional expressiveness.'[9]

As for the jazz public's reaction to the music, Coleridge Goode felt, 'a lot of people liked it. I think the majority of jazz fans liked it but, funnily enough, it was the other musicians who were dead set against it. But we used to play in Ronnie Scott's Old Place in Gerrard Street and, as we all know, a few years later free music turned out to be very much the thing to do.'[10]

One musician dead set against it was Dizzy Gillespie. Harriott recounted to *Melody Maker*'s Bob Dawbarn that at an overseas festival, possibly Antibes, he asked Dizzy to sit in and 'he said, "I don't want to play none of your damn weird music."

Dizzy was put down in just the same way when he started experimenting. When he said that to me I felt, you can play *your* music better than anyone else, but you can't play *mine*.'

He also commented that: 'Someone with a rather different attitude was Cat Anderson. He came to one of our rehearsals and stayed so long he missed a Duke Ellington rehearsal. He wanted some of our music to take back to the States with him.'[11]

Anderson, who played trumpet with the Ellington band, would sit in with Harriott's quintet at the Marquee. Joe normally chose not to present a wholly free programme. 'We'd always mix it, you see,' remembered Coleridge. 'On one of our later albums we actually did one composition where we alternated between straight and free.'[12]

Smythe thought that, in embracing the new music: 'A classical training certainly helps. I feel very restricted when we get back to playing ordinary jazz themes. The chords come off that conveyor belt – big ones, small ones and so on – and you are dominated by them. In our new music you can play the normal changes if you want to, but there is somehow more reason for it if you do.' With so much freedom, Pat was asked how discords were avoided. He answered, 'you have to concentrate the whole time. If it clashes – well, that's part of it.'[13]

Reviewer Kitty Grime felt a studio atmosphere suited the pianist. 'Pat Smythe is heard to better advantage here than in a club. He sounds beautifully controlled, with what my piano teacher mum would call a 'singing tone'. His voice is the cool one of the group, but there is always an underestimated steel in his soul.'[14]

In the face of criticism, Joe defended his ideas. 'It is a big break from the regular formula … it is abstract music, not relying on chordal structures and not affected by harmonic sequences. It is the most free and easy form of music possible – and I predict that, eventually, it will be the type of music heard a lot in the clubs. It is so unrestrictive.' He reassured those who preferred his earlier repertoire: 'I cannot dismiss the standards – but I want to create a new type of music.'[15] He predicted that people would become increasingly receptive. 'So far nobody has thrown anything at us and, in fact, [the abstract performances] go down very well.'[16]

Phil Seamen, according to Jack Cooke, had been present at Joe and Dizzy Reece's 'free' experiments in 1958 at the Marquee and he surprised many with his acceptance of free form. Peter King said, 'Phil actually liked playing the new music but typically saw the humorous side and used to call it "free ... form ... five ... six music."'[17]

Keane temporarily left the band in October 1960 to go back to London University and Les Condon took his place. A professional since 1952, Les had heard the best on the New York scene when he worked on the Cunard liners. In the fifties he had worked with, among others, Ronnie Scott, Tubby Hayes and Tony Kinsey. As well as his ability on trumpet, he had a talent for arrangement and composition and a keen sense of fun.

He presented his arrangement of a Benny Golson number to Harriott: 'The first thing I broke with the group was Golson's 'Killer Joe'. I thought it was funny with it being Joe's band, and Pat Smythe was of a similar mind. But Joe didn't have much of a sense of humour. He said he wasn't sure about it and so on. He tried to change it round and have drums throughout instead of the way I had written it. I told him he could have my arrangement or Benny Golson's but he'd have to write it down himself from scratch because I wasn't letting him alter mine. He realised how serious I was and we did it with my arrangement.'[18]

The Dave Brubeck Quartet was at the height of its popularity in Britain in 1961. Their nine day concert tour of the country promoted by Harold Davison opened in London at the Royal Festival Hall on 21 January and Harriott's quintet was the supporting band for the tour. Joe told *Jazz News*: 'We're all very pleased that we've been given this opportunity and we're looking forward to it very much. This will give us a chance to feature our 'new' music on a wider scale and in concert where it will be very effective.' Harriott sometimes thought jazz club audiences were too noisy for prolonged exposure to free form and concert conditions promised a more receptive audience.[19]

On the second night, the Brubeck and Harriott groups appeared at the Victoria Palace. Critic Benny Green, Joe's old section-mate from Ronnie Scott's orchestra, was among those listening. Although he was not attracted to Brubeck's musical vision, Green praised the quartet's altoist. 'What makes the quartet worth listening to is the fragile beauty of Paul Desmond's alto saxophone.'

Not one to allow personal friendship to gag his honesty, Benny added: 'Appearing with the [Brubeck] quartet is a local group led by an alto saxophonist very different in character from Desmond, Joe Harriott. Under normal circumstances Harriott might be expected to supply a healthy antidote to the main attraction but, unfortunately, he is currently conducting an experiment called 'free form', which consists of not acknowledging the existence of melody in music. It is hard to believe that a jazz musician as accomplished as he cannot perceive the difference between free form and no form at all.'[20]

Steve Race, jazz pianist, writer and radio presenter, attended the same concert and was pleased to note that Joe had not taken to ignoring his concert audiences. 'Was Joe Harriott's performance any less artistic or less musicianly because he used neat music stands, dressed well, announced the items and got his musicians to bow their thanks? ... No, of course not ... Mind you, even the Joe Harriott quintet has its idiosyncrasies. When the curtain rose to reveal Phil Seamen wearing a look of extreme agony and Coleridge Goode wearing a look of benign pleasure, one hardly knew whether to award the band a 'U' certificate or an 'X'. Is it necessary to look so tortured Phil?'

Race was obviously aware that Phil's heroin addiction reduced him on occasions to a state of torture. He avoided saying the Harriott programme was torture to listen to, but came close enough, commenting that it was, 'like watching a film in which all the dialogue is in Swahili: one has difficulty following the story. I found myself in sympathy with the

Ancient Mariner – entirely surrounded by water, but unable to slake my thirst.'

'Not that free form is as free as all that,' his review continued. 'If it were totally free – harmonically, melodically and rhythmically – only one man could play at a time without disastrous results. As things are, Joe Harriott's new music never rejects the basic four-in-a-bar pulse of conventional jazz, with the result that Phil Seamen can play more or less as usual. Harmonically it tends to get hung up on a chord ... so that the bass player has some chance of playing notes which are complementary to the soloist's improvised line. To some extent even free form is planned.'

Race's other problem with the music then was that it clung too much to convention. He reported Harriott as saying, 'I take my theme and write it out; there must be a statement as a starting point.' But Race challenged: 'Why Joe, if the subsequent discussion is unrelated to that statement? And if you should insist that even an unrelated theme serves to warm up both player and listener, what reason can there be for returning to it at the end of the free section?'

Race ended with a plea for a Harriott programme featuring 'two distinct types of jazz: The conventional A-B-A 'busker' in which the soloist improvises within the normal bounds of harmony and eight-bar phrase; and the free section without any restrictions as to key or metrical form, unencumbered by written statements of unrelated material.' One of the BBC's most amiably avuncular figures of the sixties, Race couldn't finish on a sour note. A genuine fan of Joe's musicianship and particularly his bebop repertoire, he added, 'P.S. I forgot to mention ... it's a great quintet!'[21]

Coleridge Goode was concerned that Phil's dependency on drugs made it hard to rely on him. Notoriously unpunctual, Phil could scarcely have chosen a worse night to miss the band call than their Brubeck tour performance at the Hammersmith Odeon. Coleridge remembered how the other members of the quintet were forced to take the stage without Seamen who then appeared suddenly from nowhere just as the performance seemed doomed. 'And there and then, in front of everybody, he was sick all over the place with Brubeck standing watching us.'[22]

Although this dreadful incident went largely unnoticed and was not reported in the music papers, it was effectively the beginning of the end of Seamen's time in the quintet. Despite Phil's great talent, Harriott knew things couldn't go on like this. As for Brubeck's recollection of the Harriott quintet, it was, happily, positive: 'Now, I am eighty-two years old and sometimes it is difficult for me to remember back as far as the sixties. I do recall being on tour with Joe Harriott and thinking at the time that he was one of England's best.'[23]

Les Condon thought the Brubeck tour was the highlight of his year with the band. 'We were working every night. Normally you'd work two nights on and have five nights off. We honed the material. The Harriott quintet became more like an American quintet. Every night we were listening to the Brubeck band and they were listening to us. Americans were more economical in their arrangements. Less was more in a way.'

Condon described his time with Harriott and Seamen as 'a solid education.' He credited the drummer with reshaping his approach and making him swing better: 'Phil was an enormous influence on Joe's quintet.' Seamen was disdainful of players who played a lot of quavers. 'He called them "iddle diddle players" and he said I was one of them,' Condon said. 'He gave me a hard time for it. He took me to hear African bands to hear how they played. That's what he was into.'

Being with Harriott put Les on a fast learning curve too: 'Joe was a fast one. A great trick was ... he'd start and you wouldn't know which number it would be – 'I'll Remember April' or 'I Remember You'. There would be the abstract numbers of course and we'd know which of those we'd be doing.' The audience reaction to the abstract numbers? 'I think they were a bit mystified but at the end they would clap,' Condon said. 'They were used to clapping solos but in abstract numbers Joe would come in right behind me or behind the piano and they'd be unsure.'[24]

In March 1961 an audience at the London Palladium had no such problems when Harriott made a guest appearance playing music far removed from free form. Chris Barber had invited Joe to appear with his band at the prestigious *Jazz News* Poll Winners' Concert. The Barber band had, by a comfortable margin, won their poll category while, the previous month, Joe had personally been voted number one altoist in the *Melody Maker* Readers' Poll.

The omnipresent Denis Preston organised a recording of the concert. In addition to his long association with Harriott, he had enjoyed commercial success in recording both Barber and clarinettist Acker Bilk, notably with Bilk's hugely popular single 'Stranger on the Shore', which spent over a year in the charts. Preston's partner Adrian Kerridge was there too, in the role of technical director.

Harriott's jaunty calypso tune 'Revival' was played at the concert. Preston saw commercial potential in releasing it as a single but found the live version was too long. When he called the Barber band into the studios to make a shorter version, Joe was unavailable and thus lost the chance to play on a successful single.

'Revival' spent four weeks in the lower top 50 in January and February 1962.[25] Adrian Kerridge spoke for many when he suggested that the tune had been much better performed at the Palladium than in the studio, 'not only because Joe 'sparked off' other musicians around him. It was a live concert and the adrenalin was flowing.'[26]

Soon after, *Jazz News* reported that the controversial Harriott quintet would embark on a ten day tour of Ronnie Scott clubs in the provinces. By 1961, the success of Scott's in London had led to the creation of a circuit of clubs all linked financially to Scott, Pete King and promoter Harold Davison. It was expected that contracts covering several bookings would attract big jazz names to the provinces. Everyone connected with the music would benefit. In Scotland, jazz clubs in Sauchiehall Street, Glasgow and at the Tempo Club at 13 High Street, Edinburgh, were earmarked for financial investment. 'Great news for modern jazz lovers! Nothing like it has been heard of since the boom days at the West End Cafe,' enthused the *Edinburgh Evening News*, as the Tempo Club prepared to open its doors on 18 April 1961 with an appearance by the Joe Harriott Quintet. Joint promoter Ian Gordon, secretary of the Sporranslitters Jazz Club, announced: 'We'll be charging 6 shillings admission for the Harriott quintet. These are the prices asked in London's West End and our opinion is that Edinburgh has never had it so good as far as modern jazz is concerned.'[27] Edinburgh did not have it so very long either: the club folded after a short season.

On 28th April, Margaret Tynski was admitted to the St John's and St Elizabeth's Hospital, St John's Wood, for an emergency operation. Harriott was away touring in the Midlands. 'When I came round after the operation [Joe] was sitting by my bedside, holding my hand with a big smile on his face. He had caught the early morning milk train south. He then travelled north again for the evening set. That was how caring and loving he could be.'

'Joe came to collect me when I was discharged from hospital and Sister – the hospital was run by nuns – called us into her office and proceeded to give us a pep talk on being married before having children, especially to consider this, being Catholic. Joe listened politely but stifled a smile.'

In August, the quintet played at the Sixth Beaulieu Jazz Festival. *Jazz News* reported that the Harriott free form compositions 'Calypso Sketches' and 'Coda' were a revelation in their 'unexpected sense of musical humour' and remarked upon how well they were received by the audience. At the end of a long day of music which also featured the bands of Tubby Hayes, Chris Barber and John Dankworth as well as American singer Anita O'Day, the jazz-loving owner of the Beaulieu estate, Lord Montagu, announced that the concerts had proved that there was a public for modern jazz in England.[28]

That same month, the Harriott quintet was invited to play free form for BBC *Jazz Club*, to be broadcast on the 24th. Joe told Max Jones that he was 'very, very pleased to have the broadcast,' and added, 'I hope it won't cause a riot.'

By this time, the group had been presenting free form for eight or nine months and Harriott noted that this would be the music's first radio airing. 'This is our chance. I'd like to play all our advanced stuff but I don't suppose I'll do that. If we include one or two of the better songs that are known, it would balance the programme.'

'It's a case of letting the listener get both sides of the picture and see where the division lies, because there is a division between accepted jazz forms and the abstract approach. To some people the absence of harmonic and other restrictions is a stumbling block. The possibilities are too vast. It strikes at their basic beliefs.' Harriott said he understood the resistance but found the response encouraging in some quarters: 'It's being given a fair hearing, and a fair reception. At times, such as at Southampton University during Festival Week, the abstract forms went over phenomenally well.'

Studying at Southampton at the time, Richard Veasey vividly recalled that night. '[Joe] started his programme with a fair number of bop numbers and then after a while said he'd like to introduce one of the free form numbers. This went down so well that the band played nothing else for the rest of the evening. It is the only jazz concert I've been to – and I've attended quite a few in the past forty years or so – where the atmosphere was so electric that one felt emotionally elated and physically exhausted at the end. The university had a very thriving jazz club at the time and I remember quite a number of people commenting on this experience.'[29]

Joe was cautiously optimistic: 'I know this music has no commercial appeal, but I think in the next five years, maybe longer, it will take over, become the thing. There are pointers that way.' As always, he tried to explain his approach further. The word 'jazz' was not important, and what the group played could just be called 'abstract music'. 'Though we are concerned with swinging, I am not thinking of jazz at all, not in the known sense. I'm thinking of an artist, a musician, free to paint sounds, colours and effects as the ideas come to him.'

His colleagues were free to play as long as they liked without reference to the theme. They could experiment at will. For each musician, Joe ventured: 'The only discipline lies in your taste and in cultivating a positive approach now that you're free to create anything – rubbish, if you like.'

'You have endless possibilities, once you've thrown off the illusion of being within certain boundaries ... the set harmonic lines. You're in open space, so you construct as you go along, paint your own picture.' By this time, he was confident in his approach: 'The only danger is to a limited imagination. If you have a positive approach to ideas, the music will make sense.'

He was also sure the other members of the group felt the same way: 'Believe me, the fellows are happiest playing these jazz abstractions. With free improvisation, when you've finished what you have to say, you can at least feel, "That was *you*." It is an individual thing primarily, but the musicians try to blend as a group. What we've found, as we play more and more together, is that when we all think in this particular way, we can often sense what the others' intentions are – very much as in conventional jazz.'30

Present during the BBC recording at the Paris Theatre, Haymarket, was Margaret Tynski. 'Lord Montague was there. He was keen on Joe's music. For some reason, I cannot remember, I was given a stopwatch to count down to the red light or green light indicating "On Air". I was petrified I would miss the second for transmission. After the broadcast Lord Montague and Joe had a lengthy conversation.'

The drummer for the *Jazz Club* broadcast was Tommy Jones. Exactly a week later, this line-up, with Shake Keane in place of Les Condon, would make a fine record under Shake Keane's name. The EP *In My Condition* featured three Keane compositions and the first appearance on record of Harriott's bright tune 'Morning Blue'.

After appearing at the inaugural Richmond Jazz Festival on

Saturday 26 August, the band made their way to the Marquee for their regular spot and then on to an all-nighter at Rik Gunnell's. At some point in the evening Joe and Margaret Tynski had a row. Their relationship was becoming strained, not least because of evidence of his infidelity. 'One time when he'd been away on tour he arrived home exhausted. He came in, emptied the content of his pockets on the chest of drawers, as usual, threw himself on the bed and fell asleep. I was tidying up and found receipts for a hotel room made out in the name of Mr and Mrs Harriott. When I challenged him he said, as he had on more than one occasion, "You're my queen. I always come home to you."

'When we were out anywhere or in company he would always make sure his hand would be round my shoulder or waist, making a statement.' Joe, always fiercely possessive of his women, did not recognise this as operating double standards. Margaret, however, did and rows became more frequent and increasingly explosive.

An appearance at Ronnie Scott's Club in September drew admiring comments from Kitty Grime in *Jazz News*. She thought Joe was one of the select few who seems 'to get better, go deeper and lose another inhibition at every hearing. He is now one of the freest musicians we have and my vote for the British jazzman with the widest emotional range. He is intensely serious, uncompromising, but fully conscious of his audience.' With Bill Eyden deputising on drums for Seamen and the audience in a chatty mode, Kitty thought Harriott was reluctant to play the usual quota of 'free' numbers. She noted: 'There was only one of Joe's abstracts, with which his group comes closest to pure music, without the usual jazz-life associations.'

Kitty praised Pat Smythe's 'refined ear' and 'reticent but not inhibited' playing, which contrasted well with the 'fierceness' of Joe's delivery. Goode's bass playing was 'amiable and sure-fingered'. In a reference to his innovative home-built pick-up, she said, 'his solos are interesting, too, and you can hear them.'[31]

Exactly a year after leaving, Shake Keane returned to the band as Les Condon resumed freelance work, bowing out before a Marquee audience on 28 October 1961. Condon left with no hard feelings. He told me, 'I started to get extremely busy after the quintet and I didn't work with them again. I was lucky to last a year. He was a difficult guy to get on with, Joe.' Les also had concerns about Harriott. 'I had bad vibes from Joe about his health. I thought, this guy isn't going to last.'[32] Shake's return came one month before a big event for the quintet: the first recording session for its new free form album.

6.

America takes notice

Just as Joe's working life was reaching a remarkable new level of success, his domestic life was descending into turmoil. Tensions were heightened by a sequence of events tersely noted in Margaret Tynski's diary in September 1961: '21st – Joe working Satire Club. He had £1 from me. 25th – Joe had a £1 from me. Did not come home. 26th – Joe had a £1 from me.' And then on 30th October – 'Met Joe at the Cottage Club. He had £5 from me.'

During 1961, with regular weekend gigs at the Marquee and Flamingo and paying gigs at seventy-five other venues including the Brubeck dates, it is mystifying why Joe should have needed to take money from Margaret unless he was locked into an expensive gambling habit. Or was this simply evidence of his need to dominate or control her?

By October, in Margaret's view, 'the relationship had become so turbulent we would have destroyed each other by staying together. Both of us were possessive.' On the night of 4 November Margaret had made up her mind. The other women, the 'borrowing' and the rows were hard to tolerate. But there was also Joe's possessive jealousy manifested by his dislike of her working and seeing her own friends. A month earlier, he had gone out after a row, leaving her locked in the house, a prisoner in her own home.

Two months pregnant now with Joe's baby, Margaret's decision to leave was heartbreaking. 'Despite the recent rows, I loved him dearly. A girlfriend and I took a flat in Kilburn. Joe said that I took everything when I left. However, I left with what I went in with, excepting a small glass Bambi, which I have to this day. He had several glass animals which he liked.

'Joe had a complex personality. Having known him over many years, I grew to know his sensitive and vulnerable side which few experienced. On three occasions he was given to tears. On Thursday 23 November Joe called me and I went to the flat in the evening to see him and collect some things. I said I would not go back. He was very upset and cried.

'On Monday 4 December I saw him at Ronnie's. He insisted I go with him back to the flat [where] he was physically violent which was a terrible experience. Immediately afterwards he was shocked and horrified at what he had done. He broke down in tears. The following day he called me at work wanting to see me. I refused. Joe came to my address with chocolates and apologies to try and make amends.

'Joe and I didn't sever contact even though we were no longer living together. It was as if we couldn't let go completely. We called each other. I occasionally went to 94a. We met at the clubs and he wanted to know how my pre-natal check-ups progressed. After the birth of Zachary [28 April 1962] Joe and I saw each other in the street on 30th May. We had a long conversation. He wanted to know how his son was and once again asked me to go back to him.

'Joe eventually realised the relationship was over. He threatened me, "If I see you in the street or anywhere, I won't recognise you." I did see him one day in Paddington. He was walking towards me and walked straight past as if he didn't know me.'

After months of this Joe relented and did see Margaret. She recalled, 'Right through to October 1962 we were dating, meeting at clubs, eating out, discussing and trying to resolve our differences. [And] my telling him if I went back nothing would change. Despite his womanising and complex character I have never stopped loving the guy. I wonder how many others he called sweetie, darlin' and monkey face. And I wonder how long the queue of broken hearts! I moved on and got on with my life, albeit with Joe not far away in memory. Contact with Joe was necessary in respect of our son on two occasions. After May 1968 all contact was severed.'

*

By the winter of 1961 Joe's quintet had Shake Keane back in its ranks as well as Phil Seamen, Coleridge Goode and Pat Smythe. It was his dream band. They started to prepare an album, *Abstract*, that would feature seven new free form pieces and an individual take on a Sonny Rollins' composition, 'Oleo'.

The quintet practised at Dineley's Rehearsal Rooms in London. According to Coleridge, 'Joe was so precise in attack. "Get it right!" he'd say, and we did. The concentration was terrific.' Asked whether Joe praised good results, Bobby Orr replied, 'he never said much. We all knew how it should go. If he wasn't happy, he would just say let's do so and so. He never shouted at anyone.'[1]

On 22 November 1961, Goode once again made the short journey from his home to Lansdowne Studios carrying his bass down the building's narrow winding staircase. Lansdowne was now known to recording engineers as 'The House of Shattering Glass' because of its clarity of sound. In 1959 it had become one of London's first stereo studios.

Phil Seamen plays on five tracks of *Abstract*. Four of these were recorded at the November 1961 session. The other, 'Modal',[2] had been recorded a year before when *Free Form* was made but was not included on the earlier album.[3] Bobby Orr, who rejoined the quintet on Seamen's departure in March 1962, was on the remaining three tracks, recorded on 10 May 1962. As was his custom, Denis Preston gave Harriott a free hand in the course of the sessions. With an artist like Joe, he knew that the best results would come without interference.

All the tracks on *Abstract* were given single word titles. One of them, 'Tonal', was previewed on BBC radio's *Jazz for Moderns*. Presenter of the programme, Steve Race, introduced the piece: 'This begins with a theme statement in the usual jazz sense but the improvised solos that follow are free in every sense. Not improvisations on the theme, but sheer flights of fancy. This puts quite a strain on the rhythm section. After all, they are accompanying music which is as unexpected to them as it is unplanned by the soloist. But the flow of the ideas is two way. Any member of the quintet can contribute a sudden idea if he wants to for musical discussion.'4

On the broadcast, Joe clicked his fingers counting in the band and they produced a competent, if unfortunately truncated, version of 'Tonal', with some strident playing from Harriott and good interplay between the others.

That *Abstract* was a very important album was confirmed when it was reviewed in America's *Down Beat*, then the premier jazz magazine in the world. The review was quite sensationally enthusiastic. Reviewer Harvey Pekar began by pinpointing differences from Coleman's music.

'There is certainly some similarity between their concepts, but there also are notable differences, the most noticeable being Harriott's use of a piano in his group. One reason that many avant-garde groups have dispensed with the piano is that the improvisers feel its absence gives them more harmonic freedom. However, a piano need not be out of place in free form playing, as long as the pianist does not establish a pre-set pattern under the soloists when they don't want to improvise on one.

'Smythe, who listens and responds to the alto and trumpet rather than trying to make them play his way, is a great asset to this group. He solos well and adds a wider range of colour and textural possibilities to its palette.'

Pekar described the opening theme of 'Subject', taken at a fast tempo. 'The pace slows for the improvised section, which has both solo and simultaneous improvisation. The mood of this section is haunting, with both horn men using vocal cries. However, their playing is within the bounds of good taste and is sometimes lyrical. Smythe provides rich accompaniment, and Goode lays down some good lines. His tone is pure and full.

"Shadows' has no steady tempo and features some not very cohesive simultaneous improvisation. Listen to the rhythm section, though: Goode has a fine arco tone, and Orr is a first rate drummer – inventive with a clean technique and crisp touch.

'Sonny Rollins' 'Oleo' is highlighted by Keane's two imaginative flugelhorn choruses that begin with a fragment of the theme. He has an attractive muffled tone and good range. Harriott spends most of his time pulling against the beat on this track and never does get into anything.

"Modal' conveys a moody feeling not unlike the modal pieces on Miles Davis' *Kind of Blue* album.

'Smythe has a luminous spot at the beginning of the track, and Keane plays poignantly, with Harriott blowing behind him. The alto man is featured near the end of the track, and his playing has a lovely pastoral quality. Most of his solo is built around a few simple figures.'

Pekar thought Shake's solo on 'Tonal', 'nicely paced – powerful but leaving no doubt that he has something in reserve. Harriott has a compelling solo, original but conveying some of the restless drive of Charlie Parker ... Smythe's solo has a striking contrast; he begins with graceful single note lines but suddenly shifts to percussive chords.

"Pictures' has two moods; it opens with a rather tame 'menacing' section and then moves into a pretty line. Smythe is the main voice here, playing thoughtfully and at one point employing Bill Evans-like voicings. Goode plays well, both pizzicato and arco.

"Idioms' is a multi-themed, multi-tempoed composition by Harriott, perhaps his best written effort on the date ... The improvising is underlain by a swinging beat. Harriott plays with great urgency; Keane is alternately serene and violent. Smythe's intriguing solo has an oriental flavour. Also dig his comping here; he is an artist.

'Excellent percussion solos and duet work by Holder and Seaman [sic] highlight 'Compound'. The latter is a brilliant musician, one of the finest in Europe.'5

Pekar gave the album the magazine's highest rating, five stars, unprecedented for a British jazz group. Orr felt particularly honoured because in the same *Down Beat* issue one of his heroes, Art Blakey, received only a three star rating for his latest release. Reverberations were quickly felt through the whole British jazz scene, creating at least as much jealousy as admiration. No recordings by senior British modernists

Dankworth, Scott or Hayes had ever achieved such critical success in the USA. Forty years later, when asked to comment on Harriott for this book, Harvey Pekar gave his opinion without a moment's hesitation. 'I thought, and still think, that Harriott and Keane were among the finest avant-garde artists playing in the early sixties.'[6]

Roger Cotterrell, who wrote the first detailed study of Harriott's work to be published after the altoist's death, summed up the album's importance: '*Abstract* is unique and one of the great jazz records. The music is more confident and varied than on the quintet's first free form album and there are many moments of absolutely exquisite collective invention. All the performances have a feeling of effortless originality – breaking conventions but sounding unselfconscious about doing so. There is no sense of anything 'experimental' because the musicians are completely comfortable in their new-found idiom. Perhaps because of that, they sound uninhibited and joyful and there is a frisson of discovery in all of the music, the idea that it could take off in any direction and still somehow find a safe landing. *Abstract* preserved very special musical moments.'[7]

Joe sounded very satisfied with his new recording and optimistic about the direction in which his band was headed. 'One reason it comes off is, I think, the great unity of our group. The music has changed a lot since we started. This is very marked on our new LP. One side was recorded a year ago and you can tell the difference. My composing has improved, for one thing, and the band is playing the music better than ever. Originally my ideas about free form were a state of mind. They became a conviction. I want to accomplish something and I am absorbed in it completely.'[8]

My own favourite among the performances on the album is 'Modal' which is undoubtedly the most spontaneous, as it happened by accident. Coleridge Goode explains: 'The drummer was packing up and Pat sat at the piano and he was sort of doodling, playing and then Phil, who was the drummer – Phil Seamen – took his cowbell. He was standing up – took his cowbell and started to play this cowbell. Pat then ... reacted to this and I felt, "Yeah, that sounds good". Nobody had any idea about this. It was absolutely instinctive. Joe had been up in the box to listen to the playback so when we started, he came down ... and he joined in. So I called to the recording engineer, I said "Run a tape! Run a tape! I think we're gonna play something." And he did. He was running. So this thing started. Shake had a tumbler in his hand walking around the studio and when the drummer did the cowbell bit he tapped his pen or something on the glass. He always had a drink, some brandy or something. And miraculously it was an octave above the cowbell. And we started to play and out came 'Modal'. It was a miracle!'9

A performance like 'Modal' showed the incredible level of empathy which the members of the quintet had reached by this time. An unnamed reporter from *Jazz News* who heard them rehearse was moved to say that Joe and Shake 'must live in each others' minds to produce such fine jazz so spontaneously.' The article concluded: 'Go and hear the group if you haven't already. This is jazz which is meant to shock.'10 That kind of comment probably did the band no harm, but there is no evidence that they intended to shock. The quintet was steeped in knowledge of jazz history, capable of playing in any genre, and able to create their own. Writing music to shock would have seemed a rather lowly aim for Joe.

The early sixties were difficult times for budding British avant-gardists. Harriott had to compromise to take his radical music to the public. In a two hour concert he would play one hour of conventional music and one of experimental. Bobby Orr, primarily regarded as a committed bebop drummer, thought that, 'with the free form stuff it became quite exciting. You let your imagination go and sometimes it came off. Sometimes it didn't. You'd be thinking: "This is a load of rubbish," but just get on with it.'11

Benny Green said of Harriott: 'He was ready to accept the fact that there would be nights when nothing much happened, but decided it would be worth it for the moments when everything cohered.'[12]

The environment of free form very much suited Shake too. Kitty Grime observed: 'Shake Keane plays like no one else, he's impulsive and often outrageous, taking full advantage of the happy accidents which occur in improvisation.'[13]

Keane found the music absorbing. 'We have found we can expect greater audience tolerance for our free form pieces,' he told Grime. 'We can make the assumption that an audience will listen carefully. Early on, I used to watch their faces to see what effect we were having, but now I'm much less aware – there is so much to occupy me in the group. When we're well received, of course, we feel encouraged to give more.'[14]

Although the Marquee audience generally enjoyed and valued whichever form of music the quintet produced, the reaction of musicians and music critics to free form often bordered on ridicule or abuse. Attitudes elsewhere in Europe seemed more open, more appreciative that radical change every so often was essential to a healthy jazz scene.

The band's participation in a three day international jazz festival in Ascona, Switzerland, in August 1963, gave a welcome break from the controversy raging around their music. As usual, the quintet played a mix of ballads, free form and hard bop.

The audience liked the free form numbers, but particularly pleasing was the enthusiasm of the great German trombonist Albert Mangelsdorff. He had enjoyed the Harriott quintet at the San Remo Festival in 1959 when hard bop and ballads were their menu. At Ascona it was the quintet's new direction that most impressed him.[15] His own experience inclined him to side with those battling against censorship and narrow-mindedness. As a twelve-year-old, in the time of the Nazis, he attended secret meetings of the banned Hot Club in Frankfurt to hear jazz. Like Harriott, he found life changed for ever after hearing Charlie Parker. The quintet's new music left almost as indelible a mark on him as Parker had. Through the awareness of influential men like Mangelsdorff, Harriott's work made a striking impact on European jazz.

Mangelsdorff was exactly the kind of person Joe had in mind when he described what was needed for free jazz. He told Val Wilmer: 'One should not attempt abstraction if one doesn't have a vivid imagination. You must also know as best you can all the jazz idioms in case you need to draw on them in improvisation. It's a mistake to ignore the jazz past because that's like starting at the top and not knowing what went on at the bottom.' He also emphasised the need to be open to 'a wide range of stimuli' and cited his own catholic tastes extending to music from all over the world.[16]

Harriott's demeanour was very formal when he talked to audiences but he was only too happy to explain his new music to them. His references were taken from painting. 'In brief, our music may be said to be an attempt to add colour in jazz; at its present stage, the music has already experienced all the possible harmonic variations and permutations. This is a period of embellishment – but to accept this fact is apparently a fence over which few are prepared to step. We in our small way are trying to make this stride. The music we produce is therefore in the same idiom as modern jazz but much more varied. Of the various components comprising jazz today – constant time signatures, a steady four-four tempo, themes and predictable harmonic variations, fixed division of the chorus by bar lines, and so on we aim to retain at least one in each piece.'[17]

Drummer Trevor Tomkins admired Harriott's new music. 'I was underage and went to hear Joe play his free stuff. He was a wonderful orthodox player. Not just his chops and technique. Later in the sixties I spent a lot of time in New York. I was among the first to hear Albert Ayler's loft sessions. I thought it was a cacophony. Joe's was far superior, broader, deeper. It ran through a gamut of emotions. The free stuff he did had structure and growth.'[18]

In this respect, Harriott was more revolutionary than Ornette Coleman because, while Coleman allowed the soloist free rein over a more formal backing, Joe's music let the whole ensemble experience freedom simultaneously, all the time listening to each other and allowing influences to pass between them. Intensive practising paid great dividends as, night after night, this highly risky group improvisation led through broken time signatures, or key and mood changes, into closing periods where the unit came together again. Chris Barber understood why Joe loved playing New Orleans jazz: in some ways it was a similar environment of ensemble improvisation, with an emphasis on listening and trying to influence the other musicians to follow your lead.[19]

Harry South, former quintet pianist, heard 'Subject' for the first time when it was played for him as a member of a 'blindfold test' panel for *Crescendo* magazine. The purpose was twofold: to test participants' recognition of individual styles and to remove personal prejudices by keeping the chosen artists anonymous.

After listening to the track, South commented: 'I know Joe pretty well and I know what he's trying to do. But I couldn't quite see how he could formulate it – and I still can't, really, quite honestly. I don't condemn it, because at least he's trying something.'

He outlined his problem with Harriott's concept: 'I couldn't see eye to eye with Joe about this. I could understand one person doing it ... painting his own picture. But I couldn't see at the time how you could group five guys together and make them do the same thing, making a point of playing together.'

'You can't,' agreed South's fellow panellist, clarinettist Sandy Brown. He felt that free form could not really be free, 'because these guys are already committed to familiar patterns whatever they're going to do. And you can hear Joe doing it, and especially the bass player. He's doing a familiar chord sequence. Now all that's going to happen is that you're going to hear this familiar pattern, which doesn't fit with another familiar pattern which the other guy's playing. If you want to do something different, then you have to invent some new way of playing. And this is something they've neglected to do.' But despite criticising Harriott's music, Brown accepted Joe's sincerity and the individuality of his thinking.[20]

The quintet's next album, *Movement*, recorded in 1963, mixed five straight jazz compositions with four free form pieces and was seen by some as a retreat to safer ground. Despite this, with its release the following year Joe sounded optimistic about audience reaction to free form. 'It is getting across now and people are asking for individual numbers by name.' Rather than marking any change of direction, it could be argued, the mix of material on the album more accurately represented the quintet's club appearances than had *Abstract* and *Free Form*.

Nevertheless, Terry Martin reviewing it in *Jazz Monthly* called it 'schizophrenic'. 'Many commentators have noted this and attributed this quality to the leader,' he added. 'It would seem however ... that the hands of a sales-marketing A-and-R man held the reins of these sessions firmly in their grasp.'

'We can cut this record in halves,' he continued, 'and I doubt if there will be many who will appreciate both equally.' Of what he called the 'straightforward items', he particularly liked the 'exceptionally polished performance in the [Miles] Davis vein' of 'Blues on Blues' written by Michael Garrick.[21]

On this track, the unison playing of alto and trumpet is beautifully melodic but when I first heard it in the course of researching for this book, I was particularly taken by the stutter-like sound from Keane's muted trumpet which introduces the theme. I wondered if this was the way it had been composed, or an invention of Shake's. Garrick told me, 'I wrote the phrasing of 'Blues on Blues' with Shake's playing in mind. It's a grace note which drops an octave before hitting the main notes. On *Movement* you get what he did as his marvellous interpretation: no one else can do it.'

Garrick was reminded of Keane's unique ability while recording with his big band in 1998. 'We spent a good fifteen minutes listening to it before recording 'Blues No End Amen' (an extended version of 'Blues on Blues') ... None of the trumpet players (or other players) could get near Shake's effect! So I left it out. When in doubt ...'

Although Terry Martin felt the assurance of the 'straight' performances on *Movement* was extremely impressive, 'the imposed limitation of concept occasionally leads to an empty formalism and excess of familiar phrases.' The four free form tracks were the 'meat of the album' because 'we find qualities lacking in the above (the straight jazz), viz mistakes and invention, irrelevance and original expression.... The outlook [here] is unflinchingly abstract and fragmentary; improvisatory elements pass ceaselessly throughout the group, there are very few solos or even horn/rhythm interactions in the post-bop sense but there is a continual kaleidoscope of voice, mood and melody unlike the work of any other new wave group. There are some dangers and drawbacks; 'Face in the Crowd' seems diffuse and fails for me to get much beyond ultra hip background music and there is some needless repetition. But in 'Movement' and particularly 'Beams' we may find signs of an exciting vein of thought as yet ignored by jazz men – the emotional springs remain the same as always, of course.'

'Beams' was discussed in another *Crescendo* blindfold session, this time featuring British bassist Jeff Clyne and American trombonist J. J. Johnson. Clyne considered free jazz more enjoyable to play than to listen to. Johnson was unfamiliar with the Harriott quintet and predictably asked if they patterned themselves after Ornette Coleman.

'With the Coleman records I've heard,' Clyne remarked, 'I don't find the rhythm section wandering too much. Whatever they do seems to have some relationship to the ensemble. There's always a regular time thing going through Ornette's music. I think there is some similarity in the basic approach of Joe's group, but – in person, anyway – they seem to get freer than Ornette, and go wherever the wind happens to take them. As far as the improvisation side of it [goes] ... it is basically experimental music, so there's no guarantee that it's going to come off every time.'[22]

Clyne tactfully refrained here from saying, as he did on a

later occasion, that 'Joe Harriott and Shake Keane were doing the free thing better than a lot of the Americans right back in the early sixties.'[23]

On 'Spaces', the remaining free form track on *Movement*, much use is made of silence. The music is fragmented, with solo improvisations following each silent interval. It is intriguing to hear the undoubtedly personal responses from each band member and compelling on first hearing, as the listener can only guess where each player will take the music. As Coleridge Goode suggested while listening to it with me, this track could have been called 'Movement' because of the way the sound moves from one musician to another.

In the liner notes, Joe took a swipe at critics and musicians who said that what he was attempting in free music was impossible. 'But we've been doing it now for three years. Getting standing ovations at university concerts – and they're still saying it can't be done.' In his accompanying notes on the record sleeve, *Crescendo* editor Tony Brown remarked on Harriott's appreciation of his collaborators. 'Joe, it should be noted, doesn't take personal credit for all the group achieves. Free form playing is a group activity in which all the musicians forget about individuality and go into the realms of spontaneous and corporate composition.'

But Coleridge Goode detected a serious change in Harriott after the release of *Movement*.[24] Joe gave up writing for the group and showed strong indications of disillusionment and depression. The band gradually dropped free form and fell back on ballads and standards: safe, tried and tested numbers that avoided controversy. While this was possible in concerts, it raised a question as to what the band would do in its next recording session. Harriott appears to have opted out somewhat, leaving the normally reticent Smythe to step into the limelight.

In September 1964 the quintet took a new and unexpected direction by recording the LP *High Spirits*. The stage musical, 'the story of a marriage and a medium', was based on Noel Coward's 1941 play *Blythe Spirit* and had been a recent hit on

Broadway and in London. As the sleevenotes point out, 'much of the credit for the individual approach displayed here must be given to Pat Smythe.' Pat studied the *High Spirits* score, decided on the instrumental approach and the tempos for each piece and wrote all the arrangements. There is a good case for regarding this as a 'Pat Smythe Quintet' recording.

Smythe's pleasure in undertaking the task shines through in his comments. 'In general we found that Hugh Martin's melodies lent themselves admirably to jazz purposes. The ones that didn't ... well, they presented an interesting challenge. We felt the album ought to be attractive to the jazz public and also to the people who liked the show and the tunes in it. We have also tried to be faithful to the songs. Tempos have not been altered, other than to give variety here and there, except for 'Something Tells Me' which seemed suited to the fast tempo we chose. People will be able to recognise the tunes.'

Smythe's keyboard touch is as sensitive as on any other recording featuring his work. His arrangements and Martin's music are ideally partnered and some of the playing is exquisite. Smythe himself said of Keane's playing on 'If I Gave You': 'I don't think I've heard Shake play better than this – and he is a player of world class.' Harriott called the album, 'an unusual assignment because we hadn't done a whole show before. Normally we do a lot of completely free improvising, but here the numbers were set up and we kept [to] them pretty strictly. It's a case of the show's the thing, so this is a slightly jazzed up version, easy on the ear, I'd say.'[25]

Terry Martin, again the reviewer for *Jazz Monthly*, was lukewarm. 'The Harriott quintet is now a precision group, having stood up to far greater challenges, a fact confirmed by the easy confidence shown here. The style of performance is that of the straight jazz face of the group, the curious amalgam of cool, at times bordering on West Coast, and post-bop approaches, that is characteristic of Harriott and a reflection of his temperament.' He suspected that Shake was more at home with this material, suggesting that Harriott's 'front line partner probably prefers orthodox material, and Keane certainly hits winning form on this disc.'

Martin suspected that Joe found, 'little appeal in the task at hand and while remaining entirely himself – producing smooth variations on 'Home' and a more forthright scratching solo during the course of 'Was She Prettier Than I?' – is not at his peak.' He thought the best track was 'Something Tells Me', where the whispering alto quickly gains ferocity and sounds fine in a stop-time passage and Shake Keane touches in some delicate melodic detail despite the clipping pace.[26]

Martin's main, if only implied, complaint, I am sure, was that free form had apparently been abandoned. But the music had plenty of charm and Bobby Orr told me that 'Was She Prettier Than I' became a much requested favourite among the quintet's followers.

One night in late 1964 or early 1965 Trevor Tomkins, drummer with the Don Rendell–Ian Carr Quintet, turned up for work at the Marquee expecting to play sets one and three opposite the other group, the Joe Harriott Quintet. However Bobby Orr's car had broken down en route and he wasn't able to make it to the club that night. 'I played the first set with Rendell – Carr and then I had to do the next set with Joe's quintet,' said Tomkins. 'I ended up playing the whole four sets that night. The Rendell–Carr Quintet stuff was demanding anyway and of course, with Joe it was full steam ahead. I was absolutely soaked. There was no air conditioning then. It felt like I had jumped into a swimming pool. I didn't even have the energy to pack my kit away at the end and I left it till the next day. I remember it nearly killed me!'

Trevor remembered Keane's playing, alongside Harriott, Smythe and Goode on that night. 'I always felt that Shake was underrated, like Kenny Wheeler, because he was modest. But he also had that honesty and commitment to the music. His music was very real.'[27]

But Keane needed more financial security than work with the quintet could offer. He felt disillusioned that the group's most imaginative work lacked recognition and acceptance. Some of the worst reactions had come from fellow modernist jazzmen. Tubby Hayes heard the Harriott quintet play an abstract piece and declared: 'If that's fucking jazz, give me trad!' That he could feel so vehemently opposed to what the band was trying to achieve three or four years after free form's inception, shows the extent of the struggle to get the music accepted.[28]

Keane, Harriott's ideal partner, left the band after the release of the album *Movement*. Their personalities were very different yet their musical compatibility was complete. In this case, as in so many others, musical and personal closeness did not go together. Shake's departure for Germany, where he gained lucrative work with the Kurt Edelhagen Orchestra, was a fatal blow to the quintet. Goode said, 'Shake was absolutely crucial, vital to the sound of the quintet. He moved partly because there was no recognition of what we were doing and the work he was being offered was regular income. He needed to play and earn a living.'

Michael Garrick felt that 'Shake deserved more of the attention. He was a very accomplished all-round musician. In many ways a deeper musical talent than Joe Harriott. He was absolutely unique in his phrasing. By going for more commercial success he gave up on his jazz career and never recovered his flair after that.' No trumpeter adequately replaced Keane in the quintet. This is not to belittle the talents at Joe's disposal; it was just that Shake was unique.

7.

poetry and jazz in concert

When Michael Garrick was expelled from piano lessons
for the sin of including a quote from 'In The Mood' during
an altogether too serious soirée, it taught him something
about attitudes in the academic world of music. Convinced
that snobbery would get in the way of his musical tastes, he
decided, instead of studying music, to opt for a degree in
English literature at University College London. He continued
to exercise his musical creativity by forming his first modern
jazz quartet while attending the college in the late 1950s and
was gradually able to bring his passions for jazz and poetry
together.

The poetry–jazz connection in America was well established
by then. The beat poets and bebop jazz musicians not only
supported each other at readings but in some cases inter-
changed roles. The beat poets derived their name from the
'beatnik' subculture and helped set modes of fashion for
American youth of the 1950s. To avoid looking 'square' one
acquired the uniform of 'cool': beret, t-shirt or huge loose knit-
ted sweater, tight jeans and omnipresent shades. The 'beats'
adored Charlie Parker and Dizzy Gillespie, perhaps as much
for the hostile reaction they drew from the older generation as
for their music.

The beat poets intuitively opposed the 'square' conventions
on which the survival of materialist society seemed to depend.
They were more cavalier than earlier poets in their use of
spoken and written language, less committed to fixed verse or
recognised meter. So they were ideal collaborators, first with

bebop, then with a burgeoning avant-garde music scene. Their counterparts in Britain were less anarchic in their art and less revolutionary in their politics than the Americans but there were some British poets willing to address the taboo subject of sexuality and to challenge the 'bomb culture' morality of the Cold War.

Across Britain, in venues of every description, jazz and poetry concerts sprang up from the beginning of the 1960s. Poet Michael Horovitz had begun staging his 'Live New Departures' arts circuses in 1959 while still a student. 'I often found myself at all-nighters – the Americana, Flamingo, and Florida Clubs – with London's Bohemian night people and loads of American GIs on weekend leave from their bases around England. Tony Kinsey, Phil Seamen and Ronnie Scott were mainstays of the all-nighters. I was a scruffy beatnik at the time. One night Dizzy Gillespie declared: "Man, you look like early pictures of Christ!"'

Horovitz often ran into Joe Harriott around the Soho jazz scene, and enjoyed his unusual interest in literature and philosophy: 'He had just as personal a take on these subjects as he did on music, apart from an apparently embedded interest in Rosicrucianism.' In November 1960 Horovitz presented an impressive line-up of poets and musicians, including the Harriott quintet, at the Institute of Contemporary Arts in London.

'The place was choc-a-bloc,' remembered Horovitz. 'Bruce Turner and Dudley Moore accompanied some of my jazz poems. I'd rehearsed a 'Funky Blues' dedicated to Charlie Parker, with Joe Harriott in an ICA dressing room upstairs before the gig and he'd responded with beautiful licks, counterpoints and trills. On the night Joe was very preoccupied with his band and he said he'd rather not do that *and* a band set. They were on last and they played amazingly. As I recall, the quintet played only free form numbers with great panache and brought the house down; the closing highspot in a marathon of highspots.'[1]

This appears to have been the only occasion when the quintet gave a wholly free form performance. *Guardian* photographer Maurice Hatton covered the event for the newspaper. His photograph of a delighted Seamen with a quizzical Harriott captures the contrasting personalities of the two musicians. Horovitz and Pete Brown are shown reading their marathon 'Blues for the Hitch-hiking Dead' with flautist Mike Berke accompanying.

Also appearing at the ICA event was William Burroughs, famed American beat writer of the nightmarish junkie novel *The Naked Lunch*, which had caused a furore on its appearance in 1959. Burroughs was a senior founding father of the beat movement, revered by younger members such as Jack Kerouac, Allen Ginsberg and Gregory Corso. His powerfully experimental writings have continued to impact on the wider literary world, somewhat paralleling the opening up of music by successive groups of jazz innovators. Horovitz noted that 'William Burroughs visibly warmed to Joe's playing.'

'I loved Joe's music before, during and after his free form period,' said Horovitz. 'I think Joe relished my associates, my company and activities partly because we shared an interest in abstract/expressionist art in several media. The ICA show at the time of our gig was just this kind of art.'[2]

Other jazz and poetry events were organised by poet and publisher Jeremy Robson. 'I was young and felt a missionary zeal to bring poetry to more people than would otherwise hear it,' he explained. His success could be measured in the audiences and media attention his concerts drew. 'Sometimes we had to turn away 400 people.' A keen jazz fan, he saw the mutual benefit in the events for poets and jazzmen, all too often the Cinderella figures of the arts. Like Harriott, he was aware of the connections between different artistic media.[3]

'It is a mistake to think of art forms as being separate. All art, whether painting, music, drama or literature contains its measure of rhythm, colour and tone,' Robson told *Jazz News*. 'Every language reflects rhythms of life and thought which in turn mirror life's preoccupations. These are experienced and expressed by the artist and communicated to audiences who, by it, may gain a greater insight into themselves and their time.'4

In June 1960, Robson attended *Jazz and Voices*, a programme devised by Michael Garrick and bassist Johnny Taylor in the old Recital Room above the Royal Festival Hall.5 He put to Garrick a proposition for touring concerts, in which poems lending themselves to jazz accompaniment would be set to Garrick's compositions. Robson's budget allowed for a quintet or sextet. Garrick needed no further persuasion and enlisted Harriott, Shake Keane and Coleridge Goode whom he knew from the early days of the Marquee Club.

Garrick's love of both poetry and music mirrored that of Keane, whom the poet Adrian Mitchell recalled informally reciting his own poetry in dressing rooms and pubs. Goode's quiet, reserved exterior belied his eagerness to take on new challenges. And Garrick liked playing with Harriott, as he told *Jazzbeat* magazine, 'particularly because of his feeling and the adventurousness it can create. Also because of a certain naivety which carries with it a spontaneity that a lot of British players fall short of. This lack of naivety and spontaneity leads to what the BBC call 'doomy sounds', long faces and so on. I like to be happy when I'm working although not a few people have associated me with doomy sounds because of the reflective way I like writing.'6

Adrian Mitchell enjoyed participating in events staged by Robson, Michael Horovitz and Pete Brown. 'I went round with both circuses,' he laughed, remembering them. 'Mike and Pete's were ramshackle, wild ... out of hand, and ended when the last people left. They always finished with their 'Blues for the Hitch-hiking Dead' which had about 400 verses. They never ended it. Jeremy's were more disciplined and allowed a quarter of an hour for each poet. The main problem was that there was never enough time to rehearse with the musicians. If there was a poem you did with jazz, it tended to always be that one. I tended to do 'Pals'. I didn't know quite how to do it, I just went along with Mike Garrick.'7

Robson was able to call on excellent musicians and some of Britain's most distinctive poets. The quirkily eccentric Stevie Smith, as well as Laurie Lee, Vernon Scannell and Ted Hughes were among those who participated.

Not all the poets wanted direct jazz accompaniment. Garrick remarked with humorous exaggeration that Dannie Abse did not want his poetry 'contaminated by jazz'. Abse put it more gently: 'I felt, as Laurie did, that poems had their own music and didn't need it.'[8]

Abse, a playwright and poet as well as a qualified doctor, remembered his unease at his first poetry and jazz event in February 1961. Robson had telephoned inviting him to participate in a poetry reading at Hampstead Town Hall where the readers would include Jon Silkin and Lydia Slater, the sister of Boris Pasternak, reading translations of her brother's poems. Abse remains sure that neither jazz nor Spike Milligan were mentioned. He approached the venue not expecting a big audience, 'so when I saw in the distance an extraordinary long queue stretching between the Odeon and the Town Hall I briefly wondered what popular film was being shown that night in the cinema.'

Negotiating his entry past an irritable doorman barking 'Full up!' Abse heard the unmistakable voice of Spike Milligan on stage saying, 'I thought I would begin by reading you some sonnets of Shakespeare – but then I thought why should I? He never reads any of mine.' No doubt already disorientated, Abse didn't like the jazz that night either: 'blaring, raucous, too near.'[9]

But it went down well with audiences and Robson soon found a momentum building for the jazz and poetry roadshow. 'The first concerts were fairly self-financing and then we started getting invited by the Arts Council, schools, etc. Then I was contacted by the playwright Arnold Wesker. He was putting on festivals with the trade unions through his organisation Centre 42 and we ended up doing a lot of concerts with him.'

Robson remembered his first meeting with Harriott. 'I'd been talking with Denis Preston at Lansdowne Studios about doing a poetry and jazz recording and he had introduced me to Joe Harriott who'd been recording one of his free form albums there. As a regular visitor to jazz clubs I was well aware of who he was. He was quite aristocratic in his manner. I remember Joe discussing free jazz with me and in doing so he mentioned 'the petals of a rose'. He said he was trying to play the feeling of the inside of the rose.'[10]

On 7 December 1962 at Lansdowne, Harriott made his first jazz and poetry recording. The Columbia EP *Blues for the Lonely* was by Jeremy Robson and a quintet led by Michael Garrick that included Joe, Shake Keane, John Taylor on bass and drummer Alan 'Buzz' Green. Garrick composed three pieces for Robson's poems: 'Cascade', 'Sketches of Israel' and 'The Day of Atonement'. The title track was accompanied by improvisations on the sequence of Miles Davis' 'Blue in Green'. Three years later the same pieces were recorded for Argo Records, with Ian Carr and Colin Barnes replacing Keane and Green.

In fact, from 1963 and for many years, Argo was the main company documenting Garrick's music, including poetry and jazz. Many of the records involved Joe Harriott. 'Argo was the brainchild of Harley Usill.' Garrick explained. 'He had been a film and sound recordist for the Central Office of Information during the war and after that he decided to start a record company. He loved railways. He was one of those steam engine buffs and he would go with his tape machine, a big heavy thing then, to all the railways and record them, all the little ones going up Welsh Mountains and so on. One side of his company was called Transacord and these were the railway engine recordings. There were a lot of them and they used to sell extremely well.'

'The other side pursued his interest in early English music and poetry. He recorded all the works of Shakespeare. He had excellent actors and actresses, and so on, and he recorded a lot of contemporary poets. When we came to do our poetry and jazz concerts at the beginning of the sixties ... I sent him a tape. He said yes and that's how it began. He was very

interested in the poetry. He didn't know very much about jazz
but he liked what we did.'[11]

As poetry and jazz bookings became more frequent,
Harriott and the other musicians spent time familiarising
themselves with Garrick's compositions at Dineley's Rehearsal
Rooms, unchanged since Ronnie Scott had struggled to knock
his big band into shape there, years before. Interior surfaces
were buried beneath thick layers of paint. Old linoleum still
dominated the corridors of this former department store,
which Garrick described as 'a rabbit warren'.

On June 10th 1963, *Poetry and Jazz in Concert* was recorded
before a live audience at Decca's Hampstead studios. It was
released by Argo in two separate albums even though, artisti-
cally, a double album might have been better. Garrick's *Blues for
the Lonely* quintet, with Colin Barnes now on drums in place of
Alan Green, supplied the music. The first album includes
Garrick's joyful 'Wedding Hymn', which as he pointed out, 'is a
bit high for trumpet, but Shake makes a valiant and victorious
assault upon it.'[12] Dannie Abse, Laurie Lee, Jeremy Robson and
Adrian Mitchell supplied the poetry.

Mitchell relished working with jazz musicians. 'Jazz was my
rebel music. We had a jazz gang at school and we'd listen to
Bessie Smith and Fats Waller. Joe and Shake were amazing personalities and wonderful musicians. I was in awe of them.
Shake was a genial, great big Father Christmas. I felt at ease
with Shake. Joe was sterner, very dedicated. For him, this was a
serious business.'[13]

The live audience was clearly intended to provide a
concert atmosphere but, on the recording, the audience seems
unsure of itself and first reactions of less intimidated members
are immediately aped by the rest. Listening to their uncertain
laughter on record, I picture them looking round at each other
to make sure they have got it right. But the musicians sound
sure of their role.

'Vishnu', a driving Garrick composition on the second LP,
has a good Harriott solo with his familiar raw-edged tone. A
walking bass leads in as Shake reaches for his flugelhorn on the

short melodic accompaniment to Robson's reading of 'Approaching Mt. Carmel'. Another Robson poem, 'The Midnight Scene', is presented with opening unison playing by Harriott and Keane followed by discordant, raucous notes and much changing of tempo. 'That phrasing,' Joe told Garrick during rehearsal, 'is full of jazz feeling.'

Those words of praise were distinctly encouraging for Garrick. 'What I scribbled down for [Joe and Shake],' he recalled, 'was devoid of any marks of expression, dynamics and so forth: I didn't know any! But what came out of those horns was a perfect understanding of what I was trying to say. Beautiful, unique.'[14]

Garrick's setting of Robson's 'A Face in the Crowd' comes close to free jazz. An anarchic section in the middle is resolved by a harmonious finale. Inexplicably, a 'Dixieland Improvisation' appears next. The steady beat and use of cymbal is like an accompaniment for the high kicking routines of the Tiller Girls at the London Palladium.

Adrian Mitchell told me his favourite story from the jazz and poetry concerts. 'We were playing a school one evening and we were backstage with some beer bottles. We were having trouble opening them but nothing stops a jazz musician, or a poet for that matter, and pretty soon someone had a bottle in the door jam. In came a man in heavy-framed spectacles and sports jacket: clearly a teacher, very stern and square. Joe and Shake were very cool people, but the rest of us, we had ourheads down.'

'"What's the problem?" the teacher inquired. On realising what was needed, he rolled up his trouser leg, put the bottle behind his knee, bent it and opened the bottle with his artificial leg. It was a moment when all of us laughed at once.'[15]

Quite apart from Garrick's projects, Harriott was involved with his own quintet in a collaborative arts entertainment in an Edinburgh Festival late-night show *Ex-Africa* at the Lyceum Theatre. Billed as 'A Black Odyssey in Jazz, Rhyme and Calypso', it presented 'many aspects of Negro culture' and ran for a week in September 1961. Devised by Jamaican dancer, actor and singer Bari Johnson, the show had been at the Royal Court Theatre, London before heading for Edinburgh. Johnson told me: 'Shake Keane I knew quite well from the theatre world in London.... They were really, really fantastic musicians and had developed their free form music which they played on stage.' The show apparently had to be cut short on its first night, 'because there were ten items more than there was time for.'

In a week when American black civil rights activists were pressuring the U.S. Congress to speed up progress on civil rights laws and in Britain the National Union of Teachers expelled a racist member, the show was described in the *Edinburgh Evening News* as depicting 'how the Negro reacted to the agonies of his various environments.'[16]

The *News* declared: 'The Joe Harriott Quintet was an integral and completely essential part of the production, playing excellent jazz throughout.' *The Scotsman* observed that, 'the quintet was 'equally at home with African themes and modern jazz'. Keane recited poems at each performance, including one of his own. *The Scotsman* duly noted that only two members of the cast were white and they, indeed, were Scots: quintet members Orr and Smythe.[17]

Perhaps the last point is not irrelevant. Bill Ashton, founder of the National Jazz Youth Orchestra, observed that, 'the greatest jazz musicians come from oppressed peoples. The blacks have their blues, the Scots, their pibroch and the Jews have their Jewish minor scales.'[18]

By the end of the week the band had made a big impact in Edinburgh. 'Harriott Group a Breath of Fresh Air' trilled the *Evening News*: 'Joe Harriott and members of his quintet ... have instilled new enthusiasm in the jazz scene in Edinburgh. Throughout the week Harriott and flugelhorn player Shake Keane and other quintet members have been regularly sitting in with Edinburgh musicians. Tenorist Jack Duff, with whom Harriott played for about an hour, said, "It was a great experience. He really made the Festival for me."'[19] Bari Johnson, too, was impressed with the passion Harriott and Keane had for playing. 'They were real musical enthusiasts.'[20]

As for poetry and jazz concerts, many were held around the country in the following years. For the poet Dannie Abse, one night stood out. It was 22 November 1963. 'We were to give a concert, sponsored by the Welsh Arts Council, at the King's Hall, Aberystwyth. Ten minutes before it was due to start I sat in a pub across the road from the King's Hall with Joe Harriott.... The [pub] radio's volume was suddenly turned up cutting through conversations. A wild voice said, "Kennedy. Kennedy. Kennedy. Shot. Assassinated. Dead. Kennedy."'

'We quit the pub and crossed the road to the stage door of the King's Hall. It was half past seven. The manager thought it too late to cancel the concert.' He decided that before it began he would announce the death of the American President. Then there would be a two minute silence. '"Yes", said John Smith, one of the poets that night, "that would be best." But someone stupidly inferred that Kennedy had probably been assassinated by a member of the Black Power movement. Joe Harriott and the trumpet player, Shake Keane, stood close together talking passionately about something beyond our hearing. We overheard the sense of it only. They suddenly were two black men and we ... [were] white.'

All the performers were called onstage for the manager's sombre announcement and his request for a two minute silence. The audience rose as requested and everyone shared the enormity of the occasion. Then, 'the silence finally snapped with the audience unaccountably clapping and clapping. They were in a theatre. And how do people express emotion in a theatre? They clap.'

Abse was convinced that the audience responses that night were heightened by the emotional atmosphere preceding the performance. The clapping was louder. The laughter more sustained.

After the performance, the manager, seeking support for his decision not to cancel the show, asked the poets and musicians: 'It was the right thing to do, don't you think?'

Harriott said simply: 'Man, the Windmill never closed,' referring to the famous theatre which defied the bombing in the wartime Blitz.[21]

Abse mentioned a bizarre incident that took place after one reading. 'Joe and I went to an Indian restaurant. There was a chap sitting at the next table, with a knife and fork, just rubbing them together, staring at us continually. You can imagine the grating sound. It was very threatening and I was relieved when Joe said he thought we should move to another table.'

As always, Harriott committed himself fully to the music at poetry and jazz events and gave no other reaction to the words spoken by the poets. But Abse was bemused by one musician's response to a poem he often performed. 'I remember the drummer Trevor Tomkins always laughing while I read 'Funland'. After we'd been doing it for years, he one day suddenly said to me: "I've just realised, that's a sad poem," which indeed, it was.'[22]

At a poetry and jazz concert in Stoke-on-Trent, Abse sat within earshot of the musicians while they discussed cannabis. He heard familiar claims that its use improved musicians' playing. As the claims extended to other qualities of the substance, he heard Joe grumble, 'it may be an aphrodisiac but it don't do much for me, man.'[23]

Flying didn't do much for Joe either. Abse remembered going to Belfast. With snow on the ground and a gale blowing, it was doubtful whether the plane would take off. 'We were at the airport but Joe wouldn't go on the plane. I said we'd probably get above the storm by plane. But he had decided he would go by sea! It was crazy!' His aversion to flying meant enduring a horrendously rough ferry crossing.[24]

Colin Barnes remembered Harriott travelling alone on the ferry for that Belfast trip. 'It wasn't really surprising that he would go on his own like that. He was a big star, a leader in his own right, and so strong-willed once he'd made his mind up. We played the concert and then did an extra impromptu date at a student jazz club because there was a festival going on. We were stranded in Belfast, I remember, because then snow came in and we couldn't get out by air or sea.'

Barnes told me that as Michael Garrick had not passed his driving test, a four-wheeled car was not an option for him. Garrick's favoured mode of personal transport was his beloved Robin Reliant. Often the butt of jokes, Reliant drivers fail to comprehend the humour their cherished chariots provoke in everyone else. Harriott always took advantage of any lifts he could get to and from gigs. For a considerable time he turned to Coleridge Goode for this courtesy until, working with Garrick, he engaged the pianist as his unpaid chauffeur. This continued until one night when, as Colin Barnes remembered, Joe emerged shaking from the Reliant following a 60 mph journey he'd found particularly harrowing. All he could say was, 'Michael Garrick – he go too fast on his one wheel!'

After that, it was Barnes who helped Harriott get to gigs. 'I had a little mini van and I'd pick Joe up at the West End. Musicians are notoriously bad time keepers, but Joe was always there right on time and very grateful for the lift.'[25]

The *Poetry and Jazz in Concert* albums were very well received. 'Everybody seemed to like them,' Garrick recalled, 'and then Harley Usill said, "Would you like to do one on your own just with the music?" Harley liked it. He was a gentleman. He wasn't a shark. So we did the one after *Poetry and Jazz*. It was *October Woman*.'

October Woman was recorded in November 1964 by Garrick with Harriott, Keane, Barnes and Coleridge Goode who had now become Garrick's regular bassist. Charles Fox, doyen of British jazz critics, found some faults with the album. Keane performed 'satisfyingly enough on the title piece, which is more or less a vehicle for his talents, but on 'Seven Pillars', 'Sweet and Sugary Candy' and 'Sketches of Israel' he conveys an impression of thinking about the changes as well as playing them. Nor, for that matter, is Joe Harriott as carefree as he normally sounds. He even seems a trifle distraught on 'Little Girl', a track which features his playing – and which is, apart from this air of spindliness, a fairly satisfying performance.'

Fox most enjoyed 'Anthem' and 'Echoes' where Harriott and Keane 'really unleash themselves' and 'where they come closest to free form jazz.' Even the ever-reliable Goode didn't escape censure. 'I'm not so happy with Coleridge Goode. He performs nicely enough in the section, but he displays a distressing fondness for these solos which involve humming (for want of a better word) as well as playing. I grew very tired of this particular gimmick almost as soon as Slam Stewart thought it up a quarter of a century ago.'[26]

More positive responses to *October Woman* came from other quarters. Dave Double in *Crescendo* magazine enjoyed the exciting 'Anthem', 'with driving solos by Harriott and Keane, often improvising simultaneously' in free form. He thought the group sounded 'completely at home in this relatively uncommon time signature (5/4 time).'

Double particularly liked Harriott's 'delicate Konitz-like sound' on 'Little Girl'. On 'October Woman', Keane soloed 'with originality on flugelhorn, wending nimble-fingered through the shifting tonal centres of the haunting [Garrick] composition.' Double concluded: 'Because the group is playing music in which it obviously believes wholeheartedly, and because the compositions have been written with their own sense of purpose, this has produced a fine jazz LP.'[27]

On 10 April 1965 the *October Woman* line-up was augmented with Simon Preston on organ and the Elizabethan Singers to record new versions of 'Anthem' and 'Wedding Hymn' for an EP. After that, the next album Harriott made with Garrick was *Promises* with trumpeter Ian Carr in place of Shake Keane and Tony Coe adding his clarinet and tenor sax to the musical palette.

Charles Fox reviewed *Promises* and the *Anthem* EP for *Jazz Monthly*. He thought *Promises* superior to *October Woman* but complained that, 'Garrick still has a tendency to devise pieces that make his musicians play out of character. On 'Parting is Such' for example, with its theme like a Johnny Hodges tune (but much wryer), Joe Harriott sounds more like Lee Konitz than the alto player we know him to be.' He thought Joe sounded like Paul Desmond in the Brubeck-like composition 'Portrait of a Lady', 'although Harriott does grow more authoritative as the track progresses.' Ian Carr, however, had probably 'never played better on record'. There was more warmth in the critic's tone when he discussed *Anthem*. 'Both Joe Harriott and Shake Keane hit their peak form, especially in 'Anthem', where the solos are surprisingly intense.' Despite his preliminary fears that the EP's attempt to fuse jazz with liturgical music would end in disaster, Fox finally commended it as 'stimulating' and expressed the 'hope that our grumpier reviewers will not dissuade Michael Garrick from following it up.'[28]

Black Marigolds, recorded in January 1966, was one of the most successful collaborations ever between poet and musicians. This was the final album Garrick recorded with Harriott and featured the poet John Smith reading his 'Jazz Nativity' and 'Jazz for Five'.

Uniquely among the jazz poets, Smith wrote poems to complement the individual styles of the musicians. 'Jazz for Five' is a sequence of five poems, each written to be accompanied by one of the members of Garrick's quintet. Smith told me: 'Curiously enough when I met Mike Garrick and began to read with the group I knew very little about jazz and spent most of my time listening to Haydn and Bartok string quartets!'

'I was a good friend and still am of Dannie Abse, both as poet and his literary agent, and also Jeremy Robson and Vernon Scannell. I also felt very at home with the musicians and spent more time with them than the other writers. I think my own poems for them were different (not better!) from theirs because I wrote for the individual players ... trying to reflect their personalities, so that in 'Jazz For Five', the first one for Mike is very calm and classical as he has a kind of Mozartian feel. Then Coleridge, of course, bowed his bass so [his poem] was more flowing. The drummer at the time was a very strict player so his was more staccato. Shake [was] a sort of golden player, sunlike and with a style to match his appearance, so his was a kind of celebration. But the one for Joe Harriott was perhaps the most personalised, much freer in performance because I was able to enter into his phrasing and try to become more emotional.'

'He was a remarkable man and an astonishing player. We could not have been more different but although I did not know him well I liked him and was stimulated in his presence – but with the others as well. Coleridge the perfect gentleman, Shake deeply distressed by the racial prejudice – worse at that time. Perhaps [he was] a musician wishing to be a poet as I, a poet, wished to be a musician.'[29]

On the album, Smith's reading of the poem he wrote with Joe in mind, the disturbing 'He Ran Out Crying', is perfectly accompanied by the forlorn sounds from Harriott's alto. 'Pent-up passion' is how Garrick described Joe's playing on this piece. On first hearing, it is simply stunning. Harrowing too, but a beautiful depiction of the isolation of grief. One feels Joe is drawing from his own experience in producing the emotion therein.

He ran out crying
He ran out crying
He said
Oh my most beautiful dear girl
Oh my most beautiful dear girl
He ran out crying
He said
All the windows, all the windows and doors are crying
The locks broken on their hinges are crying
He ran out
Oh my most beautiful
He ran out crying
The air
The air is on fire

And all Christ's tears will not quench it
(He ran out crying)
Where, Oh my most beautiful dear girl,
My most beautiful dear girl lies dying

The last word of the poem trails slowly and the other musicians join in the closing, discordant fanfare with Ian Carr's trumpet sounding suitably harsh. But this is very much Harriott's piece and well worth the hearing.

Discord eventually drove a wedge between Joe and the Garrick Group. Harriott seemed to be pining for Shake's presence on the bandstand. 'He started to play up and he didn't want to work with Ian,' explained Garrick. 'That's what it was. That's how Joe and I parted company on the stand one night. He just wouldn't play. He just stood there. When that happened I was with this group [the Don Rendell – Ian Carr Quintet] and they were getting lots of publicity, winning *Melody Maker* awards. Jeremy [Robson], who was still running [poetry and jazz events] said: "Now that Joe's being problematical, let's have Rendell–Carr." And so for the remainder, a couple of years, we had that group instead.'[30]

Reflecting decades later on his time with Harriott, Garrick said: 'It was for me a great gift to work with him and Shake and learn from their unmatchable jazz instincts. All I had to do was to scribble the barest of leadsheets – and out came the most perfect of interpretations, complete with all the inflections and feeling I could ever hope to hear.'[31]

8.

the many sides of Joe Harriott

Joe Harriott presented many faces to the world. The impression he made on people largely depended on the rapport, or lack of it, achieved with him. He polarised opinion. Those who felt rebuffed or ignored by him often conceded that he probably had good cause to distrust and be wary of people. Others, while feeling affection for him, thought that some problems he faced were of his own making. One view is that the often mentioned 'chip on his shoulder' sprang from insecurity rooted in his early childhood and eventual entry into Alpha Orphanage. Other people, well placed to know, point to rejection of him by people who wielded most influence over the jazz scene.

His personality did not endear him to certain 'movers' in jazz. Some of them provided work in clubs, radio and television to less talented musicians while neglecting him. In their defence, it could be said that he was 'an awkward customer', very self-centred and never the 'clubbable' type. It seemed to many that he deliberately chose the path of the loner. After all, he knew with absolute certainty that his immense talent dwarfed that of most of his contemporaries.

'He was fiercely proud,' explained Michael Garrick. 'He wouldn't play the hanging-in game. He wouldn't hang around at Ronnie Scott's to be seen. He thought himself above all that, so he didn't make any effort to become one of the lads, and that's very important in British jazz ... you're either in with the crowd or you're not. He was never in.'[1]

Garrick himself had experienced the cold shoulder when beginning his career at the Marquee. A sympathetic observer told him that among jazzmen he was being derided as the 'college boy'. The fact that he received an educational grant made him cosseted in their eyes, compared to his fellow musicians whose livelihood depended purely on performances. Innovative playing by Garrick was criticised as 'too clever by half'.

Harriott found it very hard to form close relationships. As well as his orphanage experience, being black in Britain brought its difficulties. He was described by Denis Preston as, 'not a lonely man but an alone man.'[2] Many people who knew Joe would agree with this distinction. For most of his life he seemed self-contained and self-reliant. Of the hundred and more people who spoke to me about Joe, hardly anyone claimed to know him well. Ian Carr said: 'You couldn't get close to him. He never shared secrets. You have to share secrets to get close to people. He was passionate about everything and he had suffered humiliations which he felt keenly.'[3]

Garrick found him an egocentric character, explaining: 'You couldn't have a constructive argument with him.' On one occasion a musician friend of Garrick had been given an old recording of Charlie Parker playing a concert at Carnegie Hall, New York, on Christmas Day 1949. It was on a Voice of America transcription. The musician knew Parker's discography thoroughly and was clear about what had been released. The transcription was obviously very rare. At Garrick's house, having something to eat after a concert at Camberley, the friend produced the recording saying, 'Joe, you must hear this. This will surprise you.'

But Joe seemed loath to provide the expected response: 'Oh, I know that one. I know all them Parker things.'

Dismayed and deflated, the musician protested: 'No, Joe, you don't. You can't. It's never been released.'

Quickly manoeuvring the conversation in a different direction, Harriott added one of his much repeated favourite sayings, 'Parker? He can play a few aces. But there's them over *here* will surprise you.'[4]

Garrick recognised this response as a common Harriott

practice: 'He would simply start talking about another subject.'
The priority for Joe was simply to derail the argument he faced
losing.

Club owner Jeffrey Kruger's impression was that Joe was
a suspicious introvert: 'He thought everybody was out to do
him in. He was very slow to trust people, perhaps with good
reason. And this isn't to denigrate him. That's just the way he
was. I saw him weekly over a long period of time and not once
did I hear him string more than two sentences together to anybody. I was never his manager but he was such a great artist, we
used him whenever we could.'[5]

Like many musicians, Harriott was not generally well disposed to club owners or record producers. He resented what
he considered poor financial return for his stage appearances.
He felt that he suffered financially from the unavailability of
much of his recorded work and, in the view of some of his associates, his relationship with Denis Preston was soured by this
perception.

He was intensely guarded about his background and Kruger
was one of those who, in spite of knowing him for a long time,
learned nothing at all about his early days. Joe never made any
reference to his youth. Jack Cooke, a jazz writer friend whose
home Harriott often visited, once met a Jamaican pianist and
composer who knew Joe and thought the world of him. Cooke
got the impression that they might have attended the same
school. Jack and his wife Anne invited both men to their home,
thinking that reminiscing on old times in Jamaica would be a
pleasant experience. The result was an evening that began
badly and deteriorated. Harriott avoided being drawn into conversation with his compatriot, appearing distinctly hostile,
despite the obvious warmth shown towards him. Jack had to
accept the inevitable: 'It was awkward. Joe just wasn't forthcoming. We never tried to put them together again.'[6]

In contrast to this tendency to be uncommunicative, many
refer to Joe's impeccable manners but his humour could be
childish and it was not uncommon for him to indulge in a sudden bout of playfulness. Though publicly he adhered to the

best practice in his table manners, at home he enjoyed letting his standards slip. Margaret Tynski referred to occasions when Joe would belch, giggle and say, 'I like the repeats.' He also derived fun initiating soup slurping contests.

In his stage announcements, he came across as courteous and keen to inform, but proud and superior, presenting himself strongly as the leader of his quintet. Coleridge Goode has alluded to Harriott's habit of using exclusively the first person in announcements: 'I would now like to play for you ...'[7] although one recorded announcement on the CD *Genius* does use the inclusive 'we'. But on that record, as he addresses the audience, there is a palpable coolness in his delivery. His precise diction is comparable to that of the stiffest radio and television announcers of the day and the only hint of his Jamaican origins emerges in the dropped 'g' in verbs like tryin', makin' and doin'. Margaret Tynski confirmed that Joe's manner of speaking on stage was deliberate and exaggerated. 'He often used the word "one" instead of the more commonly used "you". At home he was himself, the Jamaican accent obvious. He had a way of hanging on the last letter of the word at the end of a sentence.'

With Harriott, self-doubt never had the air to breathe. Goode, when asked how decisions were made in the Harriott quintet and particularly whether there was a collective element, answered with pointed brevity: 'Joe made the decisions.' He paused for a moment to consider amplifying his answer before concluding the subject with, 'I'll leave it at that.'[8]

Joe's manner of speaking and his confidence are revealed in a 1963 interview, part of which was broadcast on the BBC's *Jazz Legends* radio series in 2002. He talked about his vision for jazz and expressed annoyance that jazz outside the United States was automatically judged inferior. 'I would like to see jazz grow and absorb all other idioms and not be completely treated as if it were an isolated art form. Like classical music has isolated itself. I also have a pet hate that one couldn't think for oneself unless one emigrated to a place like the United States. Because, well, whether one goes to the States or [is] living in the jungle, one can think.

'[It's] that one lives in the Western world and one agrees that, well, there is a standard here as opposed to somewhere else. And this, I think, has not necessarily helped people to be more inventive. They look to a place for a guide. Now this can be unfortunate, but if one is a little more lenient towards it and if, in some cases, one is able to stand back and look at the situation, one could be easily encouraged to think for oneself.

'There shouldn't be one place leading the thinking public or the musicians or aspiring artists. Because throughout history and art there is enough proof that people come from all over the place. Unfortunately, I find – I hope I am wrong about this – that jazz musicians, American and otherwise, seem to think that, well, one could only be a good musician by being in the United States. And I'm sure there is a lot of very bad musicians there like any other place. It's not the place. It's you.'9

He was a member of the Rosicrucians, a sect that encouraged followers to be strong in their beliefs and ideas, thereby boosting their self-confidence. But his self-confidence was never known to waver. As most people who spoke to me confirmed, he had a tremendous opinion of himself as a musician and thinker. Bassist Dave Willis was sure that this was no masquerade: 'Sometimes a person can come across like this, who in truth is quite insecure. I never saw this man as at all insecure. Not at all.'10

The Rosicrucian Order was not a religion but a philosophy. Members received monthly monographs to study and exercises to perform. Some time before 1958, a woman friend called Joan had introduced Joe to the Order. Occasionally he would attend Lodge meetings at 25 Garrick Street, London. As well as the Lodge system, there were other similarities with the Masonic Order including ritualistic items of apparel worn at meetings. The ring Joe wore was a Rosicrucian ring bearing the insignia of the Order.

Rosicrucians, devoted to occult lore, claim an understanding of life's mysteries: the secrets of nature, transmutation of metals, elemental spirits and magical signatures. Jazz record dealer

John Jack recalled one day bumping into Joe on Shaftesbury Avenue and listening to him for over an hour as he 'rabbited on about Rosicrucianism.'[11] Harry Klein described listening to Harriott on the subject as sleeping with his eyes open.[12] This was probably soon after Joe had discovered the system of beliefs and was excited by it, because he would not normally discuss religious beliefs with colleagues. Michael Garrick, for example, was entirely unaware of any influence Rosicrucianism had on Harriott's life. 'There was for a while a very large amount of correspondence from this organisation, I received some myself. But I never heard Joe discuss it and I don't believe it had any attraction for him.'[13]

Teddy Layton, a Southampton-based sax and clarinet player, told of another influence upon Harriott, the *I-Ching*, which he would sometimes consult, keeping a copy handy when travelling. He had the book with him on his final stay in hospital when a visiting friend, Del Southon, asked him what was its attraction. 'One has to seek the answer,' was Joe's reply.

Coleridge Goode always suspected that the beauty and wistfulness apparent in Harriott's ballad playing indicated a concealed longing for love.[14] The often-mentioned 'fire' in his playing seemed to confirm the widespread observation that he was passionate about everything. Some of his closest associates and friends thought that his music spoke more eloquently than his words of his true nature.

Les Condon put it well when he said: 'Joe was one of the most extraordinary jazzmen I ever worked with. The complexity of his character was reflected in the variety of his music. In Joe's solos could be heard the history of jazz, going back to its African roots and many other worldwide influences. His personal sound had a great range of all the emotions, being able as he was to express them fluently. He was a seriously dedicated musician, like a man with a mission. On many occasions he amazed me with the intensity of his playing, like a man on fire, about to explode. His unique contribution to jazz certainly justified the old cliché, "after him, they broke the mould".'[15]

Bobby Orr thought, like many others, that 'Joe had a chip on his shoulder. When Ronnie Scott opened his first club he was keen to have us in, but Joe stood very erect, pushed his shoulders back, and said, "I think we'll leave it this time." I thought we were keen to get bookings, but whether Joe thought he was above this ... I don't know.'[16]

Tommy Whittle said, 'Joe was an egotist,' and explained with an anecdote. One time when Harriott was playing with a local rhythm section he turned to the pianist and gave him the title of the next number he intended playing. 'Do you know it?' Joe asked.

'No,' came the reply.

'What do you mean you don't know it?' Joe made it sound like a serious gap in the man's musical education.

The floundering pianist asked who wrote it and Joe answered without humour or irony, 'I did.'[17]

His aggression came out in the competitive atmosphere of the musician's world. John Mayer, who would co-lead a band with Harriott in the late 1960s, recognises one reason their relationship was so harmonious. 'It might have helped that there was no competition between us. I was a composer and I wasn't trying to show what a fine fiddle player I was. And I always gave full credit to him for the existence of the band.'[18]

Pianist Brian Dee said, 'I remember one memorable occasion in Ronnie's Old Place in 1960 or '61. [The musicians] were like matadors on the stage. The bass player was Tony Archer – and it might have been Ginger Baker on drums – but there was Harold McNair, Peter King and Joe. I played one chorus and they were all in for another nine or ten choruses each. Afterwards, in the back office, Pete King was saying, 'Is this Wembley or what?'[19]

With Don Rendell it was a similar story. When asked whether he enjoyed playing with Harriott, he recalled a specific occasion. 'There was a gig we did. I'll never forget it. It was at the Clarendon Pub in Oxford Road, Manchester. It was the forerunner to the 43 Club Ernie Garside ran in Manchester. This would be around 1967. Michael Garrick and Ian Carr were there too. We were doing 'Webster's Mood', a slow blues Michael Garrick wrote in tribute to Ben Webster, when Joe took off. He played nineteen choruses. It was absurd. He'd said everything that had to be said. How do you follow that? I don't think it would be fair to say more than that. He was a very, very strong and creative jazz player.'[20]

Garrick said, 'I liked Joe, but then I never had any axe to grind with him. A lot of musicians were jealous of him. Most of the time he seemed to be on his guard. He was not without tenderness: his ballad playing reveals much that he otherwise kept tightly under wraps. My daughter, Miranda, then four or five years old, remembers his kindly and protective manner when they went for walks together in Tekels Park, in Camberley, where we used to live. She, of course, was non-threatening and Joe would be absolutely delightful with her.'[21]

Although Harriott had little to do with children, he had a natural way with them. His manner was more laid-back and relaxed than it was in adult company. Shake Keane told Peter Clayton in an interview that he could never have imagined Joe sitting down to a Christmas meal with a family. Sharon Atkin, who had a relationship with Joe in the late sixties, commented: 'His austere way of life and his devotion to music didn't mean that these things had no appeal for him.'[22]

Trumpeter Del Turner agreed. 'I had got to know Joe well through bookings I made for him at the RAF Honington Jazz Club. I realised that Christmas was probably a lonely time for Joe and invited him to spend the Christmas of 1962 staying with my family. My girls loved Joe. I remember he was particularly thrilled by a pair of leather gloves they gave him. He seemed really touched by their gift.' Harriott must have enjoyed the experience because the following year he again accepted Del's invitation. Turner's daughters, now grown up, remember Harriott as a kind and friendly companion of whom they were very fond. 'The other day,' Del told me, 'when I was looking among my photos for two big pictures of Joe, I realised that they were probably at my daughters' houses.'[23]

Drummer Tommy Chase also experienced Harriott's kindness. 'When I came to London,' he explained, 'there was very much an established scene, difficult for an outsider to get into.

Joe was supposed to have an abrasive personality but he was really helpful to me, always encouraging me up to play drums.'

But Chase also noted Harriott's solitariness. 'He wasn't one for surrounding himself with lots of people. We often went to the Café des Artistes in Fulham Road where he'd be playing in jam sessions.' For Chase, Harriott 'was unbelievable, phenomenal. He was out of this world. I thought his talent was wasted in this country. There were a lot of good things happening then. Dick Morrissey was playing some fantastic stuff, but a lot of solos were much of a muchness. I got the same impression with Tubby [Hayes]. I didn't walk away from Tubby gigs singing one of his solos the way I did with Joe. Joe always played with tremendous passion.'[24]

Ian Croal and Mike Travis played bass and drums together in the mid to late sixties and remembered Harriott's considerate behaviour when he was touring as a solo artist and played with them on several occasions in Edinburgh. They particularly remembered one gig: 'It was a festival jam session,' said Travis, 'and he just walked in, opened his sax case and sat in with us. We immediately tensed up.' Croal added that Joe, 'was charming and chose tunes and keys he made sure we were familiar with. After everyone else had gone home we carried on playing. Joe relaxed with a drink and played brilliantly for hours. Around 3 a.m. he said: "Let's call it a day."'

Travis recalled that they had been playing a lot of medium-tempo stuff. and 'with the brashness born of youth, I suggested an up-tempo one to finish on. Joe smiled. With a glint in his eye he replied: "You want a fast one?"' He clicked his fingers setting the beat. As he began playing 'Cherokee', his admirers realised he was playing a whole bar for each click. 'He tore through it and we were amazed,' commented Croal. 'He was a phenomenal musician.'

Travis admitted: 'I basically got taken to the cleaners. We were totally burned.' Did Joe do it with humour, or as a lesson to them? 'A bit of both really, I suppose,' said Travis. 'But a year later Joe was good enough to say during a private party we were playing at that I'd come on quite a lot.'25

Bass player John Burgess found himself chatting with Harriott after a gig. 'He was very well-educated. He told me he'd studied at Trinity College. I remember it distinctly being Trinity.'26 I contacted Trinity College of Music in London to check on this but no verification was forthcoming and it is certain Harriott's work schedule would not have allowed him to attend a degree course. There is an indirect, tenuous connection in that Dineley Rehearsal Rooms, where he spent many hours, were bought by Trinity College as an annexe prior to the College's move to Greenwich.

That many people described Joe as highly educated was a credit to the man himself because most of his learning was due to his own efforts. Alpha School had not had the resources to build an academic tradition equal to its musical achievements. After a late start in schooling with concentration on music and basic vocational skills, Harriott had left Alpha at sixteen. Some of his recorded utterances sound tortuous, with unnecessary words, as though he believed the quantity of words would enhance the content, and he often used phrases such as 'so to speak' and 'one is inclined to think'. In spite of the difficulty listeners sometimes had in understanding him, he had a poetic gift for original, utterly apt statements to describe musical experiences.

One was his observation that 'others play here in the room while what I play is *out the window.*'27 But my favourite 'Harriottism' is one that playwright Alan Plater recalled: 'I got to know Joe in the late sixties and early seventies when I was living in Hull. He'd [stay] overnight when playing gigs in the area. He loved to stay up late talking and drinking vast quantities of whisky. One night he talked about the first time he played with Dizzy Gillespie. His words, as clearly as I can remember them, went like this, in that lovely Jamaican accent: "We played a couple of numbers and Dizzy, well, he was playing OK, but just kind of going through the motions. Then

Dizzy took off and all of a sudden he was right up there in the rafters and, man, we were just like *swallows on the water*."'[28]

A most endearing feature of Joe's personality was his enthusiasm. In addition to his long-held passions for art and literature, Joe made a thrilling new discovery, by courtesy of Margaret Tynski. 'Joe had never been to the ballet and from 15 to 17 August 1960 there was a Royal Festival Hall Ballet Exhibition. Noel Coward had written a story and the music for *A London Morning*. The choreographer was Jack Carter, the costumes were by Norman McDowell and orchestration was by Gordon Jacob. I booked tickets as a surprise outing for Joe and myself. It was vibrant, colourful and so different from the traditional ballet I was used to seeing. To my knowledge this was the debut performance. But the most embarrassing thing happened because Joe hadn't been to the ballet before. We sat in our seats and he put his arm round me – and you don't do that sort of thing at the ballet or a concert hall!

'Joe was over the moon afterwards and could not stop talking about [the ballet] on the way home. I had made a note on the back of the programme, "Took Joe to see this ... and he was inspired. As soon as we got home he started composing and rang Pat Smythe to tell him about it." It was *the* topic of conversation for some time afterwards.'

Harriott's strong charisma appealed to women fans. Possessed of considerable stage presence, he would often be aware of an admiring female gaze from the front row and would go off with the woman concerned during the band break or at the end of the concert.[29] Ian Carr remembered one gig where there was a woman 'flashing at him in the front row'. After the show she offered Joe either a lift home or to her place. Joe opted for her place. She drove miles into the country down a lonely country lane and stopped to put him out, explaining, 'I must go home first to see if my husband's home or not.' As her car disappeared into the darkness, Harriott was left sitting under a bush wondering if she would come back for him. She eventually did and drove him back to her home. When Joe whipped her naked over the piano he thought, 'I hope her husband doesn't come back now.'[30]

Kenny Baxter first met Harriott at the Florida Club in London in 1955. He told me: 'Joe was appearing with the Tony Kinsey band. From the moment I heard him play I was hooked. At that time I was studying [saxophone] under the great Kathy Stobart. Kathy introduced me to Joe and from that time we became very close friends. We had an affinity with each other immediately.'

'He was a very private man. Very astute. He was a loner.' Despite this, Kenny often met him at weekends. Both sharp dressers, the two enjoyed each other's company. 'He loved my tailor, Toby, on the north end of Fulham Road. He said he couldn't afford to shop there but Joe always wore smart clothes. I have a photo of him in a white jacket. He looked great in it. I knew Joe liked me because any time I'd phone him he'd arrange to meet me.' At weekends they would meet at the Marquee or Flamingo and, after picking up women, go to hear jazz. 'Sometimes we'd go to the Caribbean Club. There would be some white women there dancing but I would often be the only white guy present. Then I'd take the milk train home to Southend-on-Sea.'[31]

Kenny Baxter told a story about Joe travelling to a post-gig party. He and Harriott were left behind when their places in a car were offered to some girls they had invited to the party. A bike was leaning against a nearby wall so they took it, Joe sitting on the saddle holding his sax while his partner pedalled. They fell off several times, collapsing in laughter.

Sharon Atkin was only twelve when she first saw Harriott after a Ray Charles concert at Hammersmith Odeon in 1963. She was at the concert with her parents, who were from Jamaica and good friends of the brother of Charles' Jamaican trumpeter Roy Burrowes. Afterwards they waited to meet Burrowes. Joe was also waiting for the same reason. Introductions were made and the group conversed. Such was Harriott's magnetism that Sharon told her mother on the way home that Joe was the man she wanted to marry. Her mother advised her not to be so foolish and that a twelve-year-old child couldn't know such a thing. Joe was thirty-five at the time.[32]

In the most repeated story of Harriott's 'pulling power', Coleridge Goode remembers packing up his bass after a gig and going to look for Joe. He found him at the entrance to the venue watching two women on the ground fighting. Each seemed likely to end the fight follically poorer. Goode asked what the trouble was, to be told: 'Don't worry, man, they're only fighting over me.'[33] Ian Carr also remembers being present and the incident is said to have taken place in Manchester, although jazz raconteurs Benny Green and Ronnie Scott also claimed to have witnessed it.

Michael Garrick was expecting Joe to stay at his home after playing a gig at Camberley Jazz Club one winter night. As the music ended Harriott disappeared with a woman admirer. Garrick's door was left off the latch for his return. The following day Joe told of his experience. The woman had asked him to wait while she checked all was quiet in her home. Harriott, with only a suit against the chill of the winter's night, tried to keep warm in the shadow of a hedge. She reappeared and beckoned him inside. As he began making advances to her she insisted that he beat her with his belt as a preliminary to sex. As Garrick recalled Joe's account of this experience he said, 'I recollect him being totally bemused by this. Not remotely turned on by it. He just wanted a shag.'

After a quintet gig at the Marquee, a fan who had been chatting with Harriott offered to run him home. Joe didn't hesitate and, on reaching his flat in Maida Vale, invited the man in for coffee. An awkward scene ensued as a young woman was discovered in the flat. Harriott's words were, 'I told you to be out of here before I got back. What do you think you are you doing?'

The woman pleaded to stay as it was now the early hours of the morning. But Harriott insisted she leave. As she made her way downstairs and into the night, Joe turned to the embarrassed fan with a businesslike: 'Besides, there's another one coming in the morning.' The fan, who later became a BBC soundman, retold his tale years later while recording a programme on Jamaican music with Michael Garrick. As Garrick put it: 'Joe was coldly logical about it.'[34]

Musician colleagues of Harriott's that I spoke to didn't associate him with any particular woman. Many saw no evidence of relationships except casual ones. Any women he was involved with were kept largely in the background and were generally not present in the audience with the wives and girlfriends of other band members. Colin Barnes recalled seeing one woman with Joe on several occasions in the sixties. 'She was a lady from Hampstead. A nice lady, but he didn't introduce her.'[35] Certainly, there were occasions when Joe was involved with married women and discretion was called for. But there was also the fact that he could be jealous and possessive.

Margaret Tynski cited an example. '[On] one occasion Phil called at the flat when Joe was out so I asked him in to wait, which he did. Phil was a lovely guy despite his problem with addiction. He wasn't stupid by any means. He had great wit and repartee and a happy-go-lucky nature. I made him a cup of coffee and I chatted with him until Joe came home. Phil and Joe discussed whatever, then Phil left. Joe was livid I had asked Phil in. He could not understand I was being polite and passing the time until he returned. Joe was very possessive.'

In her late teens Sharon Atkin began a serious relationship with Joe. She remembered an open-air jazz concert where a man persistently chatted her up at the entry gates. From a distance, Harriott surveyed the developing scene before bearing down upon the man with a very threatening look. Seething with anger, he told the interloper that the lady was with him. Then he instructed the ticket attendant to refund the man's money. As the would-be concert-goer protested, Harriott informed him bluntly that he wouldn't be gaining entry, and even if he were to succeed then Joe wouldn't be playing! There was no room for negotiation.

It was said that Harriott loved women but didn't want any responsibilities. That women were attracted to him was hardly surprising. He was an incredibly gifted, exciting musician. Tall, elegant and handsome, he could exude charm or an aloof disinterest which can intrigue and attract some women. On one occasion, it was claimed, he seduced an attractive and intelligent woman in the Clifton pub in Maida Vale by giving her the eye before any conversation got under way.

His charms were not universally appreciated, though. Marianne Wasser, wife of bassist Stan Wasser, recalls one of her birthday parties in the early sixties. A woman friend arrived with Joe as her companion. Marianne and Joe got off to a bad start when, in her words, 'he insisted on playing the latest Harriott recording on the gramophone. He also played our piano. We had a rather bad piano. His ambition, he said, was to be shot by a jealous husband at the age of eighty. I remember he succeeded in uniting us all against him.'

Her besotted friend seemed blissfully unaware of the growing hostility to Harriott who had hijacked the party atmosphere. 'Don't you think he's like a big, black eagle?' she gushed to Marianne. 'No, I think he's rather like a tatty, black vulture,' was the verdict of the party host.[36]

Kenny Baxter remarked how odd it was that in all their years of close friendship Harriott never mentioned any children. As well as Joe's Jamaica-born daughter Pauline, there were other progeny. A second daughter, Theresa, was also raised by her mother but, unlike her half-sister, did not know her natural father. This was true of Margaret Tynski's son Zachary who grew up with an adoptive surname. A second son, Christopher, emerged later as did another daughter, Amber. Each of his five children was born to a different mother. Joe, who never married, made irregular financial payments to assist at least one child's upbringing. As will be explained later, a degree of legal coercion was involved.

Amber's mother, Pat Copp recalled her relationship with Joe. 'I was living in London doing temp work as a typist. One night I was at the Marquee Club. Joe Harriott's band was playing and I quite fancied their drummer, Bobby Orr. I used to stand in front of the band and dance. I suppose I hoped he would notice me. But it was Joe who came over and talked to me. I was quite flattered. He asked me for my phone number and I gave him it.

'Next day he phoned me, and took a taxi from St John's Wood over to Parsons Green where I was staying. My flatmates were out, and we ended up in bed together.

'After that, I would usually go to his place, often after going to gigs with him. I was very naïve, and thought, "Well then, he's my boyfriend." But he wasn't affectionate at all, out of bed. He once said to me, "I must like you. I haven't been with anyone else since I've been with you." I was gob smacked! We'd only been together for three weeks! I thought, "Why would he want to?"

'I was eighteen, and inexperienced. Joe was thirty-eight, and had been around too long. His career was on the decline and he was quite bitter about it, and about some of the women he'd been involved with. He said he liked me because my "No" meant "No" and my "Yes" meant "Yes". He was not a man at peace with himself, and frequently woke up in the middle of the night to have a fag. The only times I saw a more relaxed side to him were when we went to the pub next door on a Sunday afternoon. Joe liked his Merrydown Cider, and could be very charming when he wanted to be. He was pretty obsessed with his music – which was fine with me as I thought he was a great musician.

'Before long I discovered I was pregnant. I told Joe right away. He wasn't particularly perturbed by it – it was hardly a surprise, since he wouldn't use any contraception, and I had been too inexperienced to even think about it. But after a few months, it began to cause problems for me.

'People just weren't into jazz as they had been, and work was hard to find. He was, unfortunately, just a tad arrogant in attitude to people, which didn't help much. If they offered him less for a gig than he wanted, or had been used to, he would sneer at them and refuse. That got him out of Ronnie Scott's Club, and probably quite a few others. So he wasn't in a position to help me financially (not that I would have asked though!) But I had to take time off work to go for ante-natal appointments, and that meant I didn't get paid. So in the end, I was forced to go and live with my family in Slough, because I couldn't eat properly or pay the rent.

'I used to come up to town to see Joe occasionally. An artist friend of mine lived in St John's Wood and one night she had a party. I was almost nine months pregnant. I'd been to see Joe that afternoon and we'd been to bed together. I'd helped him change the sheets after, then he went to a gig, and I went to the party. I had a great time, but got very tired and thought that rather than waiting any later to go back all the way to my friend's flat in Kilburn, I'd call Joe and stay overnight at his place, since he lived just around the corner. I kept ringing him. Eventually he answered the phone. I asked him if I could stay the night and he said, "It's not convenient." I knew he had another woman there with him and I cried for hours. I couldn't believe he would do that to me.

'Living with my parents was not easy. At one point, my mother went to see Joe and told him he should marry me – I was horrified! I didn't want to marry him!

'Because of the difficulties at home, when I'd had my baby, I was living with a friend's parents, in Eton. I rang Joe, and he came to visit us. We were kind of reconciled, and he helped me find a place to live back in London, since I couldn't move over to Kilburn yet, with my friends. He came to see me there too, and things were OK.

'Eventually, the flat in Kilburn was available, and I moved there, just up the road from Joe. During this time, he told me he was a Rosicrutionist. I'd never heard of it, but he claimed that when he was able to practise it properly, he would "get" the names of the winning horses, and would bet on them and make good money! Only, he said he wasn't very good at it, because to be "pure", you had to abstain from drink, smoking, and sex. Joe was not about to do any of that for very long! He tried to teach me to meditate, but I was too restless to do it.

'We saw one another for a while, but I wasn't all that happy, since I suspected he was seeing other women, and I didn't like it. One day I went to see him and told him I wanted more from our relationship. I guess really, I meant that I wanted to be his only woman, because he admitted he had others. He told me they helped him, gave him money, that they weren't important. He said he couldn't give me more than fifty per cent. I said that wasn't enough. I was up-front, challenging him, and he was furious. He grabbed my arm and threw me across the room. I was frightened for Amber, who was in her pram, so I left. I didn't realise he had followed us home till I got to my front door. He insisted on coming in, and stayed the night with me, saying "Ok then, we'll start the New Year new." He thought I'd get over it.

'I didn't speak to him after that. He turned up at my flat again one night. It was a shared house, and somebody let him in. They told me "Joe's here." I was nervous, as I hadn't returned his calls, and he'd been drinking.

'Amber was in her cot asleep. He went over to her and lit a lighter in front of her face to look at her. Then he picked her up and was holding her and saying that she wasn't his. I was terrified. I didn't know what he might do. He didn't hurt her though, and in the end he put her back in the cot.

'After that, I avoided him, and moved away from the area. It was seven years before I heard that he had died in Southampton Hospital. He never really knew Amber – his loss, sadly. Although he disputed that she was his, he had admitted to Social Security that she was. She even looked like him then! I think she inherited all his best qualities – she's musical, long-limbed, charming, attractive, tall, and altogether gorgeous! I think she's the best part of him, apart from his music.'

His home after leaving hospital in 1958 was at 94a Clifton Hill in St John's Wood. The Victorian villas in the area were huge houses mostly converted into flats and bedsits. For a time Phil Seamen and Kenny Graham had rooms in Clifton Hill. As fellow-musician resident Dave Willis said: 'It became a musicians' enclave quite by chance as flats became available. The bedsits were twelve foot by ten foot with a little kitchen and bathroom in each one.'

Joe lived in spartan conditions by choice. The only photograph on display was of Charlie Parker. But the respect he had for Parker was for his music and not his lifestyle. Joe's hostility to heroin was reinforced by knowing what the drug had done to Parker. He consistently made clear his view that heroin was a destructive force which could only harm his music. Close-hand experience of its effect on Tubby Hayes and Phil Seamen also contributed. Sammy Stokes, who lived under the same roof as Seamen at one time, said, 'Phil wouldn't get on with Joe. Joe was against everything that Phil was doing.'[37]

Jazz fan Jock Thomson remembered that before a November 1960 Harriott quintet gig in Edinburgh's Netherbow Church, Phil Seamen was 'out of it' in a high street fish and chip shop. He was bouncing off walls and clearly desperately in need of a fix. Heroin addiction was rare in Britain then but registered addicts, like Seamen, could collect pure heroin at a pharmacy on production of a medical prescription. London's junkies' biggest hangout was Boots the Chemist in Piccadilly. Phil's difficulty was that he was hundreds of miles north when he discovered he had forgotten his prescription.

The bass player, a dep for Coleridge Goode, tried to negotiate a remedy by having Boots in London contact their Edinburgh branch to give oral permission in the absence of paper documentation. As the time for the performance drew nearer, the bassist tried to contact a doctor to administer the dose in time. But his efforts ended in failure and the floppy, lifeless Seamen was an abject figure on the drum stool at the start of the evening. Jock Thomson saw him as 'a puppet with broken strings' but vividly recalled that, when Harriott counted in the first number, Seamen burst into volcanic action on drums. 'It was like seeing a limp figure having negative and positive electrodes attached. It was staggering!'[38] The healing power of music, or a case of Phil going on autopilot? Who can say?

In the early sixties jazz fan Jackie Docherty's spacious flat in Edinburgh New Town housed his superb record collection and was covered in photographs of jazz heroes. It was a haven for visiting and local musicians. Jackie and his friend 'Toto'

McNaughton remembered one occasion when Seamen, Les Condon and Joe retired there after their city gig. Seamen was about to give himself a fix but Les, aware of the unease Phil's preparations were causing, took the needle from him. Toto thought Seamen's heavily marked leg looked disturbingly like a pin cushion. Heroin addiction was then little known outwith the London jazz scene.[39]

Michael Horovitz found Harriott moralistic about the excesses of others, particularly Seamen, but sometimes of Shake Keane too: 'Shake could drink gallons and be underperforming. Joe was impatient with Phil and Shake.' Horovitz acknowledged that Harriott, too, liked alcohol but, 'compared with Shake, Joe was founder of the Temperance League.'[40]

Andy Hamilton and promoter Don Norman attest that Joe took no drugs whatever, but it is highly likely he smoked cannabis and made use of 'uppers' as stimulants. Bassist Dave Green recounts that when he was battling exhaustion to stay awake for a gig, Harriott handed him tablets with the advice they would help. 'There was one occasion when I played with Joe – this would be in the mid-sixties – somewhere in the south of London. I was so tired. He gave me some 'blues', which I was never into. He gave me these things and I was awake for about two days. They got me through the gig and about another two gigs after that without any sleep!'[41]

Blues, or purple hearts as they were sometimes called, were a form of amphetamine or 'speed'. Although these Drinamil tablets were a very effective stimulant, the common perception among musicians of the day was that they were all but harmless and certainly not to be classed with drugs like heroin. In Sammy Stokes' words: 'Uppers? They were like taking Aspirin.'[42]

Drummer Colin Barnes agreed that Harriott used pills: 'Joe made these tours round Coventry, Birmingham, and there was always some guy handing out tablets. One time we went down to do a gig at Bristol University in the pre-motorway days. First we went to the West Indian area there. Joe knew a guy in a cafe who gave him a package of pills. 'Blues' or yellow pills, I'm not sure which.'[43]

During the fifties and sixties Joe was a heavy smoker by anyone's standards, smoking between three and four packs of Players Senior Service plain (untipped) cigarettes a day. This was an age when the dangers of tobacco were little known or at least seriously underestimated. Margaret Tynski was fascinated by a personal routine Joe performed. 'He never used a lighter, always a box of matches. He would light a cigarette using one hand. Open the box. Take out a match. Close the box. Turn it on its side. Strike the match and light the cigarette.'

Harriott could sometimes be found in the Clifton public house where he enjoyed relaxing with a drink, sometimes playing bar billiards or the piano. The place had a friendly atmosphere and, like all good pubs, its share of characters. Norman 'the Apple' was among the most notable and a regular mirthmaker. He held court with his rambling tale of the three epic trials. The first was to shift a mountain by a teaspoon of earth at a time. The second was to drain an ocean cup by cup. The third, and hardest of all, was to borrow £5 from the barman.[44]

Sharon Atkin remembers falling under Joe's spell as he played piano for her: 'He'd compose at the piano in the Clifton. I remember him playing a number saying: "This is how a Trinidadian would play it", and then a Jamaican and so on, showing the differences in approaches.'

Harriott enjoyed scotch but generally held it well and kept its use within reasonable parameters. Frank Holder remembered that Joe hardly drank at all when first he knew him. As he grew disillusioned with the music scene Harriott would demolish a whisky bottle's contents while sitting late into the night. In the accompanying conversation he would often vent his grievances against record producers and concert promoters.[45]

Jazz Journal editor Eddie Cook, who at one time looked after Joe's instrument, said, 'he drank a lot of scotch. He used to sweat alcohol. It took all the lacquer off his instrument.'[46]

Stuart Hepburn, who ferried Harriott around London during 1969 and 1970, told me: 'I took him to this club in south London and he had about six double whiskies before he went on to play. He was the guest artist and I thought, "he'll never play." He went on and I have never heard him play so well in my life. He was just fantastic.'[47]

Joe was not astute with money but his needs were simple and financial considerations probably bored him. He could be generous and could act upon a whim, as he did when he decided to buy a celebration meal for band members after a lucrative gig. As a non-driver, ill-disposed to public transport, he found travelling costly. When a lift was unavailable, he would always elect to go by taxi if he had money in his pocket. He intensely disliked the Tube, which caused the same claustrophobic reaction as travelling by plane.[48]

Although games of poker and brag filled hours of boredom while travelling or waiting between practice and performance, card games seemed not to threaten Harriott's financial well-being in the way that horse racing and gaming machines did. Gambling was a major weakness. Jack Cooke, a friend during the late fifties, states that Joe's addiction to machines was the reason their friendship foundered. In 1960 or '61, Cooke went into the Cottage Club, off London's Charing Cross Road, to meet a friend for a drink and inadvertently stumbled on Joe there, rooted in front of a fruit machine. He was aware of Cooke's presence but remained absorbed and uncommunicative throughout his stay. Whether he ignored Cooke because he felt resentful that he had been seen indulging his weakness or whether he was simply engrossed, is a matter for speculation. But the pattern was repeated on further visits until Jack felt the ties of friendship had been severed totally.[49]

Promoter Ernie Garside, unaware of Harriott's weakness for gaming machines, told me of one of his happiest recollections of Joe. 'We got our own premises, my own club [the 43 Club in Manchester].... It was the days when you had a Durex machine, a cigarette machine, and you also had a one arm

bandit. I think you put sixpence in, in those days. Nobody ever played it. Eric Scriven [Garside's business partner] would put a quid in now and again. It paid out about eight quid, which was a decent amount in them days, I suppose. Joe walked in, and what did he do? Put sixpence in and dropped *eight quid*! But his face, man! I said, "I've been trying to hit that for weeks!" Of course, I hadn't. He'd dropped the lot. It was great to see it. And he was over the moon! He was only on a tenner for the night and he walked in, and the first thing, he pulled the handle and – eight quid!'50

9.

gigging around

Throughout his career, Joe Harriott covered an immense number of miles travelling the length and breadth of Britain. He lived for playing and was not hidebound by any notion that he should only associate with bebop or, later on, free form lineups. He thrived in diverse musical settings including African highlife, rhythm-and-blues, New Orleans jazz and – as will appear later – Indian music.

He frequently worked as a guest artist with local groups and would happily play in a pub, nightclub, sergeants' mess or concert hall. His commitment to the music never wavered, regardless of the status of the gig, the venue or the audience numbers present. The following anecdotes convey something of the variety of his gigs and the routines of his everyday life as a musician.

In 1955, Lol Coxhill was playing tenor sax with a band called Denzil Bailey's Afro-Cubans. There were no Afro-Cubans in it and Denzil's real name was Tom Bailey, but the music was the thing. They played Dizzy Gillespie and Machito compositions and arrangements. Guest musicians invited to front the band included Sammy Walker, Dizzy Reece and Harriott. 'We had a club in Aylesbury once we could play well enough,' remembered Coxhill, 'and all these people came down to play for next to nothing. They would doss on my floor. Joe Harriott got on well with my mum and dad, so he would doss at their house.' Joe would have been interested to discover that Mr Coxhill senior was a qualified bookbinder, a career that might have beckoned had he not become a musician.[1]

Kenny Baxter remembered informal sessions in the mid-fifties: 'I was … at that time running a club, Jazz at the Shrine,

in Southend-on-Sea, Essex, on Friday nights and I booked Joe.
...My piano player at the club was an ex-army officer called
[William] Haig Joyce, who later used the name of Bill Haig.
Haig and Joe got on instantly and became great friends ...
After the gig we would go back to Haig's house together with a
few young ladies, quarter bottles of light and brown ales, VP
port and chianti and carry on playing the music. Haig had a
baby grand piano and always recorded the sessions at his home
on his Grundig tape recorder.'[2]

Baxter recalled how the tracks with Haig on the *Joe Harriott:
Genius* CD were recorded. Phil Seamen had been at Jazz at the
Shrine one Friday night and afterwards, at Haig's house, he
joined the duo on brushes. The tapes emerged after Haig's
death when his son gave them to Michael Garrick. Coleridge
Goode listened to them with Garrick and recalled: 'We
thought they were marvellous. It was just Haig and Joe and
somebody else on brushes on a telephone book or something.
I said to Michael: "It will sound more full if I put a bass part
to it." So the guy came here [Goode's home] with the stuff
and we put a bass part on.' On some tracks the tape ended
abruptly, so Goode added a typical 'singing' solo to make a
neater conclusion.[3]

Some of Haig's reel to reel tapes, long thought to have been
lost, featuring Joe, Phil Seamen, Major Holley on bass and
Johnny Weed on piano, have emerged on a limited edition vinyl
record. The technical quality of the recordings is way above
what one might have anticipated after the passage of over fifty
years. But they show that even in a relaxed party setting, Joe
still sets a very high standard of performance.

Bassist Spike Heatley sometimes stayed at Bill Haig's home,
then in Ipswich, after a gig: 'I was always on the road and it
would be one o'clock in the morning when I'd roll up with my
bass. Going up the path I'd hear Joe's alto and the piano. I'd go
in and we'd be a trio. Bill was one of the finest pianists to play
with. He played sparse chords and gave lots of space which Joe
liked.'[4]

Kenny Baxter remembered Saturday evenings when he and
Harriott went to the Star Club. 'Joe would often sit in with

Alan Clare as he loved Alan's playing. Clare played some fantastic chords like Bill Evans. Joe didn't like 'busy' pianists, he liked ones who laid down chords like Bill Haig and Pat Smythe.

'On one occasion in the Star Club, Joe and I were having a pint when some of the Basie Orchestra walked in to have a jam with the Alan Clare Trio, having previously finished a gig. The Basie boys commenced their jam session. Joe sat very still and quiet. After about three numbers Joe got his alto sax out of its case and stood at the end of the line of players. In his usual 'aloof' manner, he nodded to the other players and joined in. I wish I had a picture to see their faces when Joe took his solos. He was brilliant and so were the expressions on their faces. He carried on doing a few more numbers and they were still very impressed. He then came offstage, nodded to the musicians, put his sax away, came over to me and said: "Let's go." That was Joe.'5

Guitarist Dougie Campbell's band was joined by Joe on one occasion at the Gamp, an Edinburgh jazz club. 'Everyone said he was difficult but he seemed very nice to me,' Campbell said. 'I asked him, "Is 'Stompin' at the Savoy' in five flats [B flat minor] OK?" His response was: "Great! Everybody else plays it in F."' That pleased Dougie. 'I mean, if the guy who wrote it writes it in Z, then there's a reason for that. That's how he wants it to be played. You should play it in Z. The Americans all played these numbers in the keys they were written in. It didn't matter how difficult they were. That was part of their musicianship. In his musicianship, Joe was like them.'6

Even Harriott's most modest guest appearances were sometimes noticed in local papers. In February 1958, only weeks before forming his first quintet, he performed at Southampton's Concorde Jazz Club. The local *Southern Daily Echo* reported: 'The brilliant coloured virtuoso...has a fiery tone and a forceful, intense attack. His inventive genius in improvisation was evident throughout the evening, but never once did he use it to strike phoney effects: there was logic and an odd sort of rough beauty about everything he did.'7

Harriott's guest appearance at the El Toro, a night club on London's Finchley Road was reported by Steve Race in *Melody*

Maker. Dill Jones led the resident trio and one night in May 1959 Harry Klein played with them, with Harriott joining later in the evening, probably after his Marquee spot.

Race criticised Jones' trio ('the Muzak of jazz') and Klein ('a delightful but not very extensive repertoire of baritone phrases'). But he fulsomely praised Joe. 'Harriott is not an acquired jazzman like the rest: he was born for jazz.... There is a compulsion about his work which reminds one of Bird. Joe Harriott is immeasurably our finest altoist: a true son of jazz.'[8]

Fellow altoist and future knight of jazz John Dankworth invited Joe to play as a guest artist in a Red Cross benefit concert at the Royal Festival Hall on Friday 7 July, 1961. It was billed as *An Evening with Johnnie Dankworth and his Orchestra* and Dankworth supplied his appraisal of Joe in the programme. 'Joe Harriott is another of tonight's artists linked to me by personal circumstances. Nine years ago in the *Melody Maker* he and I were nominated as the two most promising artists of the year. I laughed like a drain over that one because even in those days I had a good critical faculty. Good enough to know how talented Joe was. He was one of two saxophonists with whom I worked, the other was Ronnie Scott, who by their own unconscious example taught me how a jazz musician ought to blow his instrument.'

Harriott quintet gigs were sometimes combined with after-hours informal sessions. In mid-April 1962, the quintet played at Edinburgh's Palais de Dance. At that time, between the recording sessions that delivered *Abstract*, the band was probably at its peak. After the concert it played a jam session and a local sax player was deluded into thinking he should get up for the session. 'It was embarrassing,' a musician witness recalled. 'They were so good they just blew him away.'[9]

In September 1963, during a week of late night shows at the Edinburgh Festival, Joe played a lunchtime gig at the Edinburgh University Rhythm Club. Club treasurer Alan Anderson's most abiding memory of the occasion was Harriott's preferred payment of £30 and a half bottle of scotch. The half bottle didn't survive to the interval.[10]

A local newspaper reported that the student audience was

deeply impressed with Joe's 'searing saxophone and intense jazz' and local musicians were left 'gaping mouthed'.[11]

On another occasion in Edinburgh, Harriott and Shake Keane sat in with the Alex Shaw band at the Gamp. The club had three levels and sank deep under the main thoroughfare of the Old Town. 'You didn't see many black guys around in Edinburgh at that time,' drummer Mike Travis remembered, 'and two wee girlies were stopped in their tracks when Keane and Harriott entered the club.' Aware these imposing figures were celebrities of some kind, one girl said to her friend, without specifying which man she was referring to: 'Is that Paul Robeson?'[12]

In London, a popular jamming venue on Sunday lunchtimes in the mid-1960s was the Coleherne pub in Earl's Court. The main room was a gay bar. In the back room would be found Trinidadian pianist Russ Henderson, drummer Stirling Betancourt and bassist Clyde Davis, sometimes complemented by well-known visiting Americans. But this being an open session, a number of percussionists with their conga drums would arrive early to ensure themselves a space in the small back room. The audience needed to be dedicated. As one fan said, 'you fought your way through to the music room in the back.'[13]

Photographer Bill Smith, working for an American company in England, went to the Coleherne to hear Harriott. 'We had taken a couple that worked at the same American company for a lunchtime beer, I guess to give them another idea of what London was about. The bar had a large percentage of West Indians as customers, and one of them was celebrating the birth of a baby with a toast of free pints, and running round the pub hugging and kissing everyone. The couple we had brought to experience London life were from Georgia in the USA, so you can imagine the woman's horror at being hugged and kissed by a black man! They fled the pub. Not a memory of Joe, but part of the situation that existed and probably still does in the southern USA.'[14]

Harriott himself sometimes produced dramatic reactions. Del Turner was stationed as a serviceman at RAF Honington from 1957 to 1964 and organised the jazz club. 'We got all the big names from the London jazz scene. I got to know Joe quite well. We had him at Honington quite a few times. One Christmas we took him over to the sergeants' mess. There were lots of sergeants there, pretty drunk ... and in walks Joe: black, very smart, debonair and very serious.' Turner recounted the conversation:

'Who's he?'

'He's Joe Harriott, the great sax player.'

'Tell him to play something.'

'He wants you to play, mate.'

Harriott took out his sax, got up onto the table and played 'the most ravishing version of 'Smoke Gets In Your Eyes' I've ever heard in my life. He just tore it apart. There was a silence in the mess throughout his playing which extended seconds after it. At the end the whole place just erupted. The majority weren't even jazz fans.'

Del found Joe responded well to humour. 'At a jazz gig in Clacton, a huge person entered the room: a really enormous man! I said to Joe, "That's the biggest jazz fan in Clacton," and he fell about laughing. Another time a few of us were drinking Smirnoff cocktails and someone said: "Take that Smirnoff your face!" He laughed at that and went on using the phrase all night.'[15]

As well as their strong musical affinity, Joe and Bill Haig shared the same sense of humour. Margaret Tynski often heard them indulging in nonsense. 'I think Haig was closer to Joe than any other male friend. They were very funny together and enjoyed bantering. They would refer to whisky as "the accoutrements". Joe or Haig would say, "Have you got the accoutrements?" If one or other made a statement, the reply would be, "Oh indubitably so!" in a very exaggerated upper class English accent. Very amusing.'

Joe enjoyed unsophisticated humour particularly the slapstick variety. He and Margaret Tynski often went to the newsreel cinemas where, after Pathe News, comic fare was offered: Charlie Chaplin, Laurel and Hardy, The Marx Brothers, short films and cartoons.

*

Tommy Whittle, Harriott's predecessor in Tony Kinsey's band, remembered booking Joe for the club he ran with his wife, singer Barbara Jay. It met weekly in the Hopbine pub in Wembley: 'We ran it for years and operated a policy of promoting British jazz players. We booked solo artists and Joe was one we had every four or five months. A Hopbine regular, Ted Lyons, used to record everything we did. The tapes may still exist somewhere.' These reel-to-reel treasures may include Harriott duelling with Peter King and Harold McNair.[16]

Years later, driving by the Hopbine (now the Dog and Duck), Tommy could not resist the urge to stop and look through the glass doors. 'As I looked through the glass, memories absorbed me. In my mind's eye I saw Joe Harriott perspiring and biting on his white alto sax mouthpiece, carving through a difficult chord sequence, and then the electrifying Harold McNair on flute with the fans in ecstasy.'[17]

There were one-off gigs of a different kind. The Harriott quintet was invited to play at the Savoy Hotel in August 1962 to celebrate Jamaica's Independence. Despite never returning to his country of birth, Joe was proud to call himself Jamaican and, indeed, retained his Jamaican passport, never seeking a British one. This must have been an especially enjoyable event for him.

Alongside concerts and gigs, there were festivals of all kinds. An opportunity for jazz fans to get out of smoky cellar jazz clubs and into the fresh air was provided by Marquee Club owner and National Jazz Federation director, Harold Pendleton. The venue for his first National Jazz and Blues Festival in August 1961 was the Athletic Association Ground at Richmond, Surrey. Harriott's quintet was featured, as were those of Tubby Hayes and Don Rendell. From the other side of jazz came Ken Colyer, Alex Welsh and Chris Barber. The gathering was a success and became an annual event, paving the way for much larger ones in later years.

The 1963 festival was expanded to include events in Hamilton and Manchester as well as Richmond and the Harriott quintet appeared at all three venues. The Hamilton event was billed as the Scottish Jazz Festival and took place on a hot Saturday in June. The report in the *Hamilton Advertiser* implied that the local hack was shaken by the experience. 'Never before has Hamilton seen such an influx of weirdly dressed characters – youths in striped shirts, bowler hats and knee-length sweaters; girls wearing pigtails, ban-the-bomb badges, sunglasses and outsized striped shirts – some wearing Russian boots and most of them sporting jackets round the waist in the mode exclusive to jazz festivals. They were a colourful, often comical assortment.'

As well as performing, Harriott helped to judge the area final of a national amateur jazz band competition. Harold Pendleton and Humphrey Lyttelton were on the panel with him.

Always interested in different playing contexts, he was engaged in December 1963 to accompany American blues vocalist and harmonica player Sonny Boy Williamson II, who was touring Britain at the height of the blues boom. Williamson, whose real name was Rice Miller, had adopted the name of an earlier, much respected, blues singer who died in 1948 after being stabbed in the head on his way home from a gig in Chicago. This horrific death drew sufficient attention in the blues world to make masquerading as the original Sonny Boy an impossibility but the use of the name attracted initial interest.

Williamson had been approached to perform on the *Chris Barber Christmas Show* on BBC radio. Barber, although broadly a traditional jazz bandleader, could always accommodate other jazz idioms. But bureaucratic red tape prevented Williamson appearing and Joe took his place as featured guest on the show. 'Anything but a substitute,' were the words presenter Humphrey Lyttelton used to introduce Harriott playing Sonny Boy's blues composition 'Help Me'. The show, recorded on 19 December, featured Joe in 'Jamaica March', 'Sweet Georgia Brown' and his own 'Revival'.[18]

Early in 1965, he took part in a recording session with Williamson. While Harriott liked a generous quantity of alcohol, Sonny Boy's thirst was unquenchable. 'Twelve bars' evoked his recreational activities as much as his professional ones. His doubtful sense of timing was not improved by copious quantities of scotch. Mickey Waller, the drummer on the date, said: 'There were no rehearsals. We started at 10.00 a.m. and it was all done by 1 p.m. Also it was done completely live: there were no overdubs. We sat in a circle and played.' Williamson was supported by a quality band including tenorist Alan Skidmore and rock-hero guitarist Jimmy Page. But Waller thought the blues singer was 'all over the place'.[19]

It is highly likely that Joe, whom Waller described as being, 'a bit snooty and offhand', was irritated by Williamson's lack of professionalism. The low demand made on Joe's musicianship on this occasion typified an aspect of session work that gave it no appeal for him, even in the face of financial difficulties. 'Don't Send Me No Flowers', the title track, had a prophetic ring. Williamson died in May 1965 and Marmalade Records held the material for three years before deciding to release it.

In his own group, Harriott had to cope with the tensions that inevitably arise when strong musical personalities co-exist in a working band. His relations with Pat Smythe, and especially Phil Seamen, exemplify this aspect of his working life.

Joe certainly admired Seamen's musicianship but they had very different professional approaches. Seamen kept great time on stage but turning up on time proved virtually beyond him. 'Phil was invariably late putting his kit up,' promoter Ernie Garside recalled. 'Watching Phil put his kit together was part of the show. He made so much noise and threw cymbals around and banged about. People just couldn't get enough of Phil Seamen in any shape or form. And Pat [Smythe] would be stood with me and he'd be looking, and he'd say, "here comes Joe, now." Joe would just kind of look around and then he'd get to the piano. He would sit at the piano and he had this long intro of 'All The Things You Are'. He had several tunes but they were all Stan Kentonish, concerto type. Pat used to say, "I wish he wouldn't do that. *I'm* not late." Somehow that always happened between Pat and Joe.'

Phil would 'finally have set his kit up and off they would go. Occasionally Joe would look round at him for some reason and Phil would be staring at him and playing his ride cymbal, like real viciously, as if he was beating Joe over the head with some bloody stick. We've got Joe and we've got Phil, two egomaniacs. And Phil's so funny. He wasn't one of the most photographable blokes but he took your attention. And when he'd start pounding [his drums] and looking at Joe, everybody would be looking at Phil. Joe used to get pissed with that because he's up there and playing solos. So there was a bit of a tension but the results were fine.'

Garside recalled that forty-five minutes before a Saturday night gig he had organised at the Clarendon Hotel in Manchester, only four of the quintet had assembled for the 8 p.m. start. As the 'punters' began arriving, so too did John Malloch, in whose home Seamen was staying. Malloch told Garside, 'Phil's in bed. He said he'd get a cab down.' Malloch had no telephone, so Garside drove to the house and roared down the hallway, 'Phil!'

Seamen was sitting up in bed reading. 'Great book! I've only got ten pages to read. Won't be a minute.' At the gig his kit still had to be assembled. It was 8.10 and the tension was electric when Phil walked in, apparently oblivious to his colleagues' concern. 'Where's me tubs?' he casually asked.

Garside remembered the scene: 'Joe's on the stand playing piano. Pat's looking on. Phil begins setting up the drum kit.' Rubbing salt in the wound, he told Ernie: 'Great book this. I'll lend you it when I'm finished.'[20]

On a different occasion, Harriott showed his anger with his drummer. Coming out of a drum shop in Shaftesbury Avenue, Tommy Chase met Seamen who was carrying the first Penguin edition of J. D. Salinger's *Catcher in the Rye* under his arm. 'It had just come out and had created a bit of a stir,' Chase recalled. 'Phil was a fantastic, witty man who loved reading. On this occasion he was as high as a kite. He dragged me down to the Flamingo where he was playing that night with Joe in a quartet. Phil arrived late and Joe was doing his nut. The kit was already set up. Phil took a chair from the front and put me right in front of the drums. He had a great ego. He took a pair of brushes as Joe launched into the first number, 'Star Eyes'.' Chase was in a prime position to hear Joe, boiling with rage, turn to Seamen with the furious order: 'Fucking sticks! Fucking sticks!'[21]

Another occasion of conflict on stage was at a New Departures gig with Michael Horovitz at the ICA. Horovitz remembered Joe and Phil's adversarial relationship. 'It was socially uncomfortable but musically it created fireworks. It did produce a tremendous tension between them. Joe was very self-aware about being black. I can remember Joe coming on strong about Jim Crow but onstage on this occasion he sounded like Crow-Jim shouting, "Work! Work!" at Phil. It was a musical cue shouted quite savagely. He wanted Phil to play harder and had a hectoring tone one might imagine a sadistic slave driver using. This was only my subjective reaction though.'[22]

'It was always a real love-hate relationship,' Peter King told me. 'There was one story about Phil chasing Joe out of the Marquee and half way down Oxford Street in the middle of a tune! I only heard the story through the grapevine. I am pretty sure it's true though.... Then there was the time when Joe tried to fire Phil. Phil turned round with the classic remark: "You can't fire me, I already quit!"'[23]

Bassist Danny Thompson who played with Seamen in various groups had a tolerant view: 'Anyone working with Phil compromised with him. Women loved him. He was never a bad person. He was affected by drugs. If he was late for a gig, crashing around setting up his drums, or nodding off to sleep on the stand, [we] would laugh, but staid, gentlemanly Joe never would understand him.'[24]

Heather Smythe, Pat's widow, felt that the quintet was not a happy band but that they produced some of their best work through tension.[25] 'Possibly so,' thought Ernie Garside, 'but that tension wasn't off the bandstand. It was only on the gig. I got the distinct impression that Joe was "in public" and he

was "on exhibition" and he wanted to show that was what bandleaders did. If he got results, then fine. But all through this, Joe never put anybody down.'[26]
It was unknown for Joe to be upstaged by any other musician. However the bizarre events of 15 March 1971 rather stole his thunder. Rod Marshall, proprietor of the Anchor Inn, Brighouse, Yorkshire, was a promoter of jazz gigs in the town. A keen amateur jazz flautist, he had promoted his hero Harold McNair on several occasions. 'I was ready to open up my own jazz clubroom. A wall had been taken down which made two bedrooms into the main clubroom. I had built my own bar in a small alcove to one side and there was even a small stage. Thanks to the help of friends, I had lighting and spots, small tables and even smaller buffets. Joe seemed perfect for my opening night and he needed the work – more than I knew at the time!

'The first surprise was that on that very afternoon he rang to say he didn't have the train fare. He had been to a party and lost his wallet. I was a bit green at the time but I paid for a ticket for him at Huddersfield station and waited.

'My opening night was the very first night of the national power cuts. We had been warned that power would be cut in different areas at different times. Some places would have power when others didn't. I had dozens of candles and a wind-up gramophone to give background music if the power went off.

'Everything seemed ok as Joe went on stage without a bass player. I introduced him to the awaiting crowd. And then the lights went out and stayed out till midnight. The extractor fan didn't work and the PA didn't work. But Joe did – until someone noticed that we had competition from across the canal where a large mill was on fire, giving more light than Brighouse was used to. By this time, the crowd was beginning to feel the heat of the candles and lack of air. So everyone went out to look at the fire and I just stood around talking to Joe.'[27]

Above The Joe Harriott Quintet, 1960, at its regular Marquee Club gig. Left to right: Pat Smythe, Shake Keane, JH, Tommy Jones, Coleridge Goode (courtesy Redferns).

Below left The perfect partnership: Keane and Harriott at the Richmond Festival 1961 (photo David Redfern).
Below right At Marble Arch, London, 1966 (photo Michael Garrick).

Above JH, promoter Harold Pendleton and trumpeter Humphrey Lyttleton judging an amateur jazz band competition at the 1963 NJF Hamilton Jazz Festival. The competition sponsors, cigarette makers, made sure their product got pride of place (courtesy *Jazz Journal International*).

Below left With promoter Don Norman, late 1960s (courtesy Don Norman).

Below right John Mayer, c.1969 (courtesy Don Norman).

Above The Indo-Jazz Fusions Double Quintet rehearsing in London for a TV series, summer 1969. Left to right: John Mayer, Pat Smythe, Viram Jashani, Keshav Sathe, Coleridge Goode, Chris Taylor, Diwan Motihar, Kenny Wheeler, John Marshall, JH (courtesy John Mayer and Don Norman).

Below left Michael Garrick recording his *October Woman* LP with Shake Keane, JH and Coleridge Goode in 1964 (photo Harley Usill).

Below right 'He knew there was no money; he just wanted to blow. It was rather sad': With drummer Harry Miller, Cooks Ferry Inn, north London, 1967 (photo Bunny Austin).

Right Skip Conway at Harriott's grave, Bitterne, 1974–5 (courtesy *Southern Daily Echo*).

Left Whatever the context he put his whole heart into the music. JH gigging at Manchester's 43 Club in the 1960s (photo P. J. Ankers, courtesy Ernie Garside).

Above 'Joe Harriott? Who's he?': Altoist Martin Hathaway carrying the legacy forward with Shake Keane in the Joe Harriott Memorial Quintet organised by Michael Garrick in 1989 (photo Tony Mullett).

Right Joe Harriott's home, Clifton Hill, Maida Vale (photo Alan Robertson).

10.

proving Kipling wrong –
East meets West

Calcutta-born violinist and composer-arranger John Mayer found little support at first for an idea he had long been nurturing. 'The idea for Fusions first came from the 'Dances of India' I wrote for three Indian instruments and symphony orchestra about 1958. I'd been telling Denis Preston I wanted to make a fusion of Indian and Western techniques but he always dismissed it. In fact his secretary, Sylvia Pentlow, wrote to me saying not to get in touch with him. He was too busy.'[1]

In 1964, six months after receiving Pentlow's letter, Mayer was asked by Preston if he had a short piece in a jazz idiom. Although he hadn't, he seized the opportunity and said yes. To Mayer's dismay, Preston announced he intended to record it the following day. Mayer had to lose a night's sleep to compose a suitable piece in time. The following day, bleary-eyed, he attended the recording of his new composition, 'Nine for Bacon', at Lansdowne Studios. The session featured such prominent musicians as Don Lusher, Kenny Baker and Humphrey Lyttleton. Mayer remarked happily, 'I got £20. It was a hell of a lot of money in those days.' Worth losing a night's sleep for.[2]

'Nine for Bacon', with its combination of jazz and Indian influences, favourably impressed Ahmet Ertegun of Atlantic Records in New York when Preston played him the recording. Ertegun suggested the idea of an album blending Indian music and jazz and using jazz musicians alongside Indian instrumentalists in an integrated group.

Three months after Mayer's debut recording he received a further letter from Sylvia Pentlow asking him to call on Preston. 'I was nervous. I thought he wanted the money back,' Mayer confessed. 'As I entered his office, he said, "John, I understand your friends call you Johnny. Do you mind if I call you Johnny?"' Then, without any sense of irony, he announced: 'We have had this idea ...'

Although he found the concept very familiar, Mayer was diplomatic. 'I said, "What a marvellous idea!"'3. His 1965 meeting with Joe Harriott at Lansdowne Studio proved fateful. Harriott seemed to be unaware of Preston's guiding hand when he described the meeting with Mayer. 'The way we got together with John was more by accident than design. I had finished my third abstract album4 and was talking about the next step to record producer Denis Preston. Denis introduced me to Mayer, we exchanged ideas, and the result was the first record.'5 Mayer spent a month writing the music.

Mayer's memory of an early conversation with Harriott indicates the strength of Joe's self-belief. When the Indo-Jazz Fusions project was in its infancy, Mayer was paying the bills by playing violin with the Royal Philharmonic Orchestra, although he considered himself as first and foremost a composer. 'Joe said I shouldn't be doing it because they would pigeonhole me as a violinist not a composer.' In Mayer's case, recognition as a composer did come only after he had given up the violin position in the RPO, but he could not afford to take Harriott's advice at that time. Joe rarely considered compromise in his own life.6

Bobby Orr, who had embraced free form music to the surprise of some, was not as well disposed to the Indo-jazz repertoire, so Harriott's old associate, Allan Ganley, was the eventual choice on drums. Mayer initially used Phil Seamen as drummer but one bad experience led him to look elsewhere. Seamen 'was ill and he left the room. Phil was slurring his words and I saw him go to the toilet. When he came back out he was fine. Joe said: "He's had a fix." In my ignorance I asked: "Who fixed him?"'

Pat Smythe's response to the Indo-jazz concept was predictably enthusiastic as he had previously suggested the idea of
experimenting with Indian music to Harriott. Smythe had
made a television recording in 1965 with Seamen, bassist Peter
Ind, Larry Adler on harmonica, a sitarist and a tamboura player. Mayer said: 'I used to see Pat quite a lot. I used Pat as a liai-
son or intermediary for my [Indian] group and Joe's quintet. He
was the one.'

Tabla player Keshav Sathe, too, found much affinity with
Smythe. 'I had been to Pat's house many times. On one occasion he told me of his first plane crash. Something very funny
about how he destroyed a plane!'7 Coleridge Goode recalled:
'they got the idea – John, Pat and a sitar player – of fusing the
two, the jazz and the sort of classical Indian thing. John wrote
out the arrangements, and eventually we worked the thing out
very successfully.'8 Goode was clear that 'the prime mover in
developing the idea' was 'John Mayer who had studied Western
music and was keen to find ways of combining its techniques
with those of Indian classical music.'9

The band's first recording session was in October 1965: 'I
remember the first day we went into the studio,' Mayer said.
'We had two days recording. Carte blanche. We just went into
the studio and we put it down. And the first piece we played
was the 'Overture' which was the first piece on the first album.
And after we started the whole band collapsed. "Man," Joe said,
"Johnny, what is this? I can't play against this!"'

'I said, "Just take it easy. This is something new." This was
the first time in the history of music that you had Western
musicians and Indian musicians playing together from a written score. You must remember that everything of the Fusions
was all notated.'10

Goode relished the challenge. 'The time signatures were
very abstruse ... and the whole feel was quite different. It was a
question of playing things in certain sequences ... very absorbing, really. The bass often worked as a sort of drone, but in a
precise series of phrases that would be repeated as other things
were interweaving with it. But the time signatures were fierce!

Like 13 or 15 beats, all odd numbers in the bar; it needed a heck
of a lot of concentration – not for the tabla players, who played
that music all their lives, but certainly for me. Another problem was dynamics, because the Indian instruments were so soft
in volume compared to the brass.'[11]

Sathe, thoroughly grounded in the Indian classical tradition,
was also well disposed to jazz. 'I couldn't have done jazz if I
hadn't lived in this country,' he told me. 'I was born in Bombay
and came to Britain in 1956.' He became enamoured of jazz
through frequenting the 100 Club and the Bull's Head jazz pub
in Barnes. 'When we recorded in Lansdowne Studios that first
morning, I'd never heard an instrument like a trumpet right
next to my ear before. It was very difficult to get used to. They
had to build soundproofed screens between us. We took a
break and went for an Indian meal, which Denis Preston loved.
When we came back it all worked out.'[12]

Columbia released the album *Indo-Jazz Suite* the following
year in both Britain and America. The tactfully shared billing
was 'the Joe Harriott double quintet under the direction of
John Mayer'. In the Mayer group the leader played violin and
harpsichord, Diwan Motihar played sitar. On tamboura, providing the drone notes, was Chandrahas Paigankar and the
tabla player was Keshav Sathe. They were joined by Mayer's
RPO flautist colleague, Chris Taylor, who loved playing jazz.
Harriott's quintet consisted of Smythe, Ganley, bassist Rick
Laird, and Eddie Blair playing trumpet and flugelhorn.

Mayer talked to Charles Fox about the contributions of the
jazz improvisers. 'I gave them the notes of the particular raga
in each case. Pat Smythe stuck rigidly to them in all his piano
solos, which is why his improvisations sound so uncompromis-
ingly Indian. But Joe Harriott often moved outside the frame-
work, playing his own free form jazz. As for the flute, this is
used as a kind of intermediary, sometimes playing jazz parts.
The flute part, however, was completely written out. And I
play harpsichord a couple of times, to keep the raga line going
when the sitar is doing something else. The sound after all is
very similar.'[13]

The rhythmically most challenging piece is 'Raga Megha' with four sections, the improvising starting in the final part. The rhythm is at its most adventurous when eighteen beats are divided into three groups of six. Fox felt that, with Indo-jazz, the musicians 'were entering territory that looks likely to be explored more and more during the years to come'. He delighted in repudiating Kipling's view that East and West were a twain never to meet because 'ever since, both life and art have been proving him wrong.'[14]

While in London, Horace Silver, an old friend of the Harriott quintet, listened to 'Raga Megha' in a blindfold test for *Crescendo* in 1966. He confessed, 'I'm not that hip to Indian music but I liked that. I enjoyed Joe Harriott's playing, the piano solo was cute and, with the flute and everything, it was a nice piece of music.' Silver's bassist Larry Ridley was also present and had special words of praise: 'I used to play violin and I'm very fond of the instrument. So when I hear someone like John Mayer who can really play it, man – it knocks me out! It calls for a very unorthodox fingering to be able to play those Indian scales, the ragas and what have you, on the violin. And he played it beautifully – had a lot of control. Interesting experiment.'[15]

Did Harriott bring to the experiment any knowledge of Indian music? Mayer told me, 'Joe was a fine saxophonist whose knowledge of jazz and free form jazz was unquestionable but his knowledge of world music, or music other than his own was not very good. But why should he have been interested in Arab-Persian, Chinese or Indian music? He was a superb jazz musician.'[16]

Joe was enthusiastic about Indo-jazz when Max Jones interviewed him for *Melody Maker*: 'Obviously I don't follow the format as strictly as the Indian players do. What I try to do is paint a picture with the symbols given to me. I try to create something with the raga – you know, create something over the top.'[17]

What seemed like flexibility to Harriott paradoxically seemed the opposite to Mayer. Speaking many years later, he suggested that Joe was maybe too set in his ways to fully embrace the Indian format. 'They were all hard-boiled professional musicians ... Joe Harriott was like a tree ... I mean, when the tree's grown you can't bend it, can you?' Mayer wanted to go in a direction where Joe's 'freedom' would not release him.[18]

Jazz Monthly's Bruce King was much taken with *Indo-Jazz Suite*. 'For the past decade Harriott has been the most interesting musician on this side of the Atlantic. While the habitual shape of his phrases and melodic ideas was influenced by Parker, Harriott has always been his own man ... [and] seems through the logic of his own development to have independently worked his way from bop to free jazz.... His lines move freely through space, continually developing, creating their own form without regard to metre or harmonic structure, and yet they are rich in melodic beauty and emotional intensity.

'Jazz has always been aggressive in applying Afro-American musical techniques to seemingly unrelated musical idioms, and there is no reason why Indian music should not be brought into the fold.... This record is a pleasure to listen to, and my only objection is that Harriott does not take any extended solos. The solos he does take are magnificent.'[19]

Charles Fox agreed. Joe had 'responded nobly to the challenge. Indeed it is likely that his work here is among the finest he has ever put on record.'[20] But, as good as Harriott's work is on this album, it hardly represents his artistic peak. *Free Form* and *Abstract* remain his paramount achievement in both composition and execution.

Some jazz fans and musicians never took to the Fusions music, referring disparagingly to it as 'curried jazz'. It may well have been Phil Seamen who first dubbed the band 'Confusions' in his inimitable way. Benny Green also needed convincing: 'I confess when I first heard Harriott and Mayer working together, not only did Mayer's group sound out of tune to me, but they seemed to make Harriott's players sound out of tune also. Being a typical jazz musician and therefore something of a bigot, I wrote them off, but further hearings have suggested to me that it is just possible that it was my ear and not their playing which was at fault.'[21]

The first concert, organised by future Indo-Jazz Fusions manager Don Norman, took place in Chichester's Festival Theatre on 8 May 1966. Norman had previously booked Joe there both as a solo artist and in a quartet with Seamen and Dave Goldberg. He had also organised concerts at the Festival Theatre by the Tubby Hayes orchestra, Annie Ross and poet Christopher Logue. The Indo-jazz music was very well received and the band met with acclaim.

'I think God smiled on us,' Mayer commented. 'It was a very well integrated ensemble, the musicians got on very well with each other. Apart from being of different musical traditions the band was also a fusion of different cultures, nationalities and religious beliefs. There were four Indians, two players from the Caribbean Islands, two Londoners, a Scotsman and a Canadian. They were Moslems, a Hindu, a Rosicrucian (Joe), a Jew, a Catholic, a Protestant and an atheist.

'Although there was some unavoidable deputising at times, the ten piece group remained essentially the same at most concerts. The venues varied: theatres, universities and some less prestigious places. Travel was often by car or a hired coach and, since there were no mobile phones in those days to keep track of everyone's whereabouts, we all met at a specific time and place ready for some long journeys.

'Apart from worrying about the music, there was the concern that everyone would turn up on time. The Indians were the worst! Before Fusions gigs we'd meet at the car park of the Odeon Cinema at Swiss cottage. If we were due to meet at two o'clock, the Indian members of the group would arrive at quarter to three. Don [Norman] would always ask them to turn up an hour earlier than they were needed.

'One night we stopped [at the services on the M1 motorway] on the way home and had a drink. Setting off [again] we left Coleridge behind. You couldn't just turn around and it was thirty-five miles before we could turn back for him. This meant seventy miles in total before we got back to where we were. He said: "Where were you?" Instead of getting home at twelve o'clock we got home at one.[22]

'We used to have some wonderful and very funny times on the coach. Like the time when Joe pestered Diwan Motihar to play poker; at first Motihar declined but, when Joe insisted, he did reluctantly join the game; but cleaned the whole group out. You see, he was an expert poker player, which nobody knew. He was never asked to play again!' Mayer also mentioned an appearance at Ronnie Scott's where sitarist Motihar was a few minutes late in arriving. This presented Ronnie with a once in a lifetime chance to quip: 'Ladies and gentlemen we are sorry we are a few minutes late, but Diwan Motihar couldn't find a baby sitar.'[23]

The group played at the Marquee Club in November 1966. Bass player, composer and jazz writer Graham Collier reviewed the gig for *Crescendo*. He noted the audience's enthusiasm but commented that there were two rhythm sections in tension and not enough space in the music. Also, 'the written music generally lacked a good jazz feel. This was emphasised by the freshness of Joe Harriott's alto improvising.' Sathe, however, 'sounded like an incredibly hip bongo player' and Motihar's sitar on 'Gana' 'swung very much'. Collier felt that, 'if it ever does fuse completely, it'll be 'crazy'. Until then it provides a very interesting evening – and much food for thought.'[24]

Two further recordings, *Indo-Jazz Fusions* and *Indo-Jazz Fusions II*, were made by the Mayer–Harriott double quintet. The term 'fusion', which became the genre name, was credited by some to Denis Preston but John Mayer names Don Norman as the originator. The albums combined raga and free jazz in exciting, musically satisfying ways. *Indo-Jazz Fusions,* released in 1967, marked Harriott's last recording with Shake Keane. Joe's free form composition 'Subject' was adapted for the group. That it is jointly credited to Mayer and Harriott indicates the degree of change it had gone through, but it is still recognisably the composition from *Abstract*.

A track which did not feature Joe, but had a significant input from Goode and Smythe, was 'Acka Raga'. Originally written by Mayer for Acker Bilk, this catchy melody became recognisable across Britain as the theme tune of BBC's popular *Ask The Family* quiz show.

On *Indo-Jazz Fusions II,* Allan Ganley and Shake Keane were replaced by Jackie Dougan and Kenny Wheeler. Wheeler recalled being uncertain at the outset and asking Harriott: 'Do we have to play on the raga?' Joe's response was: 'No, I just play whatever.'[25]

Indo-Jazz Fusions toured the UK and played at large international festivals particularly in Europe. One was a four day event in Bologna. With drummer John Marshall, trumpeter Stu Hamer and Harriott as passengers, Pat Smythe drove to the festival. Disaster struck within an hour of their arrival. Joe's alto saxophone was stolen outside the band's hotel. The Italian police showed total disinterest and despite appeals on television and radio, nothing was forthcoming. A sax was borrowed from American star altoist Lee Konitz. Hamer recalled: 'It took two seconds for Joe's sax to disappear. Hank Mobley's tenor was nicked as well. I didn't let go of my trumpet. I took it everywhere with me.'

Mayer remembers going to bed after rehearsing. Goode also retired early as his fellow band members sampled the alcoholic fare in the bar. 'In the morning,' recalls Mayer, 'they were all on the balcony having a drink and saying, "come and meet Lee Konitz, Jon Hendricks, Cecil Taylor ..." I didn't know who they were.'[26] Among the revellers Konitz stood out. 'He was as straight as a die,' Hamer said. 'He wasn't getting high at all.'[27]

The concert venue was a theatre often used for opera. Keshav Sathe thought it was 'like the Leeds Gaiety Theatre. Beautiful!'[28] Marshall remarked on the hall's fine acoustics.[29] Less appealing was the hotel. 'It was a whorehouse,' Hamer candidly told me.'[30] With organised crime clearly involved, no one wanted to trust the security offered by the hotel safe. Even the fee for their festival appearance seemed at risk.

On the night before departure considerable wheeling and dealing preceded the band's payment. Boxes of paper lira were eventually delivered and early next day, with Goode and

Smythe at their driving wheels, relieved band members made a speedy exit for home.

Mayer had a surprise on waking: 'Don and all of them had left. I was taking a train later in the day and it was left to me to see the Mafia about paying for Joe's sax in the morning. I was green and that was why I was left. I went up to the room where they had all this security on the door and there the money was paid for the sax. I wasn't worried; I just went in and asked for the money. I was completely naive and that's probably why nothing happened to me. I had never harmed anyone in my life and what the eye doesn't see ... '[31] The cash given to Mayer was enough for Joe to buy a replacement sax.

There were other unpleasant occasions, such as when the group met racist hostility. Accommodation could be, and was, denied them on grounds of colour. At a jazz festival in Belfast, Don Norman was bluntly berated for 'bringing all them damn foreigners here.'[32] Mayer feels that his and Joe's experience eventually benefited later musicians in breaking down prejudice. 'Joe Harriott was a man who took all the stick, like myself. We took all the stick from everybody because I was an Indian and he was a Jamaican.'

Mayer remains adamant that 'if it hadn't been for Joe Harriott, all the [world music] people now, I won't mention their names – would not be doing what they're doing.' World music began here.[33]

A major appearance for the band was at Harold Davison's *Jazz Expo* in London on 23 October 1967. They were booked to play the second set on a bill that included Max Roach and the John Dankworth Orchestra. Sharon Atkin remembered a brief panic as she and Harriott arrived for the concert. 'I went with Joe to the Hammersmith Odeon. As we arrived there Joe turned to me and said, "I've forgotten the music!" He handed me his alto and told me to hold the dress suit. "If John Mayer comes out, tell him I'll be there in a minute."' Of course, Mayer soon did.

'Where's Joe?'

'He'll be there in a minute.'

John needed more convincing. 'You don't think he'd leave me with his sax do you?'

With that, Mayer was pacified, convinced Joe wasn't far away.[34]

Reviewing the concert, *Jazz Monthly*'s Michael James declared Indo-jazz an unsuccessful experiment. 'The jazz contributions by Harriott and his men were little better than pedestrian and the Indian parts of the proceedings, apart from an inventive violin solo, were frankly monotonous.'[35]

When the final Mayer–Harriott album *Indo-Jazz Fusions II* was released, however, Ian Carr thought it 'the most successful and satisfying to date.' Partly because of the group's heavy concert schedule, the musicians had 'become much more familiar with one another. The sitar player, Diwan Motihar, now improvises much more freely with the jazz musicians; there's a much happier fusion of the rhythm instruments; Chris Taylor, always a superb flautist, has gradually mastered the jazz idiom, and his solo work is very exciting ... and the jazz contingent, led by Joe Harriott, sound more confidently poised and less defiant.'[36]

Another reviewer, Jack Cooke, wrote: 'in this setting [Harriott's] work has a delicacy and grace that wasn't always evident before, released perhaps by these subtle structures he's working in.'[37]

The growing fascination in the late 1960s with the Indian way of life, typified by the interest of the Rolling Stones and Beatles, contributed to the band's success. Joe suggested: 'It has helped. It's not unusual for people to think Indo-jazz when they hear a sitar, though what it's playing may have nothing whatever to do with jazz.'[38]

Mayer felt the popularity of Indian music was less a fleeting success than something that had steadily progressed.[39] He and Harriott helped to spread the word about Indo-jazz outside the concert hall environment. They took part in a series of jazz workshops in London in the late sixties and Joe gave a talk to students at Leeds Music Centre around this time. One student, bassist Danny Padmore, thought the occasion revealed

Harriott as an essentially shy man who did not enjoy the lecturing situation.

Max Harrison's review of an Indo-Jazz Fusions concert at the Queen Elizabeth Hall in February 1970 was ambivalent. 'All regular groups run into stalemates,' he declared, and 'this ensemble now has its problems ... '

'Some would maintain John Mayer's and Joe Harriott's group ... have always been in a blind alley,' their 'music artfully appealing to the jazz community's strange combination of conservatism and thirst for superficial novelty, or worse still, being designed for that fringe audience which is usually attracted by freaks and hybrids. But the large number of apparently enthusiastic Indians helping pack the Hall on this, as on previous occasions, makes difficulties for such a view, and if it be asserted these were simply people who happen to like jazz besides the music of their own culture, the existence of such listeners is itself a comment on the present musical situation.' The audience 'seemed quite innocent of being a typical jazz gathering.'

Harrison concluded that Harriott and Mayer might be 'too habituated with their current methods to make further steps, and these will have to be taken by others. Yet these men should always receive credit for having made a necessary beginning.'[40]

Asked by one interviewer what Joe was like to work with, Mayer smiled. 'Bloody difficult! He was sometimes very stubborn. We argued about everything: sometimes musical things, then how we should go on the bloody coach to a gig. He was difficult.'[41]

John Marshall remembered Harriott as often morose and stubborn. On the band's coach one day, Mayer's patience with Harriott reached its limit over some issue. He raged at him: 'You drive me so mad, I am literally going to tear my hair out!' Then, in a gesture worthy of Basil Fawlty, he began tugging at his hair.[42]

Sathe recalled Joe dreading a flight to Belfast and trying to forget his anxiety by drinking. His habitual heavy drinking had not previously adversely affected his music but this time it was different. 'He was very, very drunk and could not hold the score on the stand. I think, after that, John Mayer decided that he could not use Joe again.'[43] Coleridge Goode, too, recalled that after this incident relations between Joe and John became very strained.[44]

In 1969 Don Norman brokered a recording arrangement with a new label, Sonet. When the next Indo-Jazz Fusions album, *Etudes,* was released it did not feature Harriott who remained contractually bound to Denis Preston's organisation. The excellent saxophonist Tony Coe replaced Joe but the album lacked much of the excitement of the earlier recordings. Years later, Mayer asked Preston why he had prevented Joe from appearing on it. After all, Harriott had been allowed to make a quintet album with Melodisc in June 1967. Preston's answer was unrevealing: 'Business is business.'[45]

The band broke up in 1971, around the time Harriott was telling *Melody Maker*'s Max Jones; 'Some of the music was pretty. A pity it didn't work out. I liked a lot of it, you know, and learned a lot from it. It was fun breaking some of those rules.' With such comments Joe gave Jones the impression he had moved on and felt no further attraction towards that particular project.[46]

He was hardly likely to say, as Coleridge Goode put it, that 'he had burned his boats'.[47] Nor was there any likelihood of him confessing that he didn't know where he would turn next.

In its time the Fusions band generated much media interest, initially because of the novelty of the idea, but more durably because of the freshness and virtuosity of the music. However, looking back on the financial returns from Fusions recordings, John Mayer spoke in tones bordering on disgust. 'Denis Preston promised us three per cent between the two of us on the sale of the records but the only money we made was from the concerts. Preston bought a house in the south of France on the strength of it while Joe and I were scuffling around.'[48] Trevor Tomkins thought Preston had 'pretty good vision, but was cavalier. Behind it all he was a very shrewd businessman.'[49]

Preston's colleague, sound engineer Adrian Kerridge, recalled: 'Joe always appeared to be short of money – what jazz

musician in those days wasn't? – And Denis was always generous, but I guess there comes a time when it gets taken for
granted. I cannot be sure but Denis sometimes paid the guys
"the going rate" to work on a date and if they had many solos
to play perhaps they felt they needed a slice of royalties. Artists
of that talent too could be very temperamental!'[50]

Other musicians felt grateful to Preston. Guitarist Amancio
D'Silva was championed by him. His widow, Joyce, told me:
'Amancio was fond of Denis and really grateful for the huge
opportunities he gave him. He did feel ripped off about royalties in general, but didn't want to blame Denis for this.'[51]

Singer Elaine Delmar said, 'Denis Preston was a champion.
He recorded four of my albums. He knew he'd never make a
penny out of them. He said: "We can look back on them and
say, that was a good piece of work." That's what was important
to him.'

There were further examples of his altruistic side. Elaine
recalled that when Phil Seamen's drug habit meant he was
becoming more unreliable, Denis continued to book him
against his better judgement, also booking a second drummer
just in case. After the gifted multi-instrumentalist Alan
Branscombe suffered a fractured skull falling down stairs, he
was off the scene for a long time. His confidence ebbed to an
all-time low and friends feared his career had come to a premature end. Preston booked him for a session at Lansdowne, sure
that the repertoire would appeal to him and 'bring him out'. To
Preston's credit, the plan succeeded.[52]

Indo-Jazz Fusions developed in the age of the television
variety show. Harlech TV engaged the group for a series of programmes made before a live audience. The filming was done
over a weekend during which the band was accommodated in a
Bristol hotel and, after the series was edited, six programmes
went out featuring Fusions as the resident band.[53] Star guests
included Cleo Laine, Elaine Delmar, Mark Murphy and
Georgie Fame. When I requested further information from
Harlech TV, an apologetic archive secretary said she could not

locate anything of the performances on film or in stills. She explained, 'if it was studio-based the footage would have been destroyed as soon as it was aired.'

Possibly the group's best showcase was on the prestigious *Jazz 625* series on the fledgling BBC2 television channel. The series recorded performances by Bill Evans, Thelonious Monk, Wes Montgomery and Art Blakey among other American headliners. The half-hour programme devoted to Indo-Jazz Fusions went out on 13 October 1966.

During an economy drive, BBC bosses ordered the wiping of the Fusions tape so it could be reused. Although this fate befell other *Jazz 625* recordings, it was particularly unfortunate in Joe's case. The *Jazz 625* tapes of Bill Evans and the other American stars are, of course, treasured today by the U.S. Library of Congress. One remaining hope for surviving Harriott footage may lie in Germany where the quintet was recorded in a studio while on tour in the sixties.

11.

whatever has happened to Joe Harriott lately?

Defiance in the face of overwhelming odds can be noble but is, more often, foolhardy. Tired of the struggle for wider acceptance, Joe Harriott eventually decided to abandon free form jazz. In the mid-1960s a new generation of club and concert goers was turning to beat and rhythm-and-blues groups. It was becoming harder to obtain work for Harriott's quintet and its regular members were busy with other projects.

After 1965, Shake Keane was based in Germany. Goode, Seamen and Orr were in demand for freelance work in recording studios while Pat Smythe, often leading his trio at Annie's Room or Ronnie Scott's, had developed into a superb accompanist for jazz vocalists and visiting American reedmen such as Eddie 'Lockjaw' Davis and Stan Getz. Singer Elaine Delmar explained why Pat was so special: 'There are not many people who love songs and lyrics like he did. Anything Pat touched he beautified. He would make it his own. He made tone poems out of things. He was a wonderful accompanist. He didn't have a big ego. He made *you* stand out.'[1]

Even though there were less opportunities for him in Britain at this time, America still had no pull for Harriott. He pursued club and pub gigs all over Britain as a guest solo artist and if a quintet gig became available he chose the personnel in an ad hoc manner, continuing to call on Phil Seamen in spite of the friction between them.

Trumpeter Kenny Wheeler remembers playing with Harriott and Seamen in a London pub during this period. 'Phil had decided he would 'get' Joe. There was a fast 'Cherokee' and when it came to Joe's solo, all he did was he stopped playing the drums and played on the high hat on the off-beat. Eventually, whoever you are, it gets hard to stay on the beat and Joe changed to Phil's time.' There were no angry words. As Kenny put it: 'They were fine afterwards. When Joe was playing with me I couldn't wait to get to my solo. He made you really want to play.'²

Ian Carr recalled that some time in the second half of the sixties Harriott invited him to join a gig in Glasgow. A friend of Joe's with a big American car would take all of them, except Coleridge Goode who always drove his own car. 'The rendezvous was at Joe's flat where the gas, electricity and phone were cut off because he hadn't paid the bills. At the last minute Phil Seamen called to say he couldn't do the gig so Buzz Green took his place. Joe was dressed in a black suit, white shirt and primly knotted tie, very smart as opposed to the rest of us.

'By the time we got there, there was no time to eat and after the concert it was too late. We had to sleep on couches in the Students' Union. We'd had no breakfast when we set off in the morning and Joe, who was a nervous passenger, was on the edge of his seat in the car. We had to stop at an inn to have something to eat. The only other people there were a tweedy woman and her tweedy husband and daughter. Joe said, "I'll have rainbow trout." The woman was looking at us. We were an unkempt bunch along with this black guy in the smart black suit. The woman referred to us in one word: "Arty." Joe looked at the three of them and, loud enough for them to hear, uttered the word: "Agricultural."

'On the journey back someone asked how we'd been paid, cash or cheque? Joe showed us the cheque. It was suggested he should, "give the cheque to Ian. He could cash it." He eventually gave the cheque to me but then – he snatched it back! We were both tugging at it, frightened it would tear in half. Joe ended up keeping it and I can't remember if we ever got paid our share. We knew he was always on his uppers.'³

Money was increasingly a problem for Harriott. He 'could be

a bit tetchy about money,' Trevor Tomkins remembered. 'I was up front with Joe – I'd say, "Don't muck me about" and he'd pay me ... Joe preferred it that way.'4

George 'Bunny' Austin ran the door on jazz nights at the Cooks Ferry Inn in Edmonton, north London, during 1967 when Harriott made an unexpected visit. 'Freddy Randall started the club in 1946. All we did was take money on the door, pay the advertising fee to the *Melody Maker* and pay out the rest to the musicians. Joe came along there, playing with the rhythm section. They were mainstream guys including Harry Miller, who had been Freddy Randall's drummer from 1948 to 1951. We had no money to give Joe after paying the band and he was in dire straits. He said he'd realised there was no money from the outset; he just wanted to blow. It was rather sad. He was on his own at the time. He still played the avant-garde stuff. One number he played with just the bass player. That sort of music, even in a modern club, didn't catch on, though. He was a very unlucky man. Some of the musicians deserted him. He wasn't very well, either, I don't think. He was an elusive man, yet I liked him. Very nicely spoken. He didn't strike me as being embittered at the time.'5

Any chance to record under his own name was worth taking and an opportunity unexpectedly arose outwith Preston's Lansdowne operation. With Stu Hamer on trumpet and Phil Seamen on drums, a Harriott quintet album, *Swings High,* was made for Melodisc in June 1967. The recording was supervised by Doug Dobell, owner of London's best-known jazz record shop. Reviewer Jack Cooke noted that the album's sound had 'all the cleanliness and ambience that the john under [Dobell's] shop then had.' But he was pleased to see that Joe, 'was back in his favourite format, a quintet which aspired to the drive and cohesion of Horace Silver's.'6

To have Seamen on record with Harriott again was certainly welcome but Coleridge Goode, bassist on the album, saw a big deterioration in the drummer's physical condition: 'He was in a pretty bad way. We just hoped he would get through it. And he did.'7

Composer and arranger John Keating knew what Seamen's

life was like at that time. 'I used to think the heroin guys did it for the pleasure, like screwing a bird. But it wasn't like that. Once it takes them over, that's it. Phil had me round at his flat in Maida Vale for a cup of tea. We were sitting at a table below a mirror. He looked up at the mirror and said with weary resignation: "You see that? I've got to look in that every day and say: Here goes another day."'[8]

Trevor Tomkins remembered Phil speaking unemotionally about his audiences: 'They don't come to see me. They come to see Britain's biggest junkie.' Seamen obviously had regrets but didn't feel sorry for himself. He told Tomkins 'nobody makes me take this. I'm a victim of my own choice.' He made regular visits back to Burton upon Trent, his home town, to enjoy some time angling and to try to 'clean-up'.[9]

Swings High was the last recording by a Harriott quintet and there was much to be nostalgic about. Of the eight tracks, two, 'The Rake' and 'Shepherd's Serenade', were Dizzy Reece compositions. These were familiar to fans of the quintet from concerts and BBC radio broadcasts. 'Strollin' South' was a familiar Harry South tune. There were also two ballads, 'A Time For Love' and 'Polka Dots and Moonbeams', and three Harriott themes including 'Tuesday Morning Swing', previously recorded on *Southern Horizons*.

Always a perfectionist, Harriott was happy only with the nineteenth take of 'Polka Dots and Moonbeams'. Stu Hamer recalled him saying: 'I want to have another crack at it,' after a take that sounded perfect to everyone else. Hamer sat out on this number and he recalled Joe's raised hand several times terminating takes after only the first few bars. Satisfied at last with the chords, on the final take Harriott sounded unexpectedly fierce on a ballad normally treated with tenderness. By this stage he was probably giving vent to his frustration.

Hamer remarked that the sleevenotes wrongly attributed all the false starts and alternate takes to the recording of Johnny Mandel's 'A Time for Love'. He remembered that this was recorded in one take: 'If I'd had to do nineteen takes of 'A Time for Love', they'd have had to carry me out of there.' Hamer's beautiful playing on this track is a highlight of the album.[10]

At the end of the session there was still space for one more track on the record. Joe, who had drunk a bottle of whisky by then, said, 'we'll play a blues'. 'Blues in C' featured one of Coleridge's hummed and bowed bass solos.

Producing the record was hardly a model of efficiency. In addition to recording problems – Goode was particularly disappointed with the bass sound through much of the session[11] – there were errors on the label and sleeve. Joe's surname is misspelled as 'Harriot' and Phil's as 'Seaman'. On the disc's label, 'Tuesday Morning Swing' loses the third word from the title and 'The Rake' is labelled 'The Race'. The final track, listed as 'Count Twelve', is actually 'Just Goofin''. Amusingly, the sleeve-notes describe how Joe 'experimented, together with John Mayer, in a fusion of *improved* Indian classical music.'

Goode once said of Harriott, 'he got somewhat more frantic in the upper register of the instrument and it was mostly in ballads that he made any real use of the bottom notes of his alto.'[12] In Pat Smythe's view, 'his playing always had tremendous authority – at up-tempo he played with great fire and excitement, and on ballads his playing was often like a cry from the heart.'[13] Certainly, on this album, Joe's tone is so furious at times one feels he is ready to burst and it exemplifies Goode's description of him as 'a true exciter of passions'. His playing was, 'full of an intense inner passion; the notes seeming to be fighting each other to take precedence in the particular phrase he had in mind.'[14]

A few months later, Denis Preston set up an album that was obviously intended as an elaborate showcase for Harriott's all-round musical talents. Perhaps Preston hoped it would make the public recognise Joe at last as the musical star he so obviously deserved to be.

Personal Portrait presented Harriott accompanied by strings and brass under the direction of composer-arranger David Mack. Three of the jazzier tracks, including Parker's 'Now's the Time', were enlivened by Stan Tracey's piano. Most of the material – 'September Song', 'Portrait of Jenny' and 'Mr Blueshead' – gave the album a melancholy, wistful atmosphere.

Joe played beautifully and Alun Morgan, a long-term Harriott fan, declared the record, 'the best all round collection of Harriott's music.'[15]

But, in truth, the tracks with string arrangements made many of Joe's devoted fans wince. As Roger Cotterrell said: 'The ballads are scored as for a third-rate popular singer rather than a fine jazz soloist and one is tempted to speculate as to whether Mack really understands what jazz is all about. Unless, of course, the idea was to water down the music for a broad commercial appeal. Mack's 'Mr Blueshead' is a grotesque travesty of the blues and, on most tracks, an obtrusive and unswinging harpsichord plays a major role in destroying any genuine jazz atmosphere which might otherwise filter through.'[16]

One outstanding piece features Pat Smythe in a duet with Joe called 'Abstract Doodle'. This piece, Pat Smythe later confirmed was an 'on the spot improvisation'.[17] The throwaway sounding title does not prepare one for the quality of this stunning performance, which ranks with the best and most emotional of Harriott's work. In addition, it amply demonstrates why he and Smythe were such ideal creative partners, their empathy a rare treasure in improvised music. The last part of the track uses the call and answer form of the blues: Joe's tormented cries on alto answered by the sombre chords of Smythe's piano. This is Harriott at his creative, expressive best.

After *Personal Portrait*, Preston continued to provide recording opportunities for Harriott. He had been a great Ellington admirer since buying his first record, *Creole Love Call*, in 1931. To celebrate Duke's seventieth birthday he set up an album, *We Love You Madly*, featuring Stan Tracey as leader of a big band. Top soloists including Harriott, Acker Bilk, Tony Coe, Ian Carr, Don Rendell, Kenny Baker, Les Condon, Don Lusher and Chris Pyne were brought in for the session.

Preston allowed the soloists to choose their own material and thought the choices were predictable with two exceptions. 'The odd men out seem to have been Ian Carr – a very progressive player, in the most meaningful sense of the word –

choosing that old, though loved war-horse, 'I'm Beginning to See the Light' and Joe Harriott – that most viciously aggressive of modernists – the appropriately titled 'In a Sentimental Mood.'[18] The BBC unearthed footage of Joe soloing beautifully on this with the Stan Tracey Big Band. It was included in their excellent series of three programmes on British modern jazz entitled *Jazz Britannia* and it was a surprising and welcome discovery, as currently this is the only known surviving footage of Joe playing.

Towards the end of the 1960s, Joe's options were narrowing but one more innovative recording venture arose for him. It involved a remarkable Goanese guitarist named Amancio D'Silva. In 1967, D'Silva arrived in Britain seeking urgent medical treatment for his baby son, Stephano, who suffered from a rare blood condition. The baby was so ill that he kept losing consciousness during the lengthy flight from India. Hospital treatment was successful and Amancio and his wife Joyce decided to settle with their three children in the UK. D'Silva's music was jazz-influenced but rooted in the East: his lines were sitar-like and prefigured guitarist John McLaughlin's Eastern-influenced playing with Shakti a few years later. D'Silva's jazz education had begun in Bombay where there was a surprisingly vibrant jazz scene in the fifties and sixties.[19]

In Bombay, he had found that his love of jazz meant being ostracised by Indian classical musicians who were deeply distrustful of jazz influences. He was helped, however, by an influential sponsor. At the age of twenty-five, his musical gift had been noted by the Maharani of Jaipur who loved jazz and employed him as a court musician in the two years prior to his departure for the UK. He acknowledged her support when his debut album *Integration* was recorded in 1969: 'I wrote a song on my first record. I called it 'Jaipur'.... She was a very good benefactor. She bought me a good guitar and she bought a lot of jazz records so I could hear the music.'[20]

In England, D'Silva was once more fortunate in the people he met. A friend introduced him to 'Beyond the Fringe' satirist Jonathan Miller and, through Miller, he met Denis Preston who quickly made plans to record him with some of the cream of British jazz musicians. *Integration* was recorded with the Don Rendell – Ian Carr Quintet. This seven-title suite, jointly composed by Carr and D'Silva, was well received and D'Silva was quickly recognised as a promising musician with a highly distinctive style.

Preston saw potential in a collaboration between D'Silva and Harriott. A joint album *Hum-Dono* was recorded under his direction and issued by Columbia. As on most of D'Silva's albums, his own compositions dominated. *Hum-Dono* involved Bryan Spring on drums and Dave Green on bass. Both were from a younger generation of jazz players that admired Harriott. Spring said, 'it was great to play with Joe, a privilege. He is one of the greatest. I played with him quite often. His approach was that he played every gig like it was the last gig he'd play.'[21]

Ian Carr's flugelhorn and Norma Winstone's vocals are also featured on some tracks. She recalled: 'It was my first ever recording session and I was probably full of nerves.' But the record gives no such impression. On 'Stephano's Dance', named after D'Silva's son, Winstone's voice blends with flugelhorn and sax to create a beautifully smooth sound over Green's ominous, driving bass. D'Silva takes his solo last, after Carr and Harriott, emulating on his guitar the staccato brevity of sitar notes. When I asked Winstone about Harriott, she said, 'I found him very quiet, reserved. Almost stately. That was really the only time I worked with him.'[22]

The only track not penned by D'Silva is a duet by Spring and Harriott, 'Spring Low Sweet Harriott'. Its mood is deeply uneasy and there are parallels with Joe's earlier duet recordings of 'He Ran Out Crying' and 'Abstract Doodle': they all carry the suggestion of threat and are disquieting to listen to.

Harriott begins the plaintive 'Ballad For Goa' gently over Green's bowing but his solo adopts his naturally sharper tone. The Indian influence is most evident in the title track with Amancio singing his guitar notes and Spring's expert hand-drumming.

To promote *Hum-Dono,* the group performed at a series of concerts. One, at the Mermaid Theatre in London, featured Stan Tracey, Ian Carr and other top names. Joyce D'Silva recalls: 'Joe was late. The band was already on the stage and he suddenly came in and played the most magical solo. Stunning! It made the hairs on the back of your neck stand up the way they do when you know you're listening to great music... Joe didn't get his true recognition. British jazz was riddled with racism.'[23]

Amancio had the highest regard for Harriott as a musician. He once said, 'Joe was not of this planet,' and recalled that the band, with the altoist absent, would spend a week in rehearsals before a gig. Harriott would first appear fifteen minutes before the start and lock himself away to concentrate on the music. Then he would perform as though he had rehearsed with the group all week. The guitarist marvelled too at the regularity of single takes Joe produced in the studio.[24]

Joyce remembered, 'we were living in Ealing with three small children; Joe was very warm and friendly.' The D'Silvas saw only his gentler side, particularly in the way he related to their children. Amancio told *Jazz Journal,* 'he was so good with children.... Some people thought he was hostile. No way!'

In the late 1960s, John Mayer and Don Norman occasionally contacted Harriott for dates and on Sunday 31 August 1969 a reconstructed Indo-Jazz Fusions band played at the second Isle of Wight Festival. The star attraction and cause of great excitement was Bob Dylan who arrived in style by helicopter. Dylan had godlike status among his followers but had become more reclusive since a motorbike accident. His re-appearance on the concert scene guaranteed a huge crowd. Some Dylan-starved fans even chartered a plane from America.

In a largely pop/folk programme for the closing day, Fusions played in the afternoon before an audience approaching sixty thousand. Coleridge Goode recalled that a torrential downpour accompanied their appearance. Keshav Sathe remembered receiving £12.50 as his share of the band's payment. 'It was the equivalent of between £50 and £100 today. I was single then and I loved playing. I didn't worry about money.'25 Presumably Dylan received a greater reward.

In the same month, Denis Preston brought together the London Philharmonic Orchestra and many of the best jazz talents in Britain to record Laurie Johnson's large-scale, five part composition *Synthesis*. Johnson had begun his career as arranger and composer with the Ted Heath Orchestra and had contributed the arrangements for Harriott's *With Strings* EP in 1955. The soloists on *Synthesis* included Harriott, Tony Coe, Kenny Wheeler, Tubby Hayes, Stan Roderick and Don Lusher.

Three years later, Preston spoke glowingly of Joe's role in this venture. 'For a man who never really played in a [big] band, or had very much practice or experience, outside of playing his jazz solos, [he] was able to [lead the section] ... for a very big recording that I did with Laurie Johnson which involved the London Philharmonic Orchestra.... I suggested to Laurie if he wanted ... the 'booty' Count Basie sound for saxes, to get Joe Harriott to lead. Now it wasn't an easy score by any means! And Joe sat down and led that section ... I mean, it included people like Tubby Hayes ... and so forth, but he led that section as though he'd done it all his life.' He added: 'I don't think people ever gave Joe the credit he deserved as a musician.'26 But Preston contributed to the problem by not crediting Harriott as section leader anywhere in the sleevenotes for *Synthesis*.

Adrian Kerridge was the engineer for the recording of *Synthesis* at Watford Town Hall. He remembered Joe 'as an extremely talented individual who always fitted into sessions very well and [was] much respected by his peers of the day ... Simply put, a wonderful player ... ' Kerridge gave, as an example, Harriott's section work and solo playing on *Synthesis*.27

With only occasional bookings forthcoming, Joe routinely tried to make ends meet through solo appearances with local musicians. For a while there were gigs backing singer Bobby Breen. But in popular music a seismic change had taken place. By the early 1970s, modern jazz was being described as a terminal case by the music press, which had once fawned to curry favour with its musicians. Harriott still found a sympathetic ear in journalist Max Jones and told him: 'Frankly I believe the problem is not so much jazz as the personalities that play jazz. I felt very sad to read Ian Carr's quote about not putting jazz above his name. Because he can't play anything better than jazz, and he does that excellently.'[28]

Jones began one *Melody Maker* piece by asking: 'Whatever has happened to Joe Harriott lately?' narrowly avoiding the 'Where are they now?' kiss of death on a career in trouble. Harriott had 'been out of the picture publicity-wise' but Jones reported news of new Harriott compositions and a possible new recording.

Joe must have enjoyed working with Amancio D'Silva as two years after recording *Hum-Dono* he told Max Jones that he was planning a further album on which the guitarist would augment his quintet. All the compositions were to be Harriott's. He implied that the writing was at an advanced stage. 'The music will be jazz … but not the regular forms you hear. Time signatures? They vary. There's no set pattern. There are impressionistic works, not necessarily conventional. All the compositions have a story behind them. One piece I call a collage and *Collage* is to be the title of the album.'

But it was never recorded, largely because Joe's health soon began to deteriorate. His comments are tantalising as they suggest, contrary to common belief, that he had not turned his back irrevocably on experimentation or free jazz. Perhaps some written scores survive as evidence that, as late as 1971, he was still driven by the quest to break out from conventional composition.

Jones asked Harriott about the growing interest of jazz-rock bands in free improvisation. There was more than a hint of wryness in the response. 'Interesting isn't it? Today it's all freak-outs. And what was I doing ten years ago on those Columbia long players?'[29]

Jones had to admit, Joe had been freaking out eleven years before it was fashionable.

12.

free fall

During the sixties jazz in Britain had been overtaken by rhythm-and-blues and pop music in the hearts of the young. Blues-based rock music displaced modern jazz as the 'cool' music of the time and bookings for jazz musicians dried up. By the end of the decade, Joe Harriott and many other musicians had found their regular bands unsustainable.

Chris Barber, whose own band was a remarkable survivor in barren times, said of Joe: 'He seemed to struggle for work. He felt he didn't get the recognition he should have had. He didn't make the kind of stir in the world, musically speaking, that he wanted to.... But the world is impressed by success and charisma. Joe had some charisma but he didn't promote himself at all. He had his principles and his musical convictions.'[1]

The Marquee had turned from jazz in the mid-sixties to become home to the Rolling Stones, Alexis Korner and Long John Baldry. As the decade progressed, the club also turned away from blues and booked bands such as the Moody Blues and Pink Floyd. The Flamingo was changing with the times too. Georgie Fame and the Blue Flames became the house band and regulars included the Graham Bond Organisation and singer Chris Farlow. In the USA the trend was similar. Electric rock music seized the young hip audience and jazz leaders like Miles Davis, Herbie Hancock and Chick Corea responded, remodelling themselves and moving into jazz-rock territory to survive.

Members of Harriott's quintet kept busy. Coleridge Goode still played regularly with Michael Garrick and in the resident band at London's Georgian Club. Pat Smythe's sensitive playing was much in demand and the former solicitor collaborated with Kenny Wheeler and Tony Coe in a group named like a law firm: Coe, Wheeler and Co.

Shake Keane was nearing the end of his stay in Germany and about to make the momentous decision to return to St Vincent where he would become the government minister with responsibility for culture. In his creative work, he would neglect music to concentrate on poetry writing. Phil Seamen, increasingly unreliable because of his addiction, had toured as second drummer with Ginger Baker's Airforce, a brash percussion-driven big band, and was leading his own trio in a pub residency. Bobby Orr was in great demand, touring and recording with big-name American performers including Benny Goodman, Billy Eckstine, Sammy Davis and Bing Crosby as well as French composer Michel Legrand. His options were much wider than Harriott's because he was happy to work in musical styles beyond jazz.

Harriott still played in his deeply personal and committed way, adhering to his belief that 'a lot of potentially great artists never achieve that greatness because of easy money. Good business is not always good artistry.' There would be times when this disdain for 'easy money' would occasion considerable hardship.[2] As work became scarcer, his gambling and the paternity payments he had to make for a child were a constant drain on his sporadic income. Trumpeter Del Turner remembered a careworn, impoverished Joe staying at his flat around 1970. 'He asked me to lend him £600 which was a lot of money in those days. He had been served with a paternity suit. He went round tapping everybody.

'Joe had received a lot of advances. He was a bit of a maverick and fell foul of various promoters. He didn't play London, but had to tour the whole country. I think the words, "you'll never play in London again," were actually used. There was a lot of petty nastiness to the fore in the jazz scene. Some were definitely jealous of Joe's talent and there were racist elements too. A lot of complex factors caused the problem. Joe had tremendous strength of character. Egotistic certainly. He thought very highly of himself.'[3]

Other than for one Indo-jazz gig, which John Mayer told me of, Harriott hardly ever played at Ronnie Scott's Club in London's Frith Street. Scott's partner Pete King told me, 'Joe was always involved in other things. We couldn't afford the Indo-jazz group very often. There were so many of them.'4 It does seem extraordinary that one of the most original voices on saxophone ever resident in Britain should have been so notably absent from Britain's premier jazz club.

I heard from more than one source of a booking that made Harriott ill-disposed towards Scott and King. Joe's band was booked to appear at Ronnie's but, shortly before the set was due to start, there was no trace of drummer Phil Seamen and Pete King was getting agitated. Harriott went in search of Phil and was absent as Pete's decision deadline passed. King put in a replacement band at the last moment and the club's pro-gramme got underway marginally late. On Joe's return without Phil, Pete told him: 'You're not playing. You're out.'5 Harriott confronted King seeking payment for himself and his other musicians. He felt he'd done nothing wrong. 'It's the same here at Ronnie's,' King told me. 'Sometimes the staff are responsible for something going wrong ... I get shot at. Joe had a drummer, Phil Seamen, but he didn't turn up so Joe got shot at.'6

While King was immovable, Harriott was implacable, decid-ing instantly never to play Ronnie's again. As Joe's friend Del Southon put it: 'They ran Ronnie's on a shoestring budget and even if he'd wanted to, Pete wouldn't have been able to pay both bands.' So both parties felt aggrieved by the incident. When I asked if Ronnie Scott had been involved in what hap-pened, Del paraphrased Benny Green's remark on how the club operated, 'Pete did the hiring and firing and Ronnie got to choose the colour of the walls.'7

Scuffling for money, Harriott had to travel constantly to jobs that sometimes paid derisory amounts. His friend Stuart Hepburn described Joe at this time: 'He spent most of his time in the bookie's shop. He lost all his money, didn't eat much and smoked a lot.'8

Don Rendell found that when he did gigs in clubs away from

London, such as Newcastle or Wolverhampton, an approach, probably at Joe's request, would sometimes be made to him by a third party: '"Joe Harriott's in town. Do you mind if he comes and plays with you?" It was amazing how often that happened.'9

Life in Harriott's last few years grew increasingly difficult for him. He usually found accommodation with old acquaintances on the jazz circuit, often sleeping on floors or couches. In spite of the problems, he managed to make something positive out of his work as a musician. Because he was so inspirational, the experience of playing with him was very special for many young aspiring musicians. As he always had done, he sought opportunities to play with all types of jazz bands including New Orleans line-ups. He could often lift the other musicians to a higher level of performance and his influence made some play better than they believed possible. But the jobs threatened to dry up entirely.

His last recording session was for the album *Five Bridges* by the theatrical rock trio The Nice, consisting of drums, bass and the flamboyant Keith Emerson on organ. Joe walked on-stage for a live recording as part of a stellar jazz line-up including Kenny Wheeler, Chris Pyne and Brian Smith. Playing a few minutes of a repetitive riff for the album was money for old rope, hardly requiring the involvement of such talents.

Joe's personal life was also at a very low ebb when his violence against women, as experienced by Margaret Tynski and Pat Copp, finally brought him to the attention of the courts in February 1971. A forthcoming history of British jazz by Duncan Heining refers to a conviction for maliciously wounding a young woman. Joe was fortunate to find St Ives Magistrates Court in a lenient mood, fining him £25 for the assault.10

Harriott was, unusually, visibly distressed at the funeral in March 1971 of his lifelong friend Harold McNair who had succumbed, aged thirty-nine, to lung cancer after a long, brave struggle. Sharon Atkin said, 'I had never seen Joe so upset by anything before.' He had tutored McNair, three years his junior, back in Alpha Boys' School. The two had a closeness born of their love of music and performing and Harold had been like an adopted younger brother. Sharon described Harriott's playing at the funeral as, 'searing' and 'raw'.[11]

The few possibilities that arose for him now came to very little. At the end of that month, a Harriott quartet featuring Stan Tracey on piano, Dave Green on bass and an unknown drummer spent three hours in Lime Grove Studio H for BBC television.[12] No further details exist and almost certainly no recording remains. I have no information on whether the broadcast ever took place.

John Mayer was dismayed to see the decline in Harriott around this time. Mayer went to visit him one evening and found him in the Clifton pub alone, gazing into the fire, drawing on a cigarette. 'Then he'd go out and gamble. He had nothing else to do. He was a lonely man. Everybody else was getting a lot of work, and here was this great saxophonist not getting the work due to him.'[13]

Michael Horovitz described how Harriott became, 'more dissatisfied and prickly as the years went by. He would see Tubby Hayes get much more acclaim.' Horovitz spoke of the awful conflict in Joe: 'He hated feeling socially inferior but felt dependent upon white society for survival.'[14]

Frank Holder was also concerned about the change in Harriott. He could not square the image of the highly professional musician he had long respected with the story he had been told of an inebriated Joe falling backwards from a stage while performing. Holder was in no doubt that it was deep disillusionment that caused Joe's loss of control over his drinking. 'When he used to come to me in Earl's Court we'd sit late into the morning.' As Joe consumed glass after glass of scotch, the thrust of his argument was that 'he wasn't getting in.' He felt very much that it was the conscious decision of others that he was isolated from the main music scene and that this was the main cause of his dire financial plight.[15]

Margaret Tynski's view was, 'Joe must have been so unhappy, disillusioned and bitter, devoid of that rather special sense of humour he had, to have sunk into drunkenness. Ten years previously he would have abhorred such behaviour. Such a contrast to the early, vibrant years of the Joe I knew, full of enthusiasm and hope for an exciting musical career.'[16]

Harriott knew only too well the situation he was in. In 1971, a decade after he had introduced free form, he ruefully told Max Jones, 'I was a bit early it seems. Maybe if I could change my name and go out and play the same things as ten years ago, I'd make money. Perhaps the public wasn't prepared for it then, but might take it better now.'[17]

Pockets of enthusiasm for Harriott's music existed all over the country. In Winchester's Royal Oak pub, Ken Maxwell played drums every Thursday night in a small jazz group. 'Joe would hitch down or take a cheap train and play with us. We'd save our sandwiches for him and chip in ten shillings between us to give Joe some money.

'He liked eights. Eight bars for a drummer's break. He let us take a break of eight bars to feature ourselves. He'd give you an instruction by his eyes.... For Joe, the thing wasn't what we played, it was the tempo. We had to keep the tempo. If it dragged he blew his top! He had such a sense of playing, himself. It was like a jet plane. To end the tune he liked to "hit the buffers". In other words, a sudden conclusion.[18]

'Joe could be scathing on the stand. We were doing a Herbie Mann Latin American number. I couldn't get a grip of the thing. "Play the bloody thing!" he shouted at me. But you didn't take offence. You could give it back to him, but you had to choose your time. He was moody, very moody, but you could say, "Shut up, you black bugger!" and he would smile. One time at Warsash [in Hampshire], I remember the music was flying at a helluva speed. The bass player wasn't fast but was always accurate. Joe shouted at him, "If you can't do the speed, get off the damn stage!" Then he felt bad he'd said it.'[19]

Harriott had lost his rented Maida Vale flat and was homeless, reduced to looking for accommodation with friends while seeking gigs for whatever remuneration was available. 'At one stage it was even said he was going round playing organ from bingo hall to bingo hall,altoist Pete Burden recalled. 'At a jazz gig, Harriott was asked what he was trying to do these days. He said he had given up the free form and was "just trying to play pretty like Charlie Parker."[20]

Some of his friends were generous. Don Norman put him up after gigs at the Bull, near Chichester, and John Hart, a wealthy bassist who had played gigs with Harriott, helped him financially.[21]

In March 1971, Joe's old friend Ernie Garside was working with the big band of Canadian trumpeter Maynard Ferguson who had moved to Britain in the late 1960s. Ernie had turned his attention away from full-time music promotion and was playing trumpet for a living. 'I'd moved to London and got the Ferguson band going. I think we were going to Southampton or somewhere. We had this fifteen-seater bus. We were going through Notting Hill Gate down the main road to get off going south. On the other side of the road I see Joe Harriott. I wound the window down. I was actually driving myself. I went, "JOOOE!"

'His face lit up. It was really good! He went, "Ern! Where are you going?"

'I said: "It's Maynard's band. We're going on a gig. Southampton."

'He said: "Oh, I wish I could come."'

Garside soon went to America with the Ferguson band and this was his last memory of Joe.[22]

Harriott's colleague from Indo-Jazz Fusions, Keshav Sathe, owned a three-bedroom house in Tottenham, north-east London. A bachelor at that time with a steady income from his job at the Indian High Commission supplemented by earnings from music, he was in a radically different economic position from Joe. He agreed to Harriott's request to put him up for a while but confessed, 'sometimes I got fed up with him in my house.'[23] Writer Alan Plater recalled another source of grief for many who knew Joe then. 'After his visits to Hull I'd get phone calls from people saying; "I lent Joe some money" and I'd say: "No, you didn't. You gave Joe some money. Think of yourself as a little Arts Council."'[24]

Harriott visited the home of his friend Kenny Baxter, semi-professional sax player and jazz club organiser. Over the years,

'Joe would often stay at my home in Rochford, Essex, when he needed to escape from London. He felt at home as I had a piano on which he could compose. He also enjoyed home cooking. Joe loved a little gamble, especially dog racing. Hackney Dog Stadium was a favourite haunt of his.' One night it was nine o'clock when he appeared. 'He said, "I thought I'd come down for a couple of days." He never phoned or anything. He'd taken a taxi from the station. If we'd been out, I suppose he'd have just gone round and stayed at [Bill] Haig's.'[25]

In 1972, Harriott contacted Baxter, who was still living in Essex, to obtain a gig. 'I organised a session for him to play at my club in Southend-on-Sea. He played with Pete Jacobson who at that time was a very young, up-and-coming pianist. I remember Joe being very impressed with Pete's playing. He stayed with me and my wife, Toni, that night and I then realised how ill he was. We had an attic flat at the time in Leigh-on-Sea, with just one bed. We gave him our bed and slept in an armchair each as we were both worried about his state of health.

'He never moaned a lot,' Ken told me, 'but the next time I saw him was in a club in Ilford called the Club Cubana. It had a mini casino: blackjack, roulette, etc. He was very moody throughout the whole evening as he had lost some money on the card table.' But 'this did not affect the wonderful sound he produced.'[26]

George Melly spoke of a visit trumpeter Mick Mulligan had from Joe. 'He just arrived, and while he stayed at Mick's, he drank him out of house and home. Mick couldn't get rid of him. It was quite awkward. People are very shy in such instances about saying when one should go.'[27] Mulligan himself remembers that, 'he did have a few when he stayed with us a few days in Sussex.'[28]

BBC presenter Peter Clayton met Joe around this time and proposed an appearance on his radio programme, *Jazz Notes*, in which Joe could discuss his current ideas and future plans. Clayton had been a solid supporter of the quintet and it seems likely that his motivation, like that of Max Jones and Denis Preston before, was to raise Joe's profile again. It must have heartened Joe to discover that not everyone had forgotten him.[29]

Writer and broadcaster Laurie Taylor, then lecturing at York University, was ecstatic when he heard that Harriott was heading for the city: 'But then came the bad news. Joe wasn't coming with his own band. He was relying on local musicians. Even for the best players in town this was a terrifying prospect. Being asked to sit behind Joe as he screamed and soared through some of his wilder pieces of improvisation seemed about as inviting as the offer of ten rounds with Muhammed Ali.'

No venue had been arranged. Harriott 'was about to step off the train and we were running around desperately trying to find a stage.... There was only one option. Joe would have to be asked to come down to jazz night at the Spotted Cow on Wednesday and sit in... the pianist and tenor player were able, if tentative, and the drummer perfectly adequate as long as he were denied a shed-building solo. The only unfortunate member was the vocalist, who seemed unable to sing any standard without the addition of an "Oh, yeah!" after every other line.

'We needn't have worried. [Joe] listened to three numbers and then slowly strolled over to the rostrum, whispered to the pianist, and soared straight into 'Don't Get Around Much Anymore'.... For an hour and a half he played the classics the band knew and played them with a commitment rarely heard from the other professional jazzers who turned up in the city on Arts Council sponsored tours. Joe stayed in town a month.'

There were signs that he was far from well. 'During that time we realised how courageous he had been.... For £20 a night he'd blow his guts out with a pick-up band, stagger home exhausted, wash out his one nylon white shirt, and then try to find a sleeping position in bed that wouldn't aggravate the large and, as it turned out, cancerous tumour in the middle of his back.[30]

Rod Marshall, publican and jazz promoter in Brighouse, Yorkshire, was someone Joe was able to stay with when he had gigs in the area. Rod also drove Joe to and from engagements.

'Joe had called to stay with me … in the pub I ran in this small town. And I was to get him to a gig in Bradford that evening. He had arrived from Hull where he often stayed with one of his ladies.

'After I closed the pub at 3 pm we went upstairs and I went for my normal afternoon nap, leaving Joe reading. He knew that this rest period was important for me therefore what followed must have been very difficult for him. His great lump had burst and he had tried to sit in front of the toilet seat, on the floor, to let it bleed into the toilet. In doing so, he had blocked up the toilet with paper and when he tried to flush it away, it overflowed and he was forced to seek help.

'This alone must have terrible for such a proud man. I had to undress him and try and keep his trousers dry. All that I could do was to get him into the bath to bleed while I tried to sort things out before my kids arrived home from school. He was crying and full of remorse at having to call me. I managed to clean him up and he had more dressing in his bag. The lump was still very big. I dressed it and wanted to call an ambulance but he wouldn't have that.'

I have often pondered why Joe did not seek expert medical help which might have saved him or at least provided some relief from the pain he endured. Rod appears to have the answer. 'He told me that he had never paid any stamps or tax since he had been in Britain and he thought they would deport him. It was the time when the Wilson [Government] had given an amnesty to illegal immigrants but Joe said he thought that was a trick to catch people such as him. I tried for hours to tell him that hospitals didn't check up and that he could tell them almost anything. But he needed the gig that night and that was that.'[31]

Ron Burnett and his wife, art teachers in York, were accustomed to a phone call every few months from Joe. 'Hi Ron! I'm at the station. Can you pick me up?'

'I understood he had some financial troubles,' recollected Ron. 'We'd put him up and look all round York for gigs he could do. It was very small money. We'd go over to Leeds because there was more going on there.'

On one visit, Harriott had a bit of money and was keen to buy a new suit for performing in. 'We went down to the local Montague Burton [shop] and Joe looked at mohair silk Italian suits which were fashionable at the time. He took his jacket off and there was this huge lump on his back.'

'We took him down to St James Hospital in Leeds. They took this lump out, stitched him up and kept him in for three or four days. They told him to take it very easy and not to do any playing for a few weeks. After only a few days he was looking for work again.'

The warmth of feeling and the concern for Joe clearly felt by Rod Marshall is evident too, in the words of Ron Burnett: 'Joe was always a gentleman. Very smart. He was interested in all kinds of music, classical and world music. Because my wife and I were art teachers, he picked up on that, too.' They worried that Harriott didn't seem to eat. 'He was hitting the bottle then. You would make him breakfast and he would never eat it. He didn't feel like it.'[32]

Rod Marshall outlined Joe's next move. 'When he had received the treatment he stayed for a few days with a tenor player called Barry Cole who was a student at Leeds College of Music. But he turned up for a gig at Leeds University I had arranged for him weeks before. I had fixed the backing trio. Joe told me that he had sixteen stitches in his back but felt ok. He looked terrible.'

'After only two numbers he asked me to get my flute and cover while he went to the toilet. I was no Harold McNair but I played for a while. He didn't come out. I went to find him and his stitches had given way. I had to put a dressing on. I was getting very good at this by this time. He only did one number after that. He got his £25 and left.'[33]

Harriott was no longer in touch with his old musical sparring partner Phil Seamen. But the drummer's life was following a remarkably parallel downward course. Phil, effectively homeless like Joe, was 'a regular on the floor' of Alexis Korner's flat in Bayswater, London. 'You certainly didn't share his breakfast,'

Alexis' daughter Sappho noted. 'He would get up ... make Ready Brek, sprinkle a Cadbury's Flake on it and then chuck in a whole load of blues [amphetamines] and mix it up. That was his breakfast every morning.'[34] Alexis also said that 'all the while he lived with us, we rarely saw him eat anything other than his own repulsive concoction of porridge with a Dairy Flake bar crumbled into it. Hot bubbling mud!'[35]

Seamen's legendary constitution belied his light build and pale colouring. However, the years of drug abuse, often in tandem with heavy drinking, finally took their toll and he died on 13 October 1972. According to Ken Baxter, 'cheap heroin had cracked all his arteries.' Although it could scarcely have come as a surprise, the news of his death hit his many friends and admirers hard. Bassist Ken Baldock had expected to play with him at the Plough in Islington on the night he died: 'He'd weaned himself off heroin but was finding it hard to sleep. A musician's life is ridiculous. Sometimes you don't get to bed until five o'clock and you're working in the afternoon. He got some 'sleepers', Mandrax, and took two too many and didn't wake up.'[36]

Ronnie Scott spoke of his sense of personal loss: 'Underneath the facade that we all wear (knowingly or unknowingly), Phil was a warm, tragic man who was good to be with.' Fellow drummer John Stevens said in words which were equally true of Harriott: 'Like many complete artists he could be unintentionally scary and intimidating.'[37]

What was clear to everyone was that Harriott and Seamen shared a mutual respect through all their years of association.

Harriott stayed with drummer Ken Maxwell in Hampshire at this time: 'He had trouble with his spine and he was so worried that he'd be a bother to us. He never was. So polite and pleasant. The phone would ring and he'd ask, "Can I come over?" He was like a little boy in a way. The poor boy wanted to be loved. Musicians are the most insincere people. They'd stab you in the back to get the job you had and Joe ... he just needed someone to put an arm round his shoulder.'[38]

Clarinettist Ian Wheeler unexpectedly heard from Harriott in 1972. Wheeler had left the Chris Barber band in 1968 and moved to Looe, Cornwall. In their first contact in years, Joe phoned asking if Ian could fix up some gigs for him. Wheeler's own small band played regularly at the Harbour Moon jazz club. He arranged for Harriott to appear there and at a couple of other gigs. Ian saw him sitting at the bar looking downcast. 'What's the matter, man?' he asked.

'I'm not well. Bad stomach,' Joe answered, appearing to dismiss his ailment as something commonplace. Wheeler didn't know who Harriott stayed with in Cornwall.[39]

Saxophonist Teddy Layton had first met Harriott in the fifties when their bands shared a BBC radio programme. The two became friends. In 1972 he was visiting another friend, trumpeter Bobby Mickleburgh, in Bath 'when I saw this guy limping along the road. It was Joe. He told me he was suffering from sciatica and taking medication for it. I said the next time he was down Southampton way to call in.'[40]

Next to take up the story is Clem Alford. Glasgow-born, Alford had studied sitar for two years in West Bengal. On returning from the East he heard of a sitar vacancy in Indo-Jazz Fusions created by Diwan Motihar's move to the USA. Alford joined at a time when Fusions engagements were becoming scarcer. He greatly admired Harriott and, though somewhat surprised, was happy to oblige when Joe asked to stay for an unspecified time at Clem's two room flat in Bounds Green, London.

'I learned a lot of music from Joe,' said Alford. 'He stayed with me a few weeks. We were both skint. I slept on a mattress on the floor and Joe, he slept on the carpet. He didn't seem ill. He seemed quite bubbly, although his face looked strained. He never told me how ill he was. He told me he had a gig in Southampton and he wanted to know if it was OK to call in again when he got back. I said, "of course," and gave him all I could spare, which was a couple of bob and a few roll-ups to get him to Southampton. I said: "Where's your sax?" and he told me it was in the left luggage locker at Waterloo Station.'[41]

13.

in pretty dire straits

On arriving in Southampton in August 1972, Harriott made his way to Andover where he was guest of Don Vincent, founder of the Andover Jazz Circle. Discussions centred on a proposed return visit when a much-needed gig could be provided but Don was seriously concerned about Joe's health. 'It became obvious that he was not fit to walk and at the same time reluctant to seek medical treatment.' Once again, as was evident in Brighouse, Joe feared approaching the medical authorities. Don continued, 'The trouble centred on the base of the spine and we thought it was a slipped disc or some related type of dislocation. We never suspected the onset of cancer and Joe said very little other than of the pain itself and the restriction when trying to sleep.

'When I thought he might not play on this return visit I suggested writing an article or semi-interview instead and Joe was keen to assist me in this. However his general condition caused us even to put this to one side.

'The next morning, after some persuasion to see a doctor, he finally packed his things and left in a taxi we had arranged. Later we learned he had gone to visit another jazz friend.'[1]

Joe's next port of call was the home of local bandleader Teddy Layton and his wife-to-be, Marilyn. In the following weeks Joe managed to participate in a couple of local gigs. In these he was literally 'sitting-in' as he was unable to stand up whilst playing. It was obvious his condition was deteriorating fast. His mobility became very restricted and for much of the time he was virtually housebound. Marilyn worked in a bookmaker's, a 'perfect' job from Teddy's and Joe's point of view, because, 'I used to put their bets on. Joe had my keys and when

I got home I'd give him a shout to throw them down from his bedroom window.' Harriott spent a lot of his time reading. 'He used to live by this book, the *I-Ching*. He spent a lot of time with it.'[2]

'He used to make me really cross at times,' Marilyn added 'He'd shout at me like I was his wife sometimes.' The anger didn't last long and there were gentler times. 'When he was ill I used to sit by the side of his bed. I used to massage his legs with baby lotion, baby oil or cream. And he used to love it. He was in an awful way. He was thin as a wafer.'

Marilyn remembered Joe's humorous word play. He told Teddy he had nominated him as his 'next of skin'. She saw his gentleness too: 'He loved babies. He loved to hold my sister's baby.' Other people might have tentatively asked: "May I hold the baby?" Not Joe. 'He would sit there and say in a deep voice: "Give me that baby." That's why I was surprised he didn't have much to do with his own children.'

Marilyn remembered one particularly bad day with bitterness. 'He was trying to exercise and he wanted cigarettes so he walked to the local shop although he was feeling very ill. On the way back he thought he was going to faint and wanted some water. He knocked on a door and the woman who answered it saw the black face, screamed and slammed the door. Joe collapsed on her doorstep.' He finally managed to negotiate the way back to Teddy's home. On hearing what had happened Marilyn was so incensed that she promptly knocked on each door of the street to make sure that the woman, whoever she was, would know how ludicrous her response had been.

'We got married on Friday October 13, 1972,' Marilyn told me, 'and he was in hospital by then.' Teddy added: 'One day he went to the hospital, but they were going to release him that night for malingering! Then tests turned something up and they discovered he was suffering from both TB and cancer of the spine.' He was treated for TB in the isolation hospital and then returned to the Wessex Radiotherapy Unit at the Royal South Hampshire Hospital, Southampton, for cancer treatment.[3]

Chris Topley, then a nineteen-year-old working at the hospital, had attended those local jazz sessions where Joe had been obliged to play in a seated position. 'I happened to be passing through the reception area when he was brought in on a stretcher to be admitted. The receptionist was asking him the long list of questions they always did. I arrived as she said, "What religion?" His reply was, "Don't put nothin' there." I thought about shouting out "jazz" but I thought better of it.'[4]

Don Vincent received a letter, probably from Teddy Layton, telling him that Joe had been admitted to hospital and he went to visit him in September. 'He was completely bored and frustrated looking at the four walls of his hospital room, despite the good attention from nurses and staff. In between sleeping and reading he had made attempts to write a couple of compositions with titles connected with his hospitalisation. The task was soon to overcome his initial inspiration.

'We went straight out, bought him a couple of packs of cigarettes and that week's *Melody Maker* which quoted him as "languishing in a Southampton hospital". We still had no idea of Joe's medical condition or of what treatment was taking place. It was a lovely hospital if you can call it lovely when it's you that's in there. He said little of his illness but looked forward to "getting out here within a couple of months". He had received a marvellous morale booster in the shape of flowers and a card from fans at Bath and/or Bristol where he had been staying prior to his Andover visits.'[5]

Skip Conway, an artist and fixer of gigs for his local jazz club in Southampton, befriended Joe while he was in hospital. He said, 'I had seen him doing gigs over the years, very often in the old Concorde Club at the Bassett pub. When I heard from Teddy Layton that he was in hospital, I went to visit him two or three times each week. Sometimes I'd take girlfriends of mine to see him and they'd make a fuss over him, which he loved. I used to get along fine with him. Neither of us dominated the conversation. I'd say it was 50/50. I was interested in painting music through my pictures and Joe was trying to paint pictures through his music.' Conway remembered that one of the nurses wanted the patients to retire for the night at 8 p.m. Joe's response to her was: 'Do you realise, I'm a musician?'[6]

Del Southon, then an art teacher, heard of Harriott's illness while listening to Peter Clayton's *Jazz Record Requests* radio programme. Clayton told his listeners that Joe was in hospital in Southampton and would benefit from receiving some visitors. Del assumed Harriott would be inundated following the programme and put off his visit until Clayton repeated his plea on air. It was a Saturday when he made his first visit. Skip Conway was already there.

Southon remembered, 'I went to shake his hand but he held back. "You might catch what I've got," he said. I said, "you'll have to take your chance. You might catch what I've got." I visited him Monday, Wednesday and Friday night. I went in on the Monday and asked him who'd been in at the weekend, and nobody had, so I added Saturdays as well.'[7]

Southon turned up one night only to find Harriott's bed empty. 'I was told he'd been transferred to the chest hospital, on the other side of town. He was in a room on his own when I got there, sitting up in bed and very excited. He'd been told that he could get up and walk, [so then he] did so. Really alarming, because he was so frail. Then he was moved to a general ward. I went there a few nights later to find that he'd been sent back to the radiology department and a nurse there told me that was because his cancer surgeon was furious when he found out about the walking.'[8]

Soon after he was admitted to hospital, Harriott told Skip Conway of his pride at winning the prestigious Ivor Novello Award for his composition 'Revival'. Conway was stunned to hear from me that my research had produced no evidence to support Joe's claim that he won it. The British Academy of Composers which annually presents the music awards told me that Joe Harriott had never received a Novello Award, nor had the award been given to Chris Barber for his recording of 'Revival'. The story, like the one about about Harriott's Trinity College studies, seemed to have no basis in fact. I wondered if Joe had felt a need to claim both the formal musical education and the music establishment recognition he had never received. It struck Skip as a particularly sad discovery.[9]

When Del Southon gave me the chance to hear a thirty-year-old taped BBC radio recording, information supporting Harriott's claim emerged. Denis Preston, interviewed on *Jazz Notes*, told presenter Peter Clayton that Joe was 'one of the few jazz writers in this country who won an Ivor Novello Award. It was [for 'Revival'] and, indeed, as you're with me now, if you look upon the wall there, there is the Award for the Joe Harriott 'Revival'. He was runner up for … the best instrumental composition of the year. I think it earned him more money in one lump than he'd ever seen in his life.'[10]

But Lansdowne Studios' Adrian Kerridge said: 'I am not aware of him receiving an Ivor. I am a member of the Academy and have not read anything about that. Maybe Denis was just romancing. There was certainly nothing on the wall of DP's office.'[11]

At Harriott's bedside one day, Del Southon heard him say: 'If I could just hear from Denis Preston.' Joe made it clear he felt bitter not to have heard from Denis and Southon recounted, 'I rang Preston the next day, explaining that I was calling on behalf of Joe, and received a tirade of complaints to the effect that Joe owed him money. I told him of Joe's situation, gave him the address and rang off.'

Given time to reflect calmly, the record producer sent Joe a large basket of fruit with the briefest of messages attached, 'Compliments, Denis Preston.' 'Joe was furious,' Del continued. 'As he said, all he wanted was a friendly letter. There was a young woman visitor that night. She … had met Joe at a club where she worked and he was playing. She'd left her husband and family to go on the road with Joe but then he'd gone his own way again. So he gave the fruit to her.'[12]

Southon told Pete King at Ronnie Scott's about Harriott's condition and conveyed the impression the hospital staff had given him, that Joe would recover. Del also mentioned that Joe was getting annoyed with the music available on his bedside radio headphones. King, wanting to heal the rift that had grown between them, gifted Joe a cassette player and some jazz tapes. Additionally, on hearing that Harriott's sax was in a dilapidated condition – virtually unplayable with missing pads, makeshift replacements and damaged springs – Pete had it completely overhauled at Lewington's musical instrument shop. He asked Southon to tell Joe that his alto would be held for him until he was ready and able to play it at Ronnie's again.

Joe managed the words, 'Pete King actually said that?' before breaking down in tears. In Southon's view, it was the effect of Harriott's medication that made his emotions much more apparent.[13]

In addition to feeling touched by this kindness, Joe was quite delighted to receive from King a tape recording of Duke Ellington's seventieth birthday concert. He played it many times as he lay in his hospital bed. "It's nice that someone is thinking of me," Joe said as he showed Don Vincent the tape machine.[14]

On one visit Skip Conway found Joe very excited. He had received a handwritten message from Charles Mingus who had been appearing in London. Nurses informed Harriott that the mercurial American jazz star had appeared at the hospital at two o'clock that morning and was angry that hospital rules would not allow him to visit Joe then. In an interview Mingus had once been scathing about British musicians, enquiring: 'Who invented jazz? Tubby Hayes and Kenny Napper?' but had singled out for praise West Indians Harriott, Harold McNair and trumpeter Harry Beckett.[15]

Because he was sailing from Southampton that morning, Mingus had been unable to attend during normal visiting hours but he took the trouble to write a note saying he was sorry to hear of Joe's illness and sending good wishes for his recovery. Joe, aware that the bassist wanted him to go to the States and play there in his band, made a wry comment to Del Southon that it was hard enough being black in Britain.

If Mingus' intention was to boost Harriott's spirits, it worked. For a while it appeared to his visitors that he was rallying and he spoke of plans for the future. Skip Conway commented, 'Joe didn't realise he was dying. I don't think he knew he had cancer. He said to me one day: "Get rid of that dog outside the window." I'd gone over and pretended to shoo it away, but of course there was no dog. We were three floors up and Joe was hallucinating under the effects of the medication.'

'While I was visiting,' Conway remembered, 'he got a phone call from Michael Garrick who had called to say he was trying to arrange a benefit concert for him. Joe was very proud like many West Indians.' He was uncomfortable to receive an offer of charity and keen to assert himself immediately. 'Fine,' he answered, 'I just hope this is a meeting of brains.' The tears forming in his eyes showed his appreciation of Garrick's good intentions.[16]

Garrick made several visits to Harriott in hospital. He discovered that Joe had none of his own recordings to listen to so on his second visit he took tapes of records that Joe could play on the cassette recorder sent by Pete King.

Other famous jazz names came to see him. Mick Mulligan was one: 'I remember he showed me his scar. He was in a little ward and they were letting him smoke. By then they had realised he was a goner.'[17]

Another day Annie Ross arrived with Don Norman and gave Joe a bottle of whisky but he was too ill to appreciate it and gave it to the nursing staff. In the main, of course, it was not celebrity visitors but local jazz musicians and fans who rallied round him at this time. Yet, it was reportedly said in some London circles that Joe was neglected in Southampton; that, somehow, the location compounded his worsening condition; that he had no one there for him. This notion angered Teddy Layton and others, like Skip Conway, who supported Harriott with friendship and practical help.

With Christmas approaching, he was keen to find out what the hospital were having for the Christmas meal. He assigned Marilyn Layton to find out and she reported back that it was the traditional turkey dinner. She remembered: 'He put his hand on my arm and asked, "see if they'll do it with rice."' The staff were happy to organise it for him.

Later, because of the increasing doses of medication, he was often not conscious of visitors. 'Joe would be zonked out when I got there and zonked out when I left,' Del Southon told me: 'When he was made aware of this, that would make him feel worse.'

He had difficulty reading his own mail by this time. 'A letter arrived,' Southon recalled. 'He was so weak and doped up to his ears he couldn't even open it. I handed him the letter. He handed it back and said, "Can you do something about this?" It was from a woman, some kind of court official, chasing Joe for unpaid maintenance money. I rang her the following day and she really was a hard case. When I explained that Joe was in pretty dire straits she ordered me to keep her informed of any developments. Joe said it was to do with a daughter.'[18]

Sharon Atkin visited the hospital in the last week of Harriott's life. 'Teddy warned me not to be surprised when I saw Joe. There had been a rapid deterioration. Joe was in a side room in semi-darkness and lying on a sheepskin rug. He was so thin his signet ring was falling off his finger.... It was very shocking. At only twenty-one years of age, I had never seen anyone dying before. Teddy left us alone. Joe was lying there with his cigarette. He wanted a *Melody Maker*. Bobby [Breen] had died the week before and I didn't want him to see the article.'[19]

Del Southon remembered Joe was badly upset by the death of the West Indian singer. His anguish was softened by the care he received. 'There was one [nurse] he was especially fond of. They didn't know he was famous. But he still had something special, that personality. They would cut his hair and trim his beard and moustache.'[20]

As he deteriorated, Sharon Atkin detected his frustration. 'One thing he couldn't bear was that he was too weak to get his hair cut.' He had always been immaculately groomed and 'he felt that he didn't look his best with such long hair. People might think he was a Rasta or something. And, I think, he didn't want to capitulate to death. He never really gave up hope. He was working on a piece of music although it was physically very difficult for him because he had lost so much weight and he was in a great deal of pain but he started to write this 'Royal South Hants Suite'. Perhaps he remembered the days when he was in Pinewood Hospital in Crowthorne and he saw that as a similar time when possibly, if he wrote this suite of music, it might take him out. He was talking of coming out of hospital and how he'd like to get the opportunity then to work with Charlie Mingus.... And so he was still making plans right up until his death, for a recovery.'[21]

Harriott told Southon that he had finished with constant touring, that all he wanted was to have a little house and set up a music school. Conway also remembered that Joe 'wanted to start a music school in Southampton. The other plan he shared with me was that he'd like to play while I painted.'[22]

Joe Harriott died on the morning of 2 January 1973 in the Wessex Radiotherapy Unit. He was forty-four.

Del Southon had visited him just the day before. 'As I left he said: "Thanks for coming and thanks for all the times you came." He usually told me to drive carefully, winter weather being what it is. I guess his last words to me meant that he'd decided the struggle was too unequal.' Southon notified the persistent court official who had been pursuing Harriott's paternity liabilities. Her response rocked him. 'How do I *know* he's dead?' A death certificate turned out to be proof enough.

The death certificate gave Joe's address as 40 Marles Road, Botley, Teddy Layton's home. Cause of death was noted as reticulum cell sarcoma and pulmonary tuberculosis.

On 10 January, the day of Joe's funeral at Bitterne Church, prior to the service at noon, many of the local mourners met in the Red Lion pub opposite. Del Southon said, 'There was a darkly humorous aspect to the funeral. Pete King had come down from London and we were all in the bar. Suddenly the hearse turned up and someone called out to drink up as Joe had arrived. "Yeah, that's Harriott, late again!" said another voice.'[23]

At the funeral Annie Ross sang 'God Bless The Child' accompanied by Michael Garrick on organ and Dave Green on bass. John Mayer played Bach's moving 'Sarabande' on solo violin. Today Harriott's death still hangs heavy with Mayer. 'I was connected to Joe,' he says of their friendship. 'I came back from India, where my dad had been ill, and I heard from Don [Norman] that Joe was ill. I phoned the hospital and they encouraged me to visit him. When I phoned back they told me there was no need to come. Joe had died. He was 150 per cent better than anybody else. Nobody could touch him. Not Tubby Hayes. Not John Dankworth.' After Joe's death, Mayer left the jazz scene for twenty years.[24]

Responding very differently to Harriott's death, Skip Conway involved himself more deeply in the jazz scene. 'I formed the Southampton Jazz Society with the specific intention of getting gigs for other jazz musicians like Joe who were so gifted yet living on the breadline.'[25]

Trevor Tomkins found the funeral very sad, not only because of the manner of Joe's untimely passing. 'I thought it would have been busier. At Bill Le Sage's funeral [in 2001] they had as many outside as in. They couldn't get any more in. I was very sad about Joe's funeral, like he was a bit of a lost soul.'[26]

One of those paying his respects was Don Vincent. His view was very different from that of Tomkins. 'It was quite cold in the church and outside that day, but it was a moving service coupled with Annie's rendition. About forty friends, musicians and fans attended, which considering the time, the location and small amount of publicity, was over double the number that I expected. After paying respects at the graveside most of those present crossed over the road to the "local" opposite for a reassuring drink and to reminisce on personal details concerning Joe Harriott, the man and the musician.'[27]

Marilyn Layton remembered one nice touch. 'There was a West Indian lady there, all on her own. None of us knew who she was and I said: "Find out who she is".' This kindly soul had not known Joe personally but read about his death in the newspaper. 'She had come because she wanted a black face to be there at his funeral. She needed to know there was a black face there for him among all these white people.'[28]

A few weeks after Harriott's death, Teddy Layton rang Del Southon asking him over because he had to go through Joe's things and couldn't face it alone. Del found the experience depressing. 'Apart from his alto, his whole world was in one suitcase. The main item was an enormous fur coat, but the saddest things were the bills for bed and breakfast, pubs, boarding houses, sometimes three or four in a week. There was also a letter from a doctor, which Joe was supposed to take to a hospital but he'd obviously opened it, read it and done nothing about it.' Perhaps the doctor was the one who had treated him in Leeds. Maybe Harriott knew how serious his illness was and presented an optimistic facade to visitors.

His death went unnoticed editorially in the most prominent British jazz magazine of the time, *Jazz Journal*. This denial of recognition echoed his experience in much of his later career. In the magazine's January issue a review of a benefit concert for Phil Seamen's dependants misspelled the drummer's name throughout as 'Seaman'. Two world-class musicians surely deserved better.

Fortunately, others were less negligent and moves were quickly made to pay public respect to Harriott. A joint benefit concert for him and Bobby Breen, to raise funds to help with expenses, took place on 28 January at Ronnie Scott's. On 20 February a Harriott Memorial Night was held at Gullivers Club in London's Mayfair. The programme focused on Joe's music with help from quintet associates Pat Smythe, Coleridge Goode, Shake Keane and Bobby Orr. Others who contributed to a night to remember included Chris Barber, Don Rendell, Ian Carr, Annie Ross, John Mayer's trio, Eddie Thompson's trio, the Michael Garrick band with Norma Winstone and poets Jeremy Robson, Dannie Abse and John Smith. If only such a tribute could have taken place in Harriott's lifetime his sense of isolation might not have been so desperate.

Like many people, Keshav Sathe discovered more that night about the tragedy of Harriott's circumstances than the man himself had told him. He had not known that Joe had been destitute and so dreadfully ill. He reproached himself for the occasions when he had wished Harriott would leave his home to live elsewhere. 'He could have stayed in my house anytime he had liked if I had known,' was his sad reflection.[29] But this explains exactly why Joe, who disliked pity, kept so much to himself.

14.

the legacy of Joe Harriott

The passage of time has brought an increasing awareness of how special Joe Harriott was. After his death, musicians and non-musicians alike began to speculate how much more he might have achieved with support and encouragement. His achievement was enormous but he died relatively young and with much more to give. Les Condon spoke for many when he said, 'none of us realised how great he was. You don't think, when you're with somebody, they won't be there in ten years.'[1]

Shake Keane saw Joe's talent as held back by the demons in him. He told radio interviewer Peter Clayton, 'you know, he played fantastic stuff. But I have a feeling that there's a lot of thing ... inside of himself, that he didn't wish to confront and if he did it might have come out in ... a lot better jazz than he played. I mean, not to say he didn't play a lot of fantastic jazz. But ... you never know what he could have done if he'd really got hold of himself in that kind of psychological way.' When Clayton asked if there was more to Harriott than we thought we knew, Keane was unequivocal. 'I am certain of it.'[2]

Eric Dolphy, American virtuoso on bass clarinet, flute and alto sax, was asked during a period of unemployment if he would consider a life outside jazz. Dolphy's answer could well have been Joe's response to the same question: 'I'll never leave jazz. I've put too much of myself into jazz already, and I'm still trying to dig in deeper. Besides, in what other field could I get so complete a scope for self-expression? To me, jazz is like part of living, like walking down the street and reacting to what you see and hear. And whatever I do react to, I can say immediately in my music. The other thing that keeps me in jazz is that jazz continues to move on. There are so many possibilities for growth inside jazz because it changes as you change.'3 Dolphy died of undiagnosed diabetes a week after his thirty-sixth birthday.

'When I started out,' said Bassist Danny Thompson, 'I was told, "jazz is a lost cause". You've got to do it because you love it – not because it's a living.'4 Thompson drew parallels between Harriott and drummer John Stevens. Neither man sought session work, which could have seen them through financially difficult periods. Like Joe, Stevens refused to compromise. Both seemed to accept that they'd always be on the edge. Stevens, however, enjoyed success, teaching percussion in community education projects and jazz workshops until he suffered a fatal heart attack in 1994. Although Harriott might have found regular income from teaching, it is hard to imagine him earning money anywhere other than on a bandstand. The process of creation was his lifeblood and a receptive audience for his music was his idea of heaven.

Joe eloquently and succinctly explained, 'My greatest satisfaction is in playing music and creating and expressing myself fully. No one could ever pay a true price to an artist for a really great work of art. The greatest satisfaction comes from the enormous achievement of creation.'5

Pat Smythe thought that Harriott, 'was, as they say, his own worst enemy, and this was doubtless due to the fact that he was brought up in an orphanage and never knew his parents. But he had great inner strength and he faced adversity and his last illness with tremendous courage. I shall always remember him, and when I think of his ballad playing, I know beyond question that whatever front he presented to the world, this was the real Joe.'6

Kenny Baxter summed up: 'I remember Joe's smartness, his dedication to his art, the beautiful cutting tone, his genius as a saxophonist and composer. All the bands Joe led were great. I feel privileged to have been a part of his life.'7

'All these years later,' Marilyn Layton told me, 'I can see his face in my mind as clear as day. I can't even do that with members of my family that are gone – my own brothers!'[8]

Just two months after Harriott's death, a compilation album *Joe Harriott; Memorial 1973* was released. The tracks, chosen by Denis Preston, represented a cross-section of Joe's work. *Melody Maker*'s reviewer welcomed the return of 'some hard-to-find music to the current catalogue'. The article was accompanied by a striking black ink cartoon of Harriott drawn by the gifted artist and trumpeter Mal Dean. Dean, who fell victim to cancer himself at the age of thirty-two, captures in his drawing Joe's intensity and elegance.[9]

Margaret Tynski, eleven years after parting from Joe, though still very much in love with him, had been unaware of his death. 'It was a great shock to discover Joe had died when I came across a Memorial LP in the HMV Store in Oxford Street. I had not read any reports of Joe playing in London clubs and thought he had gone to Germany as he had expressed this desire in earlier years. I called Pat [Smythe] who told me of Joe's illness, hospitalisation, funeral service and where he was buried; the grave where my son and I have planted forget-me-nots.' Her verdict echoed that of Smythe's. 'Joe was his own worst enemy with a self-destruct button. He refused to do session work for survival. He would say, 'I don't want to prostitute myself playing music I don't like.' He was a loner and, I think, lonely. 'I am sure in the later years he almost gave up and lost the will.'

In 1974, Alan Plater's play, *Swallows on the Water* was produced at the Humberside Theatre, Hull. The title evoked Harriott's description of playing with Dizzy Gillespie. Plater said, 'it wasn't about Joe or jazz but it was about people who aim for the rafters and why we should take better care of them. Maybe it was about Joe after all.'[10] Plater later wrote a lyric for a song about Joe entitled 'Swallows on the Water'. This was featured in 2004 on an album jointly credited to Plater and saxophonist Alan Barnes called *Songs For Unsung Heroes*.

Almost a year after Harriott's death, a fine black African granite headstone was set over his grave in Bitterne churchyard. The stone cost £250 and was provided by individual dona-tions and funds collected at benefits. Del Southon told me he thought the money could have been better used in a fund in Joe's name to support young jazz talent, in the same way as a fund operated in Pat Smythe's memory after his death ten years later. Southon feared the gravestone would share the fate of many others: lost in a neglected, overgrown cemetery. But, in fact, Joe's resting place is in a well-kept village graveyard and easily located in its prominent position beside a path. On the gravestone his friends had his familiar proud words inscribed: 'Parker? There's them *here* can play a few aces too ...'

Years pass and perspectives change. Harriott was often an object of controversy in his lifetime, and this has continued after his death. Racism has been placed high on the list of rea-sons why he struggled against the tide for so much of his musi-cal career. Sharon Atkin cited a gross example when she recalled Joe walking out of a recording session in the 1960s because a technician said: 'You, nigger, come back in. We need to do this again.'

Atkin said that she had 'heard people say that Joe had a spiky personality. And some people said he had a chip on his shoul-der. I think it had less to do with the facts of his early life and surroundings. It certainly had very little to do with the music scene as a whole.' She felt that Harriott was very conscious of being black at a time when opportunities for black people in Britain were limited. 'He certainly wasn't hostile to white peo-ple. He didn't feel that Britain was an unwelcoming place on some levels but that, in terms of music and the industry, they didn't give the recognition to Caribbean musicians and that black people as a whole fared not too well.'[11]

Denis Preston, interviewed shortly after Joe's death, said, 'Joe suffered greatly from being a black man.' When Peter Clayton asked if he suffered more than others, Preston was emphatic. 'Certainly.'

Clayton confessed he hadn't noticed it. 'Oh you wouldn't notice it,' responded Preston, 'and certainly among other jazz players you wouldn't notice it. But in the greater world where a musician can enter and make money by doing sessions and joining big bands and so forth, there was, and I believe in my heart still is, a great prejudice.'[12]

Amancio D'Silva's widow, Joyce, wrote, 'I'm not aware of any particular racism that Joe suffered. But it certainly wouldn't surprise me. There was quite a 'white' feeling in some elements of British jazz at the time. I know Amancio was aware of it. It may have been more in the trad elements, and not universal.'[13]

Without being specific, John Mayer cited incidents that he classified as low-level abuse. Octogenarian Jamaican saxophonist Andy Hamilton, more in sorrow than in anger, said, 'I don't want to build this thing up but I think if Harriott was a white guy, he'd be more recognised, more strongly ... and you don't hear much people talk about him. And I think that's a shame, really.'[14]

It riles some white musicians when the UK jazz scene is deemed by some to have been culpable. Many of Harriott's contemporaries are scathing at the claim that racism drove Joe to despair and alcoholism. Tony Kinsey said: 'Bullshit. It wasn't like that. We never thought about colour and we'd have known if it happened that way.'[15]

Trombonist Paul Rutherford was equally dismissive. 'I knew and loved Joe Harriott's music and he was perfect, a true gentleman. He ran a mixed race band, he had no problems within the music.'[16]

Brian Dee said, 'He wasn't an easy guy to get to know.... If anything, black players were on a pedestal. Joe got away with a lot because he was so revered.'[17]

Of all the musicians in a position to know the truth of the situation, I would expect that Shake Keane and Coleridge Goode were best placed to comment. Both shared with Harriott a West Indian background and presumably met with similar levels of racism on many occasions, yet they held opposite opinions as to why Joe's last years were so difficult.

When Goode looks back over his long, successful career, it is his work with Harriott of which he remains proudest.

Despite being with Joe longer than any other musician, Coleridge was never close to him. It did not concern him because he was always blessed with a strong sense of purpose and self-identity. Although their relationship was like a business partnership, it did not preclude feelings of empathy when life became a real struggle for Joe. Goode said in his autobiography: 'In the last years I knew him he was not at all the same chap who started out. All of us involved in his projects felt his pain. We felt it was a terrible shame that the people who had the power to present, broadcast, explain and publicise his music often ignored or neglected it.

'In the end, unfortunately, one puts it down to the fact that Joe wasn't a white Englishman. Had he been one, things would have been different. There can be no other explanation.... In America, black musicians have received some recognition. They are a majority in jazz there, whereas in Britain they are a small minority and what they have done has been easier to ignore. But at least some of the music is on record.'[18]

Keane, with his strong interest in psychology, found Joe's personality incomplete or damaged. He told Peter Clayton: 'Joe was basically a musician. When you name a profession you usually think of someone behind this profession. Somebody who is actually doing something. You tend to separate the occupation from the person doing it. With Joe this was impossible. He was an alto sax player. If alto sax players could ever have been genetically developed from some sort of amoeba millions of years ago, then Joe was that. He wasn't really a person. He couldn't understand relationships. He could only understand relationships when you were playing music. So he was ... I suppose this is the most generous way of putting it ... he was an incomplete, talented artist.'

Clayton suggested: 'This explains, I suppose, the awful loneliness of the circumstances towards the end?'

Keane summed it up. 'It was on the cards. It would have been difficult to imagine Joe spending his last years ... having kids around him, friendly conversation, what not. I imagine that at the end he was thinking what he would do next on the saxophone regardless of who said no or yes.'[19]

In 1989 the news of Keane's return from the USA to Britain galvanised Michael Garrick into action. Shake had been integral to the success of the Harriott quintet and he was the final, crucial piece needed to form a 'Joe Harriott Memorial Quintet' for a concert tour in October and November. Pat Smythe had died in 1983 so Garrick himself played piano. Goode and Orr resumed their partnership in the rhythm section and a young altoist, Martin Hathaway, had the unenviable task of taking Harriott's place. Garrick told me that, on the first occasion he heard Hathaway's playing in a smoky, noisy basement, he was struck immediately by something excitingly familiar in the young altoist's tone. He asked him, 'have you been listening to Joe Harriott?' only to hear the response: 'Who's he?' As the group settled down to rehearsals, Hathaway began to find out. Garrick's recent CD, *The New Quartet*, includes a version of Harriott's free form composition 'Subject' with Hathaway playing superb alto.[20]

A particularly poignant gig took place at Southampton University where Skip Conway joined many friends of Harriott's in the audience to hear the memorial quintet. Also among the gathering was Joe's former girlfriend, Jill Sarrazin, who had moved to Southampton. Her sadness was tinged with personal regret. 'I just wish I had known Joe was here at the time. I didn't know until I read the *Echo* that he had died.' Neither knew the other was in Southampton and it upset her to think that she had lost an opportunity to see Joe again by visiting him in hospital.[21]

Michael Garrick has done much to keep Harriott's flame burning. In April 2003 he used the occasion of his seventieth birthday concert at the Queen Elizabeth Hall on London's South Bank to commemorate the thirtieth anniversary of Joe's death. The concert featured a number of Harriott compositions presented in a big band setting.

Respect for Harriott's work has been growing. In Britain,

those of his recordings that have long been out of print fetch huge sums at record collectors' fairs and auctions. But the interest in his work is not confined to jazz 'anoraks'. His free form compositions intrigue serious musicians across the globe.

Chicago reedman and bandleader Ken Vandermark, born since *Free Form* and *Abstract* were recorded, has released his interpretation of seven of Joe's free form compositions. The CD *Straight Lines* by Vandermark's Joe Harriott Project is a tribute to Joe and his quintet but in no way a mere 'revival' or imitative exercise. The Vandermark quartet features a trombonist rather than a trumpeter and there is no piano, making the sound markedly different from the Harriott quintet's. The recording is an interesting exploration of Joe's music but, I must confess, I miss the piano.

Harriott was proud of his Jamaican heritage and would have been pleased by the posthumous recognition accorded him by his country when his name was added to the Jamaican Jazz Hall of Fame. He once told Trevor Tomkins of his dismay that despite his achievements in Britain, 'in my own backyard nobody wants to know.'[22] Things have changed.

Modern musicians of Jamaican descent working in Britain pay respect to Harriott's memory and contribute to keep his achievement in the public consciousness. In 1988 Courtney Pine's twenty piece band, the Jazz Warriors, performed a special *Homage to Joe Harriott*, featuring new compositions by Harry Beckett and Herman Wilson, at Southampton's Mayflower Theatre as part of the city's jazz festival. London-born Pine, who has promoted jazz through many projects with black musicians, refers often to Harriott's influence.[23] More recently Pine has featured his composition 'The Tale of Joe Harriott' in a series of concerts. The plaintive ballad features Courtney on alto flute. 'He's a transitional figure.... We as musicians, show who our inspirations are, not just, "This is all my stuff ... I don't think so."'[24]

Bassist Gary Crosby leads Jazz Jamaica, a vibrant, exciting ensemble which features younger generation musicians alongside Joe's contemporaries Rico Rodrigues and Eddie 'Tan Tan'

Thornton. Crosby reveres Harriott as Jamaica's finest export to British jazz. For him, Joe's musical legacy retains an inspirational quality. Harriott lives on whenever his music is played.

Joe lives on in another sense. His living, breathing legacy, his own children, have emerged publicly only since his death. These are his sons and daughters fathered in Jamaica, Germany and Britain. A statement that 'he had no family' appeared in the Southampton *Southern Echo*'s report on the erecting of Harriott's headstone. This was what most people in Joe's circle believed. The existence of Pauline, his first child in Jamaica, was known to few of Joe's contemporaries. Theresa, born in Britain, was known to even fewer. But the next of his children to make an appearance did so in a way that was as sudden as it was dramatic.

Christopher Cornelsen's trip to Britain followed his hearing a German radio programme called *Joe Harriott: The Forgotten Man*. This convinced him that he should make contact with his father's friends. After first getting in touch with Coleridge Goode and Shake Keane, he was directed by Michael Garrick to Skip Conway, who was surprised to receive a phone call from a young man in Frankfurt wanting to find out more about Harriott. 'He knew something of his father but didn't know how he had died. It was left to me. I had the task of telling him,' Conway explained.[25]

He put Christopher in contact with Teddy Layton, the executor of Joe's estate. When Christopher visited him, Teddy noted that 'he looks just like his father,' and Sharon Atkin, who met Christopher later, thought the likeness so pronounced that she would have picked him out of a crowd as Joe's son. She was taken also by the way he held his cigarette: 'Exactly like Joe.'[26]

Harriott left virtually nothing in material wealth but had bequeathed Teddy his saxophone. At Layton's home, the instrument naturally became the focus of great interest for the young German, a pop video producer. 'Christopher picked it up and blew an excruciating noise!' Teddy lamented.[27]

Layton had collected all Harriott's documents, letters, cards and lists of addresses in a small suitcase, and Christopher took some of them back to Germany to show his mother. Her relationship with Joe had been short-lived and Christopher had never known his father. It was quite understandable, and possibly something Teddy anticipated, that Christopher asked if he could have Joe's saxophone. Equally understandably, Teddy resisted handing it over. Joe had given him his beloved saxophone on his deathbed, knowing that Layton would make good use of it.

Christopher wanted to know all about his father and Skip Conway spent an afternoon sharing his memories of Joe and told Christopher about his extended family. Although the two half-sisters, Pauline and Theresa, had spoken on the telephone, they met each other for the first time only thirty minutes before encountering their Frankfurt-born half-brother in 1988. While Skip felt bemused to be introducing Joe's daughters to Joe's son, the emotion of the occasion was felt by everyone present. A further daughter, Amber, living in Northampton, made herself known to her half-sisters at a later time. Pauline presciently posed the thought: 'I wonder if there are any more of us out there?'[28]

I knew of Zachary's existence only when his mother contacted me after the first publication of this biography. It is entirely possible that Joe's five known children have other siblings as yet unknown to them.

Teddy Layton, who played regularly around Southampton, had every intention of using Joe's alto in addition to his own clarinet but Del Southon told me of a peculiar development: 'It was two years before he actually played it because, as he told me, each time he picked it up to play it he couldn't stop his hands shaking.' It seems Layton found the thought of the music it had played with its inspired owner simply overwhelming. Gradually, he overcame this condition and Joe's instrument avoided becoming an encased relic only brought out for interested spectators. It became, once again, a well-maintained working tool, appropriately for an instrument which had, in Harriott's hands, created such sublime music.[29]

Since Layton's death from cancer on 19 October 2002, I have no knowledge about the current ownership or whereabouts of Harriott's alto. The saxophone, with its dull finish and considerable signs of wear, is now presumably silent.

notes

Introduction
1. Ian Carr, *Music Outside, Contemporary Jazz in Britain*, London: Latimer, 1973, republished by Northway, 2008.

Chapter 1   *Very much taken with his instrument*
1. Ivanhoe Harriott, phone conversation, 16/12/02.
2. Pauline Harriott, phone conversation, 25/11/02.
3. Velma Gray, phone conversation, 12/1/03.
4. Jamaican parishes are regions of the country and the capital of Clarendon is about 35 miles west of Kingston.
5. Val Wilmer letter to *Jazz Journal*, September 2008.
6. Velma Gray, phone conversation, 12/1/03.
7. Sister Susan Frazer, letter to the author, 17/9/01.
8. Ivanhoe Harriott, phone conversations, 10/11/02 and 16/12/02.
9. Pauline Harriott, phone conversation, 30/6/02.
10. Sister Ignatius, phone conversations, 14 and 15/5/02.
11. Eddie 'Tan Tan' Thornton, phone conversations, 13/6/02 and 16/6/02; Dizzy Reece, phone conversation, 14/5/02.
12. Sister Ignatius, phone conversations, 14 and 15/5/02.
13. Velma Gray, phone conversation, 19/1/03.
14. Eddie 'Tan Tan' Thornton, phone conversation, 13/6/02 and 16/6/02.
15. Velma Gray, phone conversation, 13/1/03.
16. Joe Harriott quoted in Val Wilmer, 'Joe Harriott: Jazz Abstractionist', *Down Beat*, 10/9/64.
17. Dizzy Reece, quoted in Robert Levin's insert notes for Reece's *Asia Minor* CD.
18. 'Harold McNair's father was a Glasgow born seafarer who had settled and married in Jamaica. Harold took music lessons at the school but did not attend Alpha. He was well educated and while Joe's accent was acquired, McNair's was natural.' Rod Marshall in phone conversation with the author, 14/5/06.
19. Eddie 'Tan Tan' Thornton, phone conversation, 13/6/02.
20. Andy Hamilton, phone conversation, 20/9/01. Hamilton had returned from working in the USA and was leading his own band in Jamaica until he departed for Britain in 1949.
21. Harry Klein, phone conversation, 25/2/03.
22. Sonny Bradshaw, obituary of Sister Ignatius, *Jamaica Observer*, 14/2/03.
23. Ivan Harriott, phone conversation, 10/11/02.
24. Sonny Bradshaw, phone conversation, 30/7/03.
25. Sonny Bradshaw, phone conversation, 10/11/02.
26. Andy Hamilton, in 'Joe Harriott Tribute', presented by Sharon Atkin on Jazz FM radio, 1/1/1991.
27. Lloyd Bradley, *Bass Culture*, London: Viking, 2000, p. 122.

28. Quoted in *bbc.co.uk./history/community/multicultural/windrush/arrival03.shtml* visited March 2002.

29. Eddie 'Tan Tan' Thornton, phone conversations, 13/6/02 and 16/6/02.

30. Herman Wilson, phone conversation, 3/3/02.

31. Pauline Harriott, phone conversation, 30/6/02.

32. Velma Gray, phone conversation, 12/1/03.

33. Pauline Harriott, phone conversation, 30/6/02.

34. Pauline Harriott, phone conversation, 24/11/02.

Chapter 2   *The London scene 1951*

1. Conversation with Herman Wilson in London 1/8/02 and by phone 3/3/02 and 4/8/02.

2. Andy Hamilton in *Joe Harriott Tribute*, Jazz FM radio, 1/1/1991.

3. Tommy Jones, phone conversation, August 2002.

4. Chester Harriott, phone conversation and letter, June 2002.

5. Laurie Morgan, phone conversation, 10/6/02.

6. Bill Le Sage, *www.jazzpiano.co.uk* visited 30/5/02.

7. Joe Harriott, quoted in Val Wilmer, 'Jazz Abstractionist', *Down Beat*, 10/9/64.

8. Joe Mudele, phone conversation, 1/9/02.

9. Jim Godbolt, *A History of Jazz in Britain 1950–70*, London: Quartet, 1989, pp. 250-2.

10. Tommy Jones, phone conversation, 19/8/02.

11. George Melly, phone conversation, 22/4/02. The story is almost identically recounted in Melly's *Owning Up*, Harmondsworth: Penguin, 1970, p. 101.

12. Ian Croall, phone conversation, 19/9/01.

13. John Smith, phone conversation, April 2002.

14. Frank Holder, in conversation with the author, London, 22/02/02.

15. Coleridge Goode, phone conversation, 20/8/01.

16. Dave Gelly, *Masters of the Jazz Saxophone*, London: Balafon, 2000.

17. Quoted in Val Wilmer, 'Joe Harriott: Jazz Abstractionist', *Down Beat*, 10/9/64.

18. Ken Baxter, phone conversation, 14/3/03.

19. Andy Hamilton in *Joe Harriott Tribute*, Jazz FM radio, 1/1/91.

20. *Melody Maker* 5/7/52.

21. Laurie Henshaw, *Melody Maker* 5/7/52.

22. Mike Nevard, *Melody Maker* 5/7/52.

23. Jim Godbolt, *A History of Jazz in Britain 1950–70*, pp. 174-5; Humphrey Lyttelton, *I Play As I Please*, London: Jazz Book Club, 1957, p. 175.

24. *Melody Maker*, 12/7/52.

25. *Jazz Journal*, February 1953.

26. Laurie Henshaw, *Melody Maker*, 6/9/52.

27. *Jazz Journal*, February 1953.

28. Chris Barber, phone conversation, 22/10/01.

29. *Melody Maker*,19/12/53.
30. Dave Keir, phone conversation, 31/7/01.

Chapter 3   *Building a reputation*

1. Extended Play records were so named because they generally ran twice as long as the singles on 45 rpm.
2. James Asman, sleeve notes for Harriott's *Cool Jazz with Joe* EP.
3. Alun Morgan, *Jazz Journal*, October 1954.
4. Harry Klein, phone conversation, 25/2/03.
5. Spike Heatley, phone conversation, 20/3/03.
6. Roger Cotterrell, 'A Joe Harriott Memorial' in Chris Blackford ed., *Joe Harriott: Forgotten Father of European Free Jazz*. Special issue, *Rubberneck*, No. 25, Basingstoke, 1997, pp. 5-6. (This essay was originally published in R Cotterrell and B Tepperman, *Joe Harriott Memorial: A Bio-Discography*, Ilford: private publication, 1974). Cotterrell visited Preston at Lansdowne Studios on 3/4/74.
7. Brian Nichols, 'The British Jazz Scene: The Modernists' in Sinclair Traill ed, *Concerning Jazz*, London: Faber, 1959, as quoted in Cotterrell, 'Joe Harriott Memorial', p. 5.
8. *Melody Maker*, 12/6/54.
9. Jeffrey Kruger, insert notes for *Best of British Jazz* CD.
10. 'Kinsey Triumph in Paris Leads to Bid for U.S.', *Melody Maker*, 12/6/54.
11. As above, *Melody Maker*, 12/6/54.
12. Brian Nicholls interview, *Jazz News*, featured in Dave Brubeck tour programme, Jan. 1961.
13. Stokes had begun his musical career in the army as a clarinettist and tenor sax player. Wounded and taken prisoner at Dunkirk, he was repatriated in a prisoner exchange in 1943, allowing him to rejoin his unit. The loss of his embouchure as a result of malnutrition led to his becoming first a vocalist and then a bass player (Sammy Stokes, phone conversations, 29/6/02 and 4/7/02).
14. Bill Le Sage and Tony Kinsey, quoted in sleevenotes for Harriott/ Kinsey, *Jump For Me* LP.
15. Newbrook who co-owned Esquire with Carlo Krahmer has since given up the recording business, daunted by the thought of transferring his company's extensive catalogue onto CD.
16. Peter Newbrook, phone conversation, 2/10/01.
17. Tony Kinsey, in conversation with the author, Sunbury on Thames, 21/2/02.
18. Roland Ramanan, *The Wire*, Issue 53, July 1988.
19. *Melody Maker*, 8/1/55.
20. This, and information in subsequent paragraphs, from conversation with Tony Kinsey, Sunbury on Thames, 21/2/02.
21. *Melody Maker*, 12/2/55.
22. Tony Kinsey, in conversation with the author, 21/2/02.
23. Jim Godbolt, *A History of Jazz in Britain 1950–70*, p. 265.

24. Denis Preston, *Melody Maker*, 13/1/73.
25. Max Harris, phone conversation, 23/1/03.
26. Phil Seamen talking on the LP *The Phil Seamen Story*.
27. *Melody Maker* 18/6/55.
28. Lita Roza, phone conversation, 8/9/02.
29. Discographer Tony Middleton and a review in *Jazz Journal*, February 1956, give the name of the bass player as Lennie Bush but the sleevenote gives the name as Sammy Stokes.
30. P.T., *Jazz Journal*, February 1956.
31. Ronnie Scott, *Melody Maker*, 13/8/55.
32. Dominic Green, *Benny Green, Words and Music*, London: London House, 2000.
33. Benny Green, programme notes for Indo-Jazz Fusions concert, date not given.
34. Benny Green, interviewed for broadcast celebrating forty years of Ronnie Scott's: *The Club That Ronnie Built*, BBC Radio 3, 1999.
35. Tony Brown, *Melody Maker*, 10/9/55.
36. Tony Brown, *Melody Maker*, 24/9/55.
37. John Fordham, *Jazz Man: The Amazing story of Ronnie Scott and His Club*, London: Kyle Cathie, 1995, p. 63; Jim Godbolt, *A History of Jazz in Britain 1950–70*, p. 111.
38. Pete King, phone conversations, 2/8/02 and 13/8/03.
39. John Fordham, *Jazz Man*, p. 63.
40. Peggy Burton, widow of trombonist Ken Wray, in conversation with the author, July 2002.
41. The only recording of the quintet, 'Manteca Suite', was made after trombonist Ken Wray had taken Joe's place. It appeared on the *Third Festival Of British Jazz* LP. Seamen's quintet, minus Goldberg, did however record two tracks as a quartet under Harriott's name. These were issued on the *Jazz Britannia* EP. See Tony Middleton, *Joe Harriott Bio/Discography*, London: TM Publications, 1996, p. 5.
42. Margaret Tynski, interviewed by the author, 21/7/08.
43. *Jazz News*, April 1957.
43. *Melody Maker*, 2/2/57.
45. *Melody Maker*, April 1957.
46. Tony Kinsey, in conversation with the author, 21/2/02.
47. Bob Efford, in email to the author, 25/1/03.
48. Tony Hall, sleevenotes for Tony Kinsey's *A Jazz at the Flamingo Session* LP.
49. The vacancy with Kinsey was filled by trumpeter Les Condon.
50. Allan Ganley, phone conversation, 9/11/01.
51. Roger Cotterrell, 'Joe Harriott Memorial', p. 6.
52. Tony Hall, sleevenotes for Reece's *A New Star* CD.
53. Frank Holder, in conversation with the author, London, 22/2/02.
54. He also had a West Indian barber and dentist. Information from Margaret Tynski.

55. Jack Cooke, phone conversation, 30/6/02.
56. Dizzy Reece, phone conversation, 14/5/02.
57. Tony Hall, phone conversation, 6/10/02.
58. Dizzy Reece, phone conversation, 14/5/02.
59. Tony Hall, sleevenotes for Reece's *Progress Report* CD.
60. Tony Hall, phone conversation, 6/10/02.
61. Tony Hall, sleevenotes for *Progress Report* CD.
62. *Jazz for Moderns*, programme 9, presented by Steve Race, BBC radio, 1961, broadcast in Belgium on 14/1/63.
63. On the LP *The Joe Harriott Quintet Swings High*.

Chapter 4   *A fence over which few are prepared to step*
1. Jack Cooke, phone conversation, 20/9/01.
2. Tony Middleton, *Joe Harriott Bio/Discography*, p. 6.
3. Jim Godbolt, *History of Jazz in Britain 1950–70*, p. 251.
4. Coleridge Goode, in conversation with the author, London, 20/2/02.
5. Doris Steel, phone conversation, 18/05/02.
6. John Marshall, phone conversation, 20/11/02.
7. Michael Garrick, phone conversation, 25/11/01.
8. Joe Harriott as quoted by Bob Dawbarn, *Melody Maker*, 23/2/63.
9. Jack Parnell, interviewed by Ken Couper, *Melody Maker*, 18/8/56.
10. Jack Cooke, review of Harriott–Mayer *Indo-Jazz Fusions II* LP, *Jazz Monthly*, June 1968. See also Jack Cooke, 'Transcending the Ordinary: Memories of Joe Harriott' in *Rubberneck* No. 25, 1997.
11. In the course of preparing his memorial booklet (Cotterrell and Tepperman, *Joe Harriott Memorial*, 1974) a few months after Harriott's death, Roger Cotterrell phoned Pat Smythe and asked about the origins of Joe's free form ideas. Cotterrell made a note of the phone conversation immediately after it took place on 20/7/73. Information from Roger Cotterrell, 5/9/03.
12. Brian Nicholls interview, *Jazz News*, featured in Dave Brubeck tour programme, Jan. 1961.
13. Shake Keane interviewed by Peter Clayton, *Jazz Notes*, BBC radio, 1973.
14. Frank Holder, in conversation with the author, London, 22/2/02.
15. *Melody Maker*, 5/7/58.
16. *Melody Maker*, 5/7/58.
17. Peter King, email to author, 22/6/02.
18. Shake Keane, interviewed by Peter Clayton, *Jazz Notes*, BBC radio, 1973.
19. Skip Conway, phone conversation, 24/11/02.
20. Kenny Baxter, letter to the author, 17/3/03.
21. *Melody Maker*, 24/1/59.
22. Bobby Orr, in conversation with the author, London, 20/2/02.
23. *Melody Maker*, 21/2/59.
24. Coleridge Goode, interviewed by Jack Massarik, *The Wire*, no. 4, 1983.
25. Bobby Orr, in conversation with the author, 20/02/02.
26. *Melody Maker* 31/10/59.

27. *Melody Maker*, 24/10/59.
28. Harold Pendelton, interviewed by Bob Dawbarn, *Melody Maker*, 21/11/59.
29. Benny Green, *Drums In My Ears*, London: Davis–Poynter, 1973.
30. Dave Green, in conversation with the author, London, 18/02/02.
31. Barry Fleming, email to the author, 18/8/02.
32. Chris Barber, phone conversation, 22/10/01.
33. Pat Halcox, phone conversation, 2/2/03.
34. Bobby Orr, in conversation with the author, Edinburgh, 29/12/02.
35. Coleridge Goode, interviewed by Jack Massarik, *The Wire*, No 4, 1983.
36. Frank Holder, in conversation with the author, 22/2/02, London.
37. Coleridge Goode, phone conversation, 8/1/02, see also Coleridge Goode and Roger Cotterrell, *Bass Lines: A Life in Jazz*, London: Northway Publications, 2002, pp. 131-2 and Coleridge Goode, interviewed by Jack Masarik, *The Wire*, Issue 4, 1983.
38. Frank Holder, in conversation with the author, London, 3/3/02.
39. Hank Shaw, phone conversation 3/3/02.
40. Quoted in Kitty Grime, *Jazz at Ronnie Scott's*, London: Hale, p. 147.
41. Shake Keane, interviewed by Peter Clayton, *Jazz Notes*, BBC radio, 1973.
42. Shake Keane, interviewed by Kitty Grime, *Jazz News*, 31/1/62.
43. According to Ernie Garside, Shake Keane preferred a perspex model of mouthpiece on his flugelhorn because it wasn't cold against his mouth. Conversation with the author, Cheadle Hulme, 18/05/02.
44. Shake Keane, interviewed by Peter Clayton, *Sounds of Jazz*, BBC radio 10/12/88.
45. Frank Holder, in conversation with the author, 22/02/02.
46. John Keating, in conversation with the author, 11/9/01.
47. Harry Klein, phone conversation, 25/2/03.
48. Bobby Orr, in conversation with the author, 20/02/02.
49. Colin Barnes, phone conversation, 29/9/02.
50. J. M., Review, *Jazz News*, 19/4/61.
51. Bobby Orr, in conversation with the author, 29/12/01.
52. *Jazz News*, undated photocopy, probably May 1960.
53. *Jazz News*, undated photocopy, probably May 1960.
54. Trevor Tomkins, in conversation with the author, 8/12/02.
55. Heather Smythe, phone conversations, 29/4/02 and 12/5/02.
56. Dave Willis, phone conversation, 6/2/03.
57. Spike Heatley, phone conversation, 20/3/03.
58. *www.zipworld.com.au/-lnbdds/home/smythepat.htm* visited on 30/4/02.
59. Stu Hamer, phone conversation, 16/4/02.
60. Shake Keane, interviewed by Kitty Grime, *Jazz News*, 31/1/62.
61. Quoted in Val Wilmer, 'Joe Harriott: Jazz Abstractionist', *Down Beat*, 10/9/64.
62. Ian Carr, phone conversations, 19/10/01 and 23/10/01.
63. Margaret Tynski had moved out of 94a in November 1961.

64. Val Wilmer, interviewed on *The Jazz Islands*, BBC radio, 3/2/2000.
65. Coleridge Goode, phone conversation, 8/1/02; and see Coleridge Goode and Roger Cotterrell, *Bass Lines: A Life in Jazz*, pp. 150-2.
66. Ernie Garside, in conversation with the author, Cheadle Hulme, 18/5/02.
67. Brian Nicholls interview, *Jazz News*, featured in *Brubeck Tour Programme*, Jan. 1961.
68. Richard Williams, *Melody Maker*, 13/1/73.

Chapter 5   *So far nobody has thrown anything at us*

1.   BBC radio Light Programme *Jazz Club*, broadcast, 17/11/60.
2.   *Melody Maker*, 19/11/1960.
3.   Ernie Garside, in conversation with the author, Cheadle Hulme, 18/05/02.
4.   Ernie Garside, in conversation, 18/05/02.
5.   Michael Garrick, phone conversation, 24/3/02.
6.   Les Condon, phone conversation, 30/6/02.
7.   Jack Cooke, letter to the author, 7/9/01.
8.   Insert notes (uncredited) for Joe Harriott's *Free Form* album.
9.   Burnett James, *Jazz Monthly*, April 1962.
10. Coleridge Goode, interviewed by Jack Massarik, *The Wire*, no. 4, 1983.
11. Joe Harriott, interviewed by Bob Dawbarn, *Melody Maker*, 23/2/63
12. Coleridge Goode, in conversation with the author, London 20/2/02
13. Joe Harriott, interviewed by Bob Dawbarn, *Melody Maker*, 23/2/63.
14. Coleridge Goode, interviewed by Jack Massarik, *The Wire*, no. 4, 1983 and see Coleridge Goode and Roger Cotterrell, *Bass Lines: A Life in Jazz*, pp. 154-6.
15. Pat Smythe, quoted by Bob Dawbarn, *Melody Maker*, 10/9/60.
16. Kitty Grime, *Jazz News*, 31/1/62.
17. *Melody Maker*, 18/2/61.
18. Joe Harriott, quoted by Bob Dawbarn, *Melody Maker*, 10/9/60.
19. Peter King, email to the author, 22/6/02.
20. Les Condon, phone conversation, 30/6/02.
21. *Jazz News*, 3/12/60.
22. Benny Green, *Drums In My Ears*, London: Davis-Poynter, 1973.
23. Steve Race, *Jazz News*, 11/2/61.
24. Coleridge Goode and Roger Cotterrell, *Bass Lines*, p. 150.
25. Dave Brubeck, email to the author, 11/3/03.
26. Les Condon, phone conversation, 16/4/02.
27. Chris Barber, *Chris Barber's Jazz Diaries*, BBC Radio 2, 11/2/02.
28. Adrian Kerridge, email to the author, 12/1/03.
29. *Edinburgh Evening News*, April 1961.
30. *Jazz News*, 9/8/61.
31. Letter to author from Richard Veasey, 12/1/04.
32. Joe Harriott, interviewed by Max Jones, 'This is Our Big Chance' *Melody Maker*, 19/8/61.
33. Kitty Grime, *Jazz News*, 20/9/61.
34. Les Condon, phone conversation, 30/6/02.

Chapter 6   *America takes notice*

1. Bobby Orr and Coleridge Goode, in conversation with the author, London, 20/2/02.
2. Coleridge Goode and Roger Cotterrell, *Bass Lines*, pp. 147-8.
3. The notes to the LP and CD issues of *Abstract* incorrectly list 'Modal' as recorded at the session on 10/5/62.
4. *Jazz for Moderns* programme 9, presented by Steve Race, BBC radio, 1961, broadcast in Belgium on 14/1/63.
5. Harvey Pekar, *Down Beat*, 21/11/63.
6. Harvey Pekar, phone conversation, 17/1/03.
7. Roger Cotterrell, email to the author, 31/5/03.
8. Joe Harriott, quoted by Bob Dawbarn, *Melody Maker*, 23/2/63
9. Coleridge Goode, talking on BBC Radio 3, *The Jazz Islands*, 19/2/02; see also Coleridge Goode and Roger Cotterrell, *Bass Lines*, pp. 147-8.
10. *Jazz News & Review*, 31/1/63.
11. Bobby Orr, in conversation with the author, Edinburgh, 29/12/01.
12. Benny Green, undated Indo-jazz programme notes, John Mayer collection.
13. Kitty Grime, *Jazz News*, 31/1/62.
14. Shake Keane, interviewed by Kitty Grime, *Jazz News*, 31/1/62.
15. Coleridge Goode and Roger Cotterrell, *Bass Lines*, pp. 157-8.
16. Quoted in Val Wilmer, 'Joe Harriott: Jazz Abstractionist', *Down Beat*, 10/9/64.
17. Joe Harriott, sleevenotes to *Abstract* album.
18. Trevor Tomkins, phone conversation, 8/12/02.
19. Chris Barber, phone conversation, 2001.
20. Blindfold test for *Crescendo*, 1963; and www.jazzprofessional.com/blindfold_tests/south_deuchar.htm visited 2/2/02.
21. T. E. Martin, *Jazz Monthly*, September 1964.
22. Disc Discussion, Blindfold Test for *Crescendo* 1964 conducted by Les Tomkins, *www.jazzprofessional.com/blindfold_tests/johnson_murphy.htm* visited 2/2/02.
23. Jeff Clyne, quoted in Kitty Grime, *Jazz at Ronnie Scott's*, p. 147.
24. Coleridge Goode and Roger Cotterrell, *Bass Lines*, pp. 160-1.
25. Joe Harriott, quoted in sleevenotes to his *High Spirits* LP.
26. T. E. Martin, *Jazz Monthly*, April 1965.
27. Trevor Tomkins, phone conversation, 8/12/02.
28. Jim Godbolt, phone conversation, 11/12/02.

Chapter 7   *Poetry and jazz in concert*

1. Michael Horovitz, in letters, 5/3/03, 7/4/03 and phone conversation, 3/3/03.
2. Michael Horovitz, in letter, 5/3/03 and phone conversation, 3/3/03.
3. Jeremy Robson, phone conversation, 14/4/02.
4. Jeremy Robson, interviewed for an investigation into jazz and poetry by Giorgio Gomelsky, *Jazz News*, 27/12/61.

5. The Poetry Library and Voicebox now occupy the space that was formerly the Recital Room.
6. Michael Garrick, *Jazzbeat*, March 1965.
7. Adrian Mitchell, phone conversation, 10/3/03.
8. Dannie Abse, phone conversation, 2002.
9. Dannie Abse, *Goodbye Twentieth Century*, London: Pimlico, 2001.
10. Jeremy Robson, phone conversation, 14/4/02.
11. Michael Garrick, in conversation with the author, August 2002; and phone conversations, 25/11/01 and 24/3/02.
12. Michael Garrick, interviewed by Julian Joseph, *Jazz Legends: Joe Harriott*, BBC Radio 3 broadcast, 22/3/02.
13. Adrian Mitchell, phone conversation, 10/3/03.
14. Michael Garrick as above, note 11.
15. Adrian Mitchell, phone conversation, 10/3/03.
16. Bari Johnson, phone conversation, 23/3/03; *Edinburgh Evening News*, 3/9/63.
17. *The Scotsman*, 3/9/63.
18. Bill Ashton, phone conversation, March 2003.
19. *Edinburgh Evening News*, September 1963.
20. Bari Johnson, phone conversation, 23/3/03.
21. Dannie Abse, *Goodbye Twentieth Century*, 2001.
22. Dannie Abse, phone conversation, 4/5/02.
23. Dannie Abse, *Goodbye Twentieth Century*, 2001.
24. Dannie Abse, phone conversation, 4/5/02.
25. Colin Barnes, phone conversation, 29/9/02.
26. Charles Fox, *Jazz Monthly*, August 1965.
27. Dave Double, *Crescendo*, August 1965.
28. Charles Fox, *Jazz Monthly*, February 1966.
29. John Smith, letter to the author, 10/4/02.
30. Michael Garrick, as above, note 11.
31. Michael Garrick, insert notes for Joe Harriott, *Genius*.

Chapter 8 *The many sides of Joe Harriott*

1. Michael Garrick, in conversation with Kevin Le Gendre, *Independent*, 13/11/98.
2. Denis Preston, in conversation with Peter Clayton, *Jazz Notes*, BBC radio broadcast, 1973.
3. Ian Carr, phone conversation, 2001.
4. Michael Garrick, phone conversation, 25/11/01.
5. Jeffrey Kruger, phone conversation, August 2001.
6. Jack Cooke, phone conversation, 8/11/01.
7. Coleridge Goode and Roger Cotterrell, *Bass Lines*, p. 116.
8. Coleridge Goode, phone conversation, 20/8/01.
9. Joe Harriott (interviewed in 1963), broadcast on BBC Radio 3, *Jazz Legends: Joe Harriott*, presented by Julian Joseph, 22/3/02.
10. Dave Willis, phone conversation, 6/2/03.

11. John Jack, phone conversation, 3/4/02.

12. Harry Klein, phone conversation, 25/2/03.

13. Michael Garrick, as above, Chapter 7, note 11.

14. Coleridge Goode and Roger Cotterrell, *Bass Lines*, p. 120.

15. Les Condon, insert notes for Joe Harriott, *Genius* CD.

16. Bobby Orr, in conversation with the author, 29/1/01.

17. Tommy Whittle, phone conversation, August 2002.

18. John Mayer, interviewed by Duncan Heining in *Jazz UK*, August 2001.

19. Brian Dee, phone conversation, 19/8/02.

20. Don Rendell, phone conversation, 16/4/02.

21. Michael Garrick, phone conversation, 2001; and see Garrick, 'Joe Harriott', *Jazz at Ronnie Scott's*, Jan-Feb 2003, p. 20.

22. Sharon Atkin, phone conversation, 26/11/02.

23. Del Turner, phone conversation, 12/11/01.

24. Tommy Chase, in conversation with the author, 29/4/02.

25. Ian Croall, phone conversation, 20/9/01; and Mike Travis, phone conversation, 6/10/01.

26. John Burgess, phone conversation, February 2003.

27. Peter Clayton, BBC radio, *Jazz Notes*, 1973; and in a slightly diffent form in Michael Garrick's sleevenote for his *For Love of Duke and Ronnie* CD.

28. Alan Plater, email to the author, 1/7/02; and see Coleridge Goode and Roger Cotterrell, *Bass Lines*, p. 130.

29. Goode and Cotterrell, *Bass Lines*, p. 118.

30. Ian Carr, phone conversation, 2002.

31. Kenny Baxter, phone conversations, 2/2/03, and letter to the author, 17/3/03.

32. Sharon Atkin, phone conversations, 28/10/01 and 26/11/01.

33. Coleridge Goode and Roger Cotterrell, *Bass Lines*, p. 130; Jim Godbolt, *A History of Jazz in Britain 1950–70*, p. 112; Ian Carr, phone conversation, 19/10/01.

34. Michael Garrick, in conversation with the author, 2002.

35. Colin Barnes, phone conversation, 21/9/02.

36. Marianne Wasser, phone conversation, 26/5/02.

37. Sammy Stokes, phone conversation, 23/1/03.

38. Jock Thompson, in conversation with the author, summer 2001.

39. Toto McNaughton, in conversation with the author, Edinburgh, 30/11/02.

40. Michael Horovitz, phone conversation, 3/3/03.

41. Dave Green, in conversation with the author, 18/02/02.

42. Sammy Stokes, phone conversation, 23/1/03.

43. Colin Barnes, phone conversation, 21/9/02.

44. Peggy Burton, in conversation with the author, 2002.

45. Frank Holder, in conversation with the author, Carshalton on the Hill, 22/2/02.

46. Eddie Cook, phone conversation, Autumn 2001.

47. Stuart Hepburn, in conversation with the author, Edinburgh, April 2002.

48. Sharon Atkin, phone conversations, 28/10/01 and 26/11/01.

49. Jack Cooke, letter to the author, 7/9/01.
50. Ernie Garside, in conversation with the author, Cheadle Hulme, 18/5/02.

Chapter 9   *Gigging around*
1. Lol Coxhill, interviewed in *Avant*, No. 5, Winter 1998, p. 22.
2. Kenny Baxter, letter to the author, 17/3/03.
3. Coleridge Goode, in conversation with the author, London, 20/2/02.
4. Spike Heatley, phone conversation, 20/3/03.
5. Kenny Baxter, letter to the author, 17/3/03.
6. Dougie Campbell, in conversation with the author, 30/11/02.
7. *Southern Daily Echo*, 3/2/58.
8. Steve Race, 'Jazz at the El Toro', *Melody Maker*, 6/6/59.
9. Tom Finlay, in conversation with the author, autumn 2001.
10. Alan Anderson, in conversation with the author, autumn 2001.
11. Undated press cuttings from the collection of Mike Travis.
12. Mike Travis, phone conversation, 19/1/03.
13. Neal Aptaker, phone conversation, 27/5/02.
14. Bill Smith, email to the author, 28/11/02.
15. Del Turner, phone conversation, 25/11/02.
16. Tommy Whittle, phone conversation, 19/8/02.
17. Tommy Whittle, in *Jazz Rag*, No. 13, autumn 1990.
18. The broadcast was issued on CD as *Chris Barber at the BBC with special guest Joe Harriott.*
19. Bob Brunning, *Blues in Britain: The History: 1950s–1990s*, London: Blandford, 1995.
20. Ernie Garside, in conversation with the author, 18/5/02.
21. Tommy Chase, phone conversation, 29/4/02.
22. Michael Horovitz, phone conversation, 3/3/03.
23. Peter King, emails to the author, 22 and 24/6/02
24. Danny Thompson, phone conversation, 18/1/03.
25. Heather Smythe, 12/5/02.
26. Ernie Garside, in conversation with the author, 18/5/02.
27. Letter to the author from the late Rod Marshall, 3/8/05.

Chapter 10   *Proving Kipling wrong – East meets West*
1. John Mayer, in conversation with the author, 31/7/02.
2. John Mayer, interviewed by Duncan Heining, *Jazz UK,* August 2001.
3. John Mayer, in conversation with the author, 31/7/02.
4. He is referring to the *Movement* album, part of which is made up of free form pieces.
5. Joe Harriott, quoted by Max Jones, *Melody Maker* 14/10/67.
6. John Mayer, in conversation with the author, 31/7/02. Quotes from Mayer in the following two paragraphs are also from this source.
7. Keshav Sathe, phone conversation, 25/11/02.
8. Coleridge Goode, interviewed by Jack Massarik, *The Wire*, No.4, 1983.
9. Coleridge Goode and Roger Cotterrell, *Bass Lines*, p. 175.

10. John Mayer, talking in 'Joe Harriott Tribute', Jazz FM radio broadcast, 1/1/91.
11. Coleridge Goode, interviewed by Jack Massarik, *The Wire*, No. 4, summer 1983.
12. Keshav Sathe, phone conversation, 25/11/02.
13. John Mayer, quoted in notes to Harriott–Mayer *Indo-Jazz Suite* album.
14. Charles Fox, notes to Harriott–Mayer *Indo-Jazz Suite* album.
15. Blindfold Test, conducted by Les Tomkins, *Crescendo*, December 1966.
16. John Mayer, letter to the author, 25/7/01.
17. Joe Harriott, quoted by Max Jones, *Melody Maker*, 14/10/67.
18. John Mayer, quoted in Robin Broadbank's insert notes for Mayer's *Asian Airs* CD.
19. Bruce King, *Jazz Monthly*, July 1966.
20. Charles Fox, notes to Harriott–Mayer *Indo-Jazz Suite* album.
21. Benny Green, programme notes for Indo-Jazz Fusions concert, undated.
22. John Mayer, in conversation with the author, 31/7/02.
23. John Mayer, letter to the author, 22/8/01.
24. Graham Collier, 'Joe Harriott's Indo-Jazz Fusions at the Marquee', *Crescendo*, December 1966.
25. Kenny Wheeler, phone conversation, 11/12/02.
26. John Mayer, in conversation with the author, 31/7/02.
27. Stu Hamer, phone conversation, 12/8/03.
28. Keshav Sathe, phone conversation, November 2002.
29. John Marshall, phone conversation, 20/11/02.
30. Stu Hamer, phone conversation, 12/8/03.
31. John Mayer, in conversation with the author, 31/7/02.
32. Don Norman, phone conversation, 8/9/02.
33. John Mayer, 'Indo-Jazz Fusions', *Avant*, No. 15, Spring 2000.
34. Sharon Atkin, phone conversations, 28/10/01 and 26/11/01.
35. Michael James, *Jazz Monthly*, December 1967.
36. Ian Carr, notes for Harriott–Mayer *Indo-Jazz Fusions II* album.
37. Jack Cooke, *Jazz Monthly*, June 1968.
38. Max Jones, 'Music to Blow the Minds of All Jazz Fans', *Melody Maker*, 14/10/67.
39. John Mayer, in conversation with the author, 31/7/02.
40. Max Harrison, *Jazz Monthly*, April 1970.
41. John Mayer, interviewed by Kevin Le Gendre, 'Too Good to be Forgotten', *Independent*, 13/11/98.
42. John Marshall, phone conversation, 20/11/02.
43. Keshav Sathe, phone conversation, 25/11/02.
44. Goode and Cotterrell, *Bass Lines*, p. 179.
45. John Mayer, in conversation with the author, 31/7/02.
46. Joe Harriott, talking to Max Jones, *Melody Maker*, 6/2/71.
47. Goode and Cotterrell, *Bass Lines*, p. 179.
48. John Mayer, in conversation with the author, London, 31/7/02.
49. Trevor Tomkins, phone conversation, 8/12/02.

50. Adrian Kerridge, email to the author, 12/1/03.
51. Joyce D'Silva, email to the author, January 13/3/03.
52. Elaine Delmar, in conversation with the author, August 2002.
53. Don Norman, phone conversation, 8/9/02.

Chapter 11   *Whatever has happened to Joe Harriott lately?*
1. Elaine Delmar, in conversation with the author, August 2002.
2. Kenny Wheeler, phone conversation, 11/12/02.
3. Ian Carr, phone conversation, 19/10/01.
4. Trevor Tomkins, phone conversation, 8/12/02.
5. Bunny Austin, phone conversation, 10/12/02.
6. Jack Cooke, *The Wire*, No. 90, August 1991.
7. Coleridge Goode, in conversation with the author, London, 20/2/02.
8. John Keating, in conversation with the author, Edinburgh, 11/9/01.
9. Trevor Tomkins, phone conversation, 8/12/02.
10. Stu Hamer, letter 9/10/02, and phone call, 12/8/03.
11. Coleridge Goode, in conversation with the author, London, 20/2/02; and Coleridge Goode and Roger Cotterrell, *Bass Lines*, p. 172.
12. Coleridge Goode, in programme notes for *Joe Harriott Memorial Night*, Gullivers Club, London, 20/2/73.
13. Pat Smythe, 'Jazz Scene', *Melody Maker*, 13/1/73.
14. Coleridge Goode, insert notes for Joe Harriott, *Genius* CD.
15. Alun Morgan, *Jazz and Blues*, March 1973.
16. Roger Cotterrell, 'Joe Harriott Memorial', p. 12.
17. Pat Smythe in a phone conversation with Roger Cotterrell, 20/7/73.
18. Denis Preston, sleevenotes for Stan Tracey's *We Love You Madly* LP.
19. Chukwunyere Kamalu, 'The Forgotten ones: Amancio D'Silva', *Jazz Journal*, August 1996.
20. Amancio D'Silva, quoted in Kamalu, 'The Forgotten Ones: Amancio D'Silva', *Jazz Journal*, August 1996.
21. Bryan Spring, phone conversation, 30/6/02.
22. Norma Winstone, phone conversation, 25/11/01.
23. Joyce D'Silva, phone conversation, 29/11/02.
24. Kamalu, 'The Forgotten Ones: Amancio D'Silva', *Jazz Journal*, August 1996.
25. Keshav Sathe, phone conversation, 26/11/02.
26. Denis Preston, interviewed by Peter Clayton, BBC radio, *Jazz Notes*, 1973.
27. Adrian Kerridge, email to the author, 12/1/03.
28. Joe Harriott, talking to Max Jones, 'Joe Harriott: Ten Years After', *Melody Maker*, 6/2/71.
29. Quoted in Max Jones, 'Joe Harriott: Ten Years After', *Melody Maker*, 6/2/71.

Chapter 12 *Free fall*

1. Chris Barber, phone conversation, 22/10/01.
2. Brian Nicholls interview, *Jazz News*, featured in *Brubeck Tour Programme*, Jan.1961
3. Del Turner, phone conversation, 2001.
4. Pete King, phone conversation, 13/8/03.
5. Del Southon, phone conversation, 5/12/02.
6. Pete King, phone conversation, 13/8/03.
7. Del Southon, phone conversation, 5/12/02.
8. Stuart Hepburn, in conversation with the author, Edinburgh, April 2002.
9. Don Rendell, phone conversation, 16/04/02.
10. Duncan Heining, *Trad Dads, Dirty Boppers and Free Fusioneers – British Jazz in the 1960s*, Equinox (forthcoming).
11. Sharon Atkin, in conversation with the author, Streatham, February 2002.
12. Dave Green, diary entry quoted in letter, 7/3/03; Tony Middleton, *Joe Harriott Bio/Discography*, p. 18 (session 29/3/71).
13. John Mayer, talking in 'Joe Harriott Tribute', Jazz FM radio broadcast, 1/1/91.
14. Michael Horovitz, phone conversation, June 2003.
15. Frank Holder, in conversation with the author, 22/2/02.
16. Letter to author from Margaret Tynski, 19/1/04.
17. Joe Harriott, quoted in Max Jones, 'Joe Harriott: Ten Years After', *Melody Maker*, 6/7/71.
18. Ken Maxwell, phone conversation, 12/8/03.
19. Ken Maxwell, phone conversation, 10/12/02.
20. Pete Burden, phone conversation, September 2002.
21. Dave Willis (bassist who sometimes depped for Hart with Indo-Jazz Fusions), phone conversation, 6/2/03.
22. Ernie Garside, in conversation with the author, 18/5/02.
23. Keshav Sathe, phone conversation, November 2002.
24. Email to author from Alan Plater, 3/2/04.
25. Kenny Baxter, letter to the author, 17/3/03.
26. Kenny Baxter, phone conversation, 13/3/03.
27. George Melly, phone conversation, 22/4/02.
28. Mick Mulligan, phone conversation, 9/9/02.
29. Peter Clayton, BBC radio, *Jazz Notes*, 1973. Harriott's illness impeded the plans and, instead of a radio appearance, a memorial programme was broadcast after his death.
30. Laurie Taylor, *New Statesman*, 26/2/99.
31. Letter to the author from the late Rod Marshall, 4/7/05
32. Ron Burnett, phone conversation, 9/7/02.
33. Letter to the author from the late Rod Marshall, 4/7/05
34. Quoted from Harry Shapiro, *Alexis Korner: The Biography*, London: Bloomsbury, 1997, p. 127.
35. Alexis Korner, 'Phil', *The Wire*, No. 2, Winter 1982/3.

36. Ken Baldock, phone conversation, 2/2/03.
37. Ronnie Scott and John Stevens, 'Phil'. *The Wire*, No. 2, Winter 82/83.
38. Ken Maxwell, phone conversation, 10/12/02.
39. Ian Wheeler, phone conversation, 23/1/03.
40. Teddy Layton, phone conversation, 28/10/01.
41. Clem Alford, phone conversation, 28/10/02.

Chapter 13   *In pretty dire straits*

1. 'The Beginning and the End – Personal Notes on Joe Harriott' by Don Vincent, dated 30/11/75.
2. This and subsequent quotations from Marilyn Layton are from a phone conversation, 4/4/03.
3. This and subsequent quotations from the late Teddy Layton are from a phone conversation, 28/10/01.
4. *http://forums.allaboutjazz.com/showthread.php?t=9582* visited 10 May 2008
5. 'The Beginning and the End – Personal Notes on Joe Harriott' by Don Vincent, 30/11/75.
6. Skip Conway, phone conversation, 7/11/01.
7. Del Southon, phone conversation, 5/12/02.
8. Del Southon, letter, 8/12/02.
9. Skip Conway, phone conversation, 27/11/02.
10. Denis Preston, interviewed by Peter Clayton, BBC radio, *Jazz Notes*, 1973.
11. Adrian Kerridge, email to the author, 11/1/03.
12. Del Southon, letter to the author, 8/12/02, and phone conversation, 8/12/02.
13. Del Southon, in conversation with the author, 5/12/02.
14. 'The Beginning and the End – Personal Notes on Joe Harriott' by Don Vincent, 30/11/75.
15. Jim Godbolt, 'Mingus Big Band', *Jazz at Ronnie Scott's*, No. 12, May-June 1998.
16. Skip Conway, phone conversation, 7/11/01.
17. Mick Mulligan, phone conversation, 9/9/02.
18. Del Southon, letter to the author, 8/12/02.
19. Sharon Atkin, phone conversations, 28/10/01 and 26/11/01.
20. Del Southon, phone conversation, 5/12/02.
21. Sharon Atkin, *Joe Harriott Tribute*, Jazz FM radio broadcast, 1/1/91.
22. Skip Conway, phone conversation, 25/1/02.
23. Del Southon, letter to the author, 8/12/02.
24. John Mayer, in conversation with the author, London 31/7/02.
25. Skip Conway, phone conversation, 27/5/02.
26. Trevor Tomkins, phone conversation, 8/12/02.
27. 'The Beginning and the End – Personal Notes on Joe Harriott' by Don Vincent, 30/11/75.
28. Marilyn Layton, phone conversation, 4/4/03.
29. Keshav Sathe, phone conversation, November 2002.

Chapter 14   *The legacy of Joe Harriott*
1.   Les Condon, phone conversation, 24/3/02.
2.   Shake Keane, interviewed by Peter Clayton, BBC radio, *Sounds of Jazz*, 10/12/88.
3.   Eric Dolphy, quoted in Nat Hentoff's sleevenotes to Dolphy's *Far Cry* CD.
4.   Danny Thompson, phone conversation, 18/1/03.
5.   Brian Nicholls interview, *Jazz News*, featured in *Brubeck Tour Programme*, Jan. 1961.
6.   Pat Smythe, 'One of the Few Unique Jazz Voices Nurtured by Britain Has Been Stilled', *Melody Maker,* 13/1/73.
7.   Kenny Baxter, letter to the author, 17/3/03.
8.   Marilyn Layton, phone conversation, 4/4/03.
9.   *Melody Maker*, 17/3/73.
10. Alan Plater, email to the author, 1/7/02.
11. Sharon Atkin, *Joe Harriott Tribute*, Jazz FM radio broadcast, 1/1/91.
12. Denis Preston, interviewed by Peter Clayton, BBC radio, *Jazz Notes*, early 1973.
13. Joyce D'Silva, email to the author, 13/1/03.
14. Andy Hamilton, talking in *Joe Harriott Tribute*, Jazz FM radio broadcast, 1/1/91.
15. Tony Kinsey, phone conversation, 2001.
16. Paul Rutherford, in 'Unsung Hero – Paul Rutherford', by Mark Wastell, *Avant*, No.5, Winter 1998.
17. Brian Dee, phone conversation, August 2002.
18. Goode and Cotterrell, *Bass Lines*, p. 181.
19. Shake Keane, interviewed by Peter Clayton, BBC radio, *Jazz Notes*, 1973.
20. Michael Garrick, phone conversation, 24/3/02; and insert notes for his CD *The New Quartet.*
21. *Southern Echo*, October/November 1989.
22. Trevor Tomkins, phone conversation, 8/12/02.
23. *Southern Evening Echo*, undated cutting, 1988.
24   Courtney Pine interviewed by Selwyn Harris in *Jazzwise*, February 2009.
25. Skip Conway, phone conversation, 27/5/02.
26. *Southern Evening Echo*, undated cutting.
27. *Southern Evening Echo*, undated cutting, 1988.
28. Pauline Harriott, phone conversation, 30/6/02.
29. Del Southon, letter to the author, 8/12/02.

records

Recorded in London except where otherwise indicated. Joe Harriott plays on all records other than those indicated by [*].

Chris Barber, *Chris Barber at the BBC with special guest Joe Harriott*, Upbeat Jazz URCD 158, CD issue, 2000, of 1963 recordings.

Chris Barber, *Chris Barber at the London Palladium*, Columbia 33SCX1346 LP, recorded 1961.

Chris Barber's Jazz Band, *Classic Concerts, Berlin/Copenhagen/London*, Lake Records LACD210, double CD, reissue, 2005, of recordings from 1958–61.

Alan Barnes and Alan Plater, *Songs For Unsung Heroes*, Woodville Records WVCD 106, CD, 2004. [*].

Acker Bilk with Stan Tracey Big Brass, *Blue Acker*, Columbia Two 230, LP, recorded 1968, reissued 2005 on Lake Records LACD 218, CD (also includes selected tracks from *We Love You Madly*).

George Chisholm, *Chis – The Art of George Chisholm*, Vocalion CDLF 8116, CD, issue, 2005, of 1956 recordings.

Amancio D'Silva, *Integration*, Columbia SCX6322, LP, recorded 1969, reissued 2004 on Universal 9866893, CD [*] .

Eric Dolphy with Booker Little, *Far Cry*, Original Jazz Classics OJCCD 400-2, CD, reissue, 1989, of 1960 New York recordings [*].

Allan Ganley Quartet, *Gone Ganley*, Nixa NJE 1046, EP, recorded 1957.

Michael Garrick Trio with Joe Harriott & Shake Keane, *Poetry & Jazz In Concert – Records 1 and 2*, Argo ZDA 26 and 27, LPs, recorded 1963, reissued 2006 on Vocalion 2CDSML 8416, double CD.

Michael Garrick Quintet, *October Woman*, Argo ZDA 33, LP, recorded 1964, reissued 2005 on Vocalion CDSML 8413, CD.

Michael Garrick Quintet, *Anthem*, Argo EAF / ZFA92, EP, recorded 1965, reissued 2005 on *October Woman*, Vocalion CDSML 8413, CD.

Michael Garrick Sextet, *Promises*, Argo ZDA 36, LP, recorded 1965, reissued 2008 on Vocalion CDSML8440, CD.

Michael Garrick Septet, *Black Marigolds*, Argo SDA 88, LP, recorded 1966, reissued 2005 on Vocalion CDSML8411, CD.

Michael Garrick Orchestra, *For Love of Duke ... and Ronnie*, Jazz Academy JAZA 4, CD, recorded 1995–6 [*].

Michael Garrick, *The New Quartet*, Jazz Academy JAZA 7, CD, recorded 2001 [*].

Michael Garrick Jazz Orchestra, *Big Band Harriott*, Jazz Academy JAZA 10, CD, recorded 2004. [*].

Kenny Graham's Afro Cubists, 'The Continental' / 'Blues in the Night', Esquire 10-377, single, recorded 1954.

Kenny Graham's Afro Cubists, 'Fascinating Rhythm' / 'Cottontail', Esquire 10-387, single, recorded 1954.

Joe Harriott Quartet, *Joe Harriott Quartet*, Columbia SEG 7665, EP, recorded 1955.

Joe Harriott Quintet, *Blue Harriott*, Columbia SEG 7939, EP, recorded 1959, and Joe Harriott Quintet, *A Guy Called Joe*, Columbia SEG 8070, EP, recorded 1960. These recordings were also released as *Southern Horizons*, Jazzland JLP 937S, LP.

Joe Harriott Quintet, *Free Form*, Jazzland JLP 949S, LP, recorded 1960, reissued 1998 on Redial 538-184-2, CD.

Joe Harriott Quintet, *Abstract*, Columbia 33SX 1477 / Capitol 10351, LP, recorded 1961–2, reissued 1998 on Redial 538-183-2, CD.

Joe Harriott Quintet, *Movement*, Columbia 33SX 1627, LP, recorded 1963.

Joe Harriott, *Live at Harry's 1963*, Rare Music RM 029, CD issue, 2006, of previously unissued 1963 recordings.

Joe Harriott Quintet, *High Spirits*, Columbia 33SX 1692, LP, recorded 1964.

Joe Harriott – John Mayer Double Quintet, *Indo-Jazz Suite*, Columbia SX 6025 / Atlantic SD1465, LP, recorded 1965, reissued 1999 on Koch Jazz KOC CD8512, CD.

Joe Harriott – John Mayer Double Quintet, *Indo-Jazz Fusions*, Columbia SX 6122 / Atlantic SD1482, LP, recorded 1966, reissued 1998 on Redial 538-048-2, CD.

Joe Harriott – John Mayer Double Quintet, *Indo-Jazz Fusions II*, Columbia SX 6215, LP, recorded 1967, reissued 1998 on Redial 538-048-2, CD.

Joe Harriott Quintet, *Swings High*, Melodisc SLP 12-150, LP, recorded 1967, reissued 2004 on Cadillac SGC/MELCD203, CD.

Joe Harriott, *Personal Portrait*, Columbia SCX 6249, LP, recorded 1967.

Joe Harriott / Amancio D'Silva, *Hum-Dono*, Columbia SCX 6354, LP, recorded 1969.

Joe Harriott, *Joe Harriott Memorial 1973*, One Up OU 2011, LP, 1973 reissue of recordings 1962–9.

Joe Harriott, *Genius*, Jazz Academy JAZA 6, CD issue, 2000, of live recordings of the Joe Harriott Quintet 1961, Michael Garrick 1960s groups, etc.

Joe Harriott, *Killer Joe! Birth of a Legend*, Giant Steps Recordings / Cherry Red Records GSCR 020, double CD, reissue, 2007, of Harriott recordings 1954–56 with his own groups and with the Tony Kinsey Trio, Ronnie Scott Orchestra, Jazz Today Unit, Lita Roza, and Buddy Pipp.

Laurie Johnson Orchestra, *Lock Up Your Daughters*, Pye NEP 24156, EP, recorded 1960.

Laurie Johnson, *Synthesis*, Columbia SCX 6412, LP, recorded 1969.

Shake Keane Quintet, *In My Condition*, Columbia SEG 8140, EP, recorded 1961.

Tony Kinsey Quartet, *Fascinating Rhythm*, Harkit Records, HRKCD 8212, CD, reissue of 1955/56 recordings.

Tony Kinsey Quintet, *A Jazz at the Flamingo Session*, Decca LK 4207, LP, recorded 1957, reissued 2003 on Vocalion, CDLK 4213, CD (part of double CD set).

John Mayer's Indo-Jazz Fusions, *Asian Airs*, Nimbus NI 5499, CD, recorded 1996 [*].

Melody Maker All Stars, *All The Winners*, Nixa NJE 1046, EP, recorded 1957.

The Nice, *Five Bridges Suite*, Charisma CAD 1014, LP, recorded 1970.

Buddy Pipp's Highlifers, 'Positive Action' / 'Ackee Blues', Lyragon J730, single, recorded 1954 ('Ackee Blues' reissued on *Killer Joe* CD, above).

Buddy Pipp's Highlifers, 'Sway' / 'Ghana Special', Lyragon J730, single, recorded 1954.

Dizzy Reece, *A New Star*, Jasmine JASCD 615, CD, reissue, 2001, of 1955–6 recordings [*].

Dizzy Reece, *Progress Report*, Jasmine JASCD 620, CD, reissue, 2001, of 1956–8 recordings [*].

Dizzy Reece, *Asia Minor*, New Jazz / Original Jazz Classics OJCCD-1806-2, CD, reissue, 1992, of 1962 New York recordings [*].

Jeremy Robson with the Michael Garrick Trio and Joe Harriott and Shake Keane, *Blues for the Lonely*, Columbia SEG 8224, EP, recorded 1962, reissued 2006 on *Poetry & Jazz In Concert*, Vocalion 2CDSML 8416, CD.

Jeremy Robson with the Michael Garrick Quintet, *Before Night / Day*, Argo EAF 115, EP, recorded 1965,

Lita Roza, *Love is the Answer / Listening in the After Hours*, Vocalion CDLK 4126, double CD, reissue, 2001, of 1955 recordings.

Phil Seamen, *The Phil Seamen Story*, Decibel BSN 103, LP, recorded 1973 [*].

Stan Tracey Big Brass, *We Love You Madly*, Columbia SCX 6320, LP, recorded 1968.

Ken Vandermark's Joe Harriott Project, *Straight Lines*, Atavistic ALP115, CD, recorded 1998 [*] in Chicago .

Various artists, *Jazz Britannia*, MGM EP615, EP, recorded 1956, including two tracks by the Joe Harriott Quartet.

Various artists, *Third Festival Of British Jazz*, Decca LK4180, LP, recorded 1956 [*].

Various Artists, *The Best of British Jazz*, Ember EMBCD 012, CD, reissue, 2000, of recordings made in the 1950s &1960s.

Various Artists, *Impressed with Gilles Peterson*, Universal 064 749 2, CD, compilation, 2002, including 'Jaipur' from 1969 *Hum-Dono* LP.

Sonny Boy Williamson, *Don't Send Me No Flowers*, Charley CD80, recorded 1965.

acknowledgements

I would like to thank everyone who contributed to the first and more recently to the second edition of my biography of Joe Harriott. It was a source of great pleasure for me to meet so many fascinating and helpful people in the course of my research. In total, hundreds of people contributed stories, news cuttings, photographs and even, in some cases, recordings. Through this patchwork of impressions a clearer picture emerges of a brilliant, complex and increasingly troubled individual.

It is impossible to thank everyone by name, but two people who deserve special mention are Derek Martin and the late Skip Conway. I was fortunate to be given access to Derek's staggeringly comprehensive collection of music newspapers, jazz radio recordings and rare album sleevenotes. The time he devoted was beyond price. Skip was a constant support throughout the research stage and his optimism sustained me when I wondered if the task would ever reach fruition. He lived to see the book published but died only weeks before a marvellous Joe Harriott Tribute Concert, given by a Gary Crosby quintet in Southampton. It was fitting that Gary began the evening by dedicating the band's performance to Skip, a true friend to Joe and a stalwart supporter of jazz in the Southampton area.

The following people, some of whom are no longer with us, deserve my deep gratitude: Dannie Abse, Sharon Atkin, Bunny Austin, Kenny Baxter, Billy Bond, Peggy Burton, Ian Carr, Gary Crosby, Ernie Garside, Coleridge Goode, Kitty Grime, Mr and Mrs Frank Holder, Michael Horovitz, Christiane Keane, Jason Koransky (editor of *DownBeat*), Ken Maxwell, David Nathan (of the National Jazz Archive), Bobby Orr, Ron Simpson (of *Jazz Rag*), John Smith, Del Southon, Laurie Taylor and Les Tomkins (formerly of *Crescendo* magazine). I must thank Michael Garrick, Tony Kinsey and the late John Mayer who cast their expert eyes upon the draft chapters in which they featured heavily.

I am indebted to Roger Cotterrell and Chris Blackford whose writings on Joe I discovered in Chris' excellent magazine, *Rubberneck*. Roger has provided valuable additional information since my book was drafted for publication. To have had his continuing help throughout the editing process has been a bonus indeed. I must also thank my editor, Ann Cotterrell, for her patient, thorough and conscientious application in editing the sometimes muddled efforts of this first time author.

Since publication in 2003 I have been in receipt of numerous and significant pieces of new information, hence the appearance of this new edition. Two important new informants are Margaret Tynski and Pat Copp: the names they were known by when they became romantically involved with Joe. I commend them for their honesty and courage in sharing experiences which must have been unsettling and poignant to recall. A darker, emotionally turbulent side of Joe emerges as a result of their harrowing stories.

I am very sad that Rod Marshall, Brighouse publican, amateur flautist and great supporter of Harriott during his final years, did not survive to see his memories recorded in this edition. His vivid reminiscences left me in no doubt that Joe was fortunate to have such a reliable, caring friend.

My thanks also must go to my immediate family. Joe Harriott's story placed increasing demands on my spare time and other duties had to be put on hold or, more often, undertaken by my wife, Lorna. She showed commendable tolerance.

Finally, to the members of the Harriott family across three generations, a huge thanks for your assistance. My sincerest wish, and prime aim in producing this book, is that it will contribute towards a growing awareness that Joe Harriott was a musical genius.

Alan Robertson
30 January 2011

The editors are grateful to the following for their help with photos and information for the first edition: Bunny Austin, Ken Baxter, Bill Bond, Peggy Burton, Skip Conway, Ernie Garside, Nick Jones, Janet and Eddie Cook of *Jazz Journal International*, Tony Kinsey, Derek Martin, John Mayer, Tony Mullett, David Nathan, Don Norman, David Redfern and the *Southern Daily Echo*.

John Smith generously gave permission to include his poem. Special thanks to Lin Cotterrell for her assistance and to Michael Garrick for his consistent and enthusiastic support for this project.

index

Jazz Books from Northway

Alan Plater, *Doggin' Around*

Coleridge Goode and Roger Cotterrell,
Bass Lines – A Life in Jazz

Peter King, *Flying High – A Jazz Life and Beyond*

Ian Carr, *Music Outside – Contemporary Jazz in Britain*

Leslie Thompson with Jeffrey Green, *Swing from a Small Island*

Graham Collier, *The Jazz Composer – Moving Music off the Paper*

Mike Hennessey, *The Little Giant – The Story of Johnny Griffin*

Peter Vacher, *Soloists and Sidemen – American Jazz Stories*

Derek Ansell, *Workout – The Music of Hank Mobley*

Vic Ash, *I Blew It My Way: Bebop, Big Bands and Sinatra*

Jim Godbolt, *A History of Jazz in Britain 1919–50*

Chris Searle, *Forward Groove: Jazz and the Real
World from Louis Armstrong to Gilad Atzmon*

Digby Fairweather, *Notes from a Jazz Life*

Ronnie Scott with Mike Hennessey,
Some of My Best Friends Are Blues

John Chilton, *Hot Jazz, Warm Feet*

Join our mailing list for details of new books, events
and special offers: write to Northway Books,
39 Tytherton Road, London N19 4PZ
or email *info@northwaybooks.com*
www.northwaybooks.com